GREAT
ADVENTURERS
OF THE TWENTIETH CENTURY

RON TAGLIAPIETRA

Bob Jones University Press
Greenville, South Carolina 29614

Library of Congress Cataloging-in-Publication Data

Tagliapietra, Ron, 1956–
    Great adventurers of the twentieth century / Ron Tagliapietra.
        p.   cm.
    Includes bibliographical references and index.
    ISBN 1-57924-073-9 (paperback)
        1. Adventure and adventurers—History—20th century. I. Title.
    G525.T26 1998
    910.4—dc21

                                                            98-12291
                                                                CIP

Cover photo credits: The central climber (Corel Corp.) symbolizes adventure as he nears his remote Yukon summit. Top left photo (Zbigniew Bzdak): Piotr Chmielinski and Joe Kane paddle down the Amazon. Lower left photo (Corbis-Bettmann): Lt. Helmer Hanssen poses at the South Pole upon arrival with Roald Amundsen in 1911. Top right photo (Corbis): Returning from the North Pole, Robert Peary stops at Indian Harbor, Labrador, on September 5, 1909. Lower right photo (Corbis-Bettmann): Matthew A. Henson, trekked to the pole with Peary. Back photo (Zbigniew Bzdak): the last Inca Bridge hangs over the the Apuríimac River and Chmielinski's kayaks.

NOTE:
The fact that materials produced by other publishers are referred to in this volume does not constitute an endorsement by Bob Jones University Press of the content or theological position of materials produced by such publishers. The position of Bob Jones University Press, and the University itself, is well known. Any references and ancillary materials are listed as an aid to the reader and in an attempt to maintain the accepted academic standards of the publishing industry.

Great Adventurers of the Twentieth Century

Designed by Rich Cutter
Project Editor: Don Harrelson

©1998 Bob Jones University Press
Greenville, South Carolina 29614

ISBN 1-57924-073-9

15   14   13   12   11   10   9   8   7   6   5   4   3   2   1

This book is dedicated to the Lord Jesus Christ who gave life to these adventurers and enabled me to write about them. Secondarily, it is dedicated to friends in high school who helped me develop my writing skills. Each member of our personal writing club, the Amalgamated Writer's Guild, read my monthly stories and greatly influenced me. Thank you to Gary Poplawski, Rich Hutchinson, John Pasurka, Mark Vormittag, and Mike Helford.

CONTENTS

Preface

Christians can learn a lot from the great adventurers of the twentieth century. Even though many of these adventurers were unsaved, each accomplished a notable feat in the history of the world. In addition to learning more about the world in which the adventurers lived, Christians can appreciate how hard each worked to reach his goal. Such a willingness to suffer adversity on long journeys for a temporal goal should inspire Christians to sacrifice for the Lord Jesus Christ in order to spread the gospel: "Thou therefore endure hardness, as a good soldier of Jesus Christ" (II Tim. 2:3). Before it is possible to serve Christ sacrificially, one must know Him. "Believe on the Lord Jesus Christ, and thou shalt be saved" (Acts 16:31).

What makes someone a "great adventurer"? First, he must successfully achieve one of the most notable goals in a field and be the first to do so. Scores of adventurers climb mountains every year—and many still make first ascents—but a "great adventurer" made the first ascent of Mount Everest, the highest of all. A great adventurer successfully accomplishes his notable goal (even if it requires several attempts or if he later dies on some other adventure). For example, a few people think that Mallory and Irvine may have reached Mount Everest's summit before Sir Edmund Hillary did. However, even if Mallory and Irvine reached the summit, they died in the attempt rather than retreating for a later attempt.

Some may be surprised that man's first walk on the moon is not in this book. The purpose of this book is to present human achievements made without engines. This means that the adventurer must have used a balloon or glider rather than an airplane or spaceship. Sailboats, kayaks, and bathyscaphs are preferred to motorboats, ships, and submarines. Dogsleds, horses, bicycles, and camels replace cars, snowmobiles, and motorcycles. Of course, treks on foot are always best.

You may also miss famous names such as Dr. Livingstone ("I presume") and John Wesley Powell. Although these men were great adventurers, their adventures were too early in history for this book: *Great Adventurers **of the Twentieth Century.***

You may notice that there are more mountain climbers and polar treks than any other type of adventures. These were the primary challenges of the twentieth century. More people attempted such feats (and more lives were lost) than in other types of adventures. Ocean crossings and cave explorations probably rank not too far behind.

Some achievements have obvious importance: the reaching of the two poles and the climbing of Mount Everest. Others, such as the climbing of Nanda Devi, may not be so obvious until you read the account. What is arguably the greatest human achievement of each decade is included.

Decade	Year	Event
1900s	1909	North Pole reached
1910s	1911	South Pole reached
1920s	1922	cave sump dive achieved
1930s	1936	Nanda Devi, highest peak yet climbed
1940s	1947	raft sailed across Pacific
1950s	1953	summit of Mount Everest climbed
1960s	1960	bottom of Mariana Trench reached
1970s	1972	Mammoth Cave system explored
1980s	1986	Amazon kayaked
1990s	1990	Antarctica crossed

Of course, there were other great adventurers of the century besides those selected. Many of the great adventurers had partners who were great adventurers themselves. In such cases, the author selected one so that stories would not be repeated. The one selected tended to be the leader of the party, the more famous one, or the one who had other key adventures that should be related. See the partner's story in such cases as Matthew Henson (with Peary), Eric Shipton (with Tilman), Tenzing Norgay (with Hillary), and Pat Crowther (with Wilcox).

Finally, I would like to thank some of the adventurers and their families for providing unpublished information. Piotr Chmielinski provided considerable information during two telephone interviews and follow-up e-mail correspondence. Patrick Morrow also provided key biographic detail by e-mail. Both Mrs. Wilcox and Mrs. Schoening provided details about their husbands over the phone. Finally, Ray Shaffer contributed information about his uncle Earl including "Uncle Earl's Trail Slides," a videotape of the slide program that Earl Shaffer presents at public speaking engagements about his famous hike.

It is my prayer that as Christians read of the admirable qualities of these great adventurers (see the Appendix for more information on character qualities), they will be stirred to similar feats as missionaries and servants of the Lord Jesus Christ.

—Ron Tagliapietra

TERMS

arete: (uh RATE; French) a narrow and serrated ridge with steep cliffs formed by glaciers carving out cirques on both sides

ballast: (BAL ist; English) heavy items placed in a balloon for stability that can be thrown overboard to control altitude

belay: (be LAY; English) to secure a rope or a climber at the end of a rope on a mountain

bivouac: (BIV oo wak; German) a makeshift temporary camp with minimal provisions and often without a tent

cache: (cash; French) a place where food and other supplies have been hidden or stored for later use

cairn: (karn; Scottish) a rock pile or mound marking a trail, especially where there are no trees to mark with blazes

calve: (cav; English) glaciers calve icebergs into the sea when large ice chunks split off from the glaciers and then float

carabiner: (kar a BEE ner; German) an oblong metal ring with a clip used to attach a rope to a piton

cirque: (surk; French) a steep basin scooped out of the side of a mountain by a glacier

col: (kol; French) a high pass or gap through the mountains, especially in Europe and Asia

cornice (KORE nis; English) the protecting tip of a snowdrift, especially one hanging over a mountainside and prone to break off with added weight

couloir (kool WAHR; French) a steep gully on the side of a mountain

crampons: (KRAM pohnz; English) a set of metal spikes attached to boots for walking on snow and especially ice

crevasse: (creh VAHS; French) a deep chasm in a glacier

crevice: (CREH vis; English) a narrow crack in arock or cliff face

cwm: (koom; Welsh) the upper end of a steep mountain valley

drain: (DRANE; English) a natural cave passage with a running stream

floe: (floh; Norwegian) a section of the ice pack that has broken off; floes can reach five miles across

gondola: (gon DOH la; italian) a basket or enclosure for passengers suspended below a balloon. With a helium balloon the gondola rotates but not with a hot-air balloon.

lead: (leed; English) the channel between ice floes in polar seas that shift, widen, narrow, or close, depending on currents

kayak: (KYE ak; Eskimo) a watercraft smaller than a canoe and designed for one person who kneels in the center. The craft is covered and watertight and steered with a double-bladed paddle.

mush: (English) to travel by dogsled

nunatak: (NOON uh tak; Eskimo) a barren rocky peak or outcropping poking up through an icecap in Antarctica

piton: (PEE tohn; French) a spike that can be driven into a cliff face in order to support a rope or climber

portage: (POR tij; French) to carry a watercraft overland between waterways or around waterfalls

sastruga: (sah STROO guh; Russian) a hardened snow ridge in polar areas with the appearance of windblown waves (plural is sastrugi)

sérac: (seh RACK; French) an ice pinnacle formed where crevasses intersect

scree: (SKREE; English) loose rocks covering a mountainside

snow blindness: (English) temporary loss of vision resulting from bright sunlight and ultraviolet rays reflecting off snow or ice

spelunking: (spe LUNK ing; English) the exploration of caves

sump: (suhmp; English) a pool at the end of a cave passage where the passage continues underwater below the water table

through-hike: (English) hiking a long-distance trail without returning home (rather than hiking sections over several years)

trek: (trek; Dutch) a long arduous journey, especially on foot

FREDERICK COURTENEY SELOUS
Safaris of the Greatest Hunter

South Africa

Fred Selous spurred his horse to a gallop in pursuit of the fleeing giraffe. It was the first one he had seen since coming to South Africa in 1872. Reins in one hand and a rifle in the other, Selous chased the giraffe for an hour. Suddenly, his right leg scraped a tree. Selous fell off his horse and rolled around in pain. Inspecting his leg, he decided it was not broken, but he realized that he had lost both his giraffe and his companions.

Selous, born Frederick Courteney Selous in London on December 31, 1851, remembered the diaries of the African hunters that had inspired him as a boy of thirteen. Charles Baldwin and Gordon Cumming had been his heroes; missionary David Livingstone was added to the list a few years later. He now found himself in the settings he had so often dreamed about.

Selous cut grass for a bed as Baldwin had done and slept in the bush. He had no food or water, his leg ached, and he had used the last of his gunpowder trying to start a fire. His face still hurt from an explosion days before, when ash from a companion's cigar had fallen in the gunpowder. Selous slept soundly.

All the next day he searched for his companions but bedded down at the end, once again hungry and lonely. When he awoke, his horse had strayed; now he was completely alone. He walked all day, seeing no one, and then slept again. He could tell he was getting weak. The next morning he met a Bushman boy who traded him milk and water for his knife. After a fourth night alone in the bush, he finally found his companions. Instead of discouraging the would-be elephant hunter, this ordeal had excited him.

Zimbabwe

Elephants were becoming scarce in South Africa, so Selous soon obtained permission from Lobengula, king of the Matabele, to hunt in Rhodesia (now Zimbabwe). He set off into the tsetse fly region on foot. During the next three years, he killed seventy-eight elephants and became one of the greatest ivory hunters in all of Africa. His elephant hunting taught him that shots to the lung were more lethal than those to the heart. He had been a good shot even as a boy in England, but he improved further in Africa. One time, while on horseback with a leopard in close pursuit, he had turned and fired, bringing the leopard down with a single shot.

Selous had his share of tough times. On a rhino hunt, he suffered a broken collarbone, which he had to set himself. He also suffered a concussion while hunting eland. A buffalo once flipped his horse into the air and then butted the fallen rider's shoulder. Another time, a half-inch wood chip lodged in the back of his nose for a year from a musket accident. He often spent evenings cleaning up the gashes caused by lions' claws on his horses rumps or dressing the wounds of his African gun bearers who were also attacked by lions. Once he found his dog, Blucher, mauled by a leopard and had to shove the intestines back in before stitching up the wound.

In 1881, Selous published *A Hunter's Wanderings in Africa,* while hunters and would-be adventurers admired the book, the conservationists of the time criticized it. The criticisms made him more conscious of his own growing concerns. Hunting safaris had begun in 1836, but already Selous recognized the tragic loss of wildlife that they had caused. He had never hunted rhino for sport and frequently argued that no one should. Also, even though during his life he killed thirty-one lions, he did so only for skins, meat, or defense. In fact, he had never killed any animal just for sport as happened on many safaris but only for work, food, or self-defense. Usually the Africans made use of all the meat and fat from the elephant carcasses left by his ivory hunting work, but he regretted the times that he had hunted solely for the tusks. He now decided to hunt only when the meat could be used as well as the ivory. This became easier with income from his book and from wages from Englishmen looking for safari guides. In 1887, the first time he worked as a guide, he and his clients discovered an underground lake in the caves at Sinoia.

*   *   *   *

"In three days, you will die!" said the enraged Barotsi warriors. The Barotsi wanted no Europeans invading their land. Indeed, two nights later, Selous found his camp surrounded by Barotsi warriors. He fled through the night on foot, armed with only his knife. For weeks he braved the dangers of wild animals across three hundred miles of bush, traveling by night to avoid the enemy warriors.

The hero of H. Rider Haggard's *King Solomon's Mines* and its sequel, *Allan Quatermain,* modeled after Fred Selous and published shortly after Selous's first book, brought even more attention to the African hunter. Haggard's later books, such as *She,* continued to fasten British interest on African adventure. Meanwhile, Selous became embroiled in the war between the British and the Africans that led to the founding of Rhodesia.

Selous published his second book, *Travel and Adventure in Southeast Africa,* in 1893. After getting married in 1897, he published *Sunshine and Storm in Rhodesia.* His wife lived with him on his farm at Bulawayo. His own books and Haggard's novels combined with his great hunting prowess and cave discovery to increase his fame further. He was considered the greatest hunter and outdoorsman in the world.

After Selous and his wife moved to Surrey, England, he still took hunting trips. He hunted in Norway, Iceland, Transylvania, the Yukon Territory in Canada, and Wyoming in the United States. In 1902, he took his first trip to East Africa.

In 1908, the century of safaris from 1836 to 1939 was drawing to a close. The ungoverned landscapes became more civilized, the desire for discovery waned, and the once-abundant big-game animals became endangered. By the end of the safari period after World War I, game spotting from planes and shooting from vehicles would divest the safaris of any shred of adventure. Old-timers angrily halted such methods, but cars and land rovers continued to simplify transportation, even though clients could not shoot from vehicles. In spite of the decline, the most famous safari of the twentieth century was about to be enacted under Selous's guidance.

East Africa

The lion charged Teddy Roosevelt. He had chased it on horseback until it turned to charge; then he had jumped off the horse to face it. Even as he faced death, Roosevelt considered this 1909 safari with Fred Selous the high point of his private life. He fired as the lion closed in on him, but the wound simply enraged the lion further.

The lion, only thirty yards away now, was closing in quickly. Roosevelt knew that with a speed of forty miles per hour, the lion could cross the gap in two seconds. He fired and missed. He fired again and hit the beast again.

Roosevelt stood transfixed by the lion's blazing eyes, now only ten yards away, as it hurtled toward him. He remained cool, though, and shot again. His twenty-year-old son Kermit and his friend Alfred also shot. The three simultaneous shots brought the king of beasts down.

Roosevelt, having completed his second term as president, had taken a year off for a safari. He arrived in Mombasa on April 21, 1909. On the first day of his safari, the largest ever in Kenya, Roosevelt had wounded two wildebeests at long range. Kermit pursued the bull for seven miles before finally bringing it down. Another man on the safari, Pease, finally got the cow at sunset. Now two weeks later, Roosevelt had killed six lions.

From the Kapiti Plains, the safari continued to Nairobi and Lake Naivasha, where Roosevelt bagged two hippos. After seeing Mount Kenya and Mount Elgon, Roosevelt's party headed for Lake Victoria.

The fifty-seven-hundred-square-mile Serengeti National Park now protects all five of the famous African big-game animals: lion, elephant, rhinoceros, buffalo, and leopard. In Selous's day, though, Roosevelt was privileged to hunt all five. Since the Serengeti Plains contain more wildlife than any other place in the world, it was a dream come true for the hunter and wildlife lover. Roosevelt enjoyed seeing the great variety of creatures and bringing specimens back to America. Antelopes there included the giant eland, the smaller impala and topi, and the tiny dik-dik. The plains thrived with stork, egret, flamingo, vulture, hyrax, monkey, baboon, wild dog, fox, Grant's gazelle, Thompson's gazelle, zebra, wildebeest, giraffe, hyena, jackal, and cheetah.

In Uganda, after taking a steamer across Lake Victoria, a man on another safari became sick. Roosevelt volunteered his doctor to perform the needed operation. He talked with the man during the operation to calm him and held the bandages for the doctor. Soon, everyone on the safari came down with fevers or dysentery, but no fever could stop Roosevelt's hunting. He bagged a hippo that day. He also got an eland and a sitatunga while in Uganda. To his face, the natives called him *Bwana Mkubwa,* meaning "Great Master," a name more appropriate for the safari's financier. Behind his back, though, his portliness earned him the nickname *Bwana Tumbo,* "the Stomach." At Lake Albert, Roosevelt was almost trampled by an elephant before another steamer took them toward Sudan.

At the White Nile, Roosevelt bagged a white-eared kob, a heavy-horned antelope. Then he sailed down the Nile to Khartoum where the safari ended on March 14, 1910. His first-class preferences and the expenses of preserving thousands of animal skins had made it a very expensive safari, and he had cabled home for another $30,000 before he completed it. He and Kermit bagged a total of 512 creatures, including 17 lions, 20 rhinoceros, 11 elephants, 10 buffalo, and 80 other species. He later mounted a few of the animals for his Trophy (North) Room at Sagamore Hill, but he gave most of the animals to the National Museum in Washington, D.C. In fact, the final count of specimens donated by the safari to the Smithsonian came to 4,900 mammals; 4,000 birds; 2,000 reptiles; and 500 fish.

Professional hunters, such as Fred Selous, considered it a disgrace if a wounded animal got away. They always stalked or chased animals to get in close range and carefully aimed shots guaranteed to bring the animal down. Inability to finish a kill was the mark of a poor hunter. However, Roosevelt took long-range potshots frequently and even expressed the idea that if he shot enough he was bound to get something. With such shooting, he often hit the wrong animal, once accidentally shooting a lion cub. Kermit also mistakenly bagged a baby bongo. Perhaps worse, animals that escaped lived out their lives crippled. Such tactics disgusted the professional hunters, who felt that it gave hunting bad publicity. The hunters deplored the excesses of the safari too. Roosevelt knew the dwindling status of the white rhino but indulged himself in the slaughter of twenty of them anyway.

On the other hand, Roosevelt did not let the specimens rot in the field but rather gave them to museums. His book *African Game Trails* drew attention to Africa. Further, no one doubted his strong interest in conservation. As president he had created fifty-five wildlife refuges, declared the first national monuments, expanded the national parks, organized conservation conferences, and become America's leading proponent of conservation

Roosevelt's contagious enthusiasm and courage in the face of danger made him easy to like. Those who hunted with him loved him in spite of his excesses. Fred Selous and Teddy Roosevelt became very good friends and shared another hunting trip in North America soon after. They corresponded closely until Selous returned to military service. Selous died in action near Kisaki south of Morogoro, Tanganyika (now Tanzania), on January 4, 1917.

ROBERT EDWIN PEARY
To the North Pole

Greenland

Ice crunched as the ship's rudder struck a large floating chunk. The wheel jerked from the captain's hands, and the tiller swung violently. Robert Edwin Peary had just walked to the stern of the ship, and the tiller crashed into his leg. Pain surged through Peary as he heard bone breaking.

Peary was born in 1856 in Cresson, Pennsylvania, but had later moved to Portland, Maine. His first major adventure had been surveying the jungles of Nicaragua for a possible canal route, but the canal was eventually built in Panama instead.

Ice drifted as far as Peary could see, reminding him of his only previous trip to Greenland in 1886. He had failed to cross the interior of Greenland that time, and before he could try again, Fridtjof Nansen of Norway crossed it in 1888.

Peary had brought six people with him for his second Greenland expedition of 1891-92. The team consisted of ornithologist Langdon Gibson; adventurer John Verhoeff; Norwegian Eivind Astrupl; expedition doctor, Frederick Cook; his best friend, Matt Henson; and Peary's wife, Josephine. It was on this expedition that he broke his leg on the ship and spent six weeks strapped to a board. As the break healed, he spent the time learning from Eskimos about dog teams and fur clothing. The Eskimos call themselves the Inuit, but at the time the rest of the world knew them only as Eskimos.

By the spring, John Verhoeff had disappeared while mineral hunting. He was never found again. With Eivind Astrup, Peary traveled five hundred miles and reached Independence Bay by early July. Thinking they had found the northeast tip of Greenland, they returned to base in early August.

Peary had met Matthew Henson in a shop in Washington, D.C., and had hired him immediately. Henson, born on August 8, 1866, in Maryland, had signed on as a cabin boy on a ship to China at age thirteen. Since then he had sailed to Japan, the Philippines, North Africa, Spain, France, and Russia and later accompanied Peary to Nicaragua. He had also joined him on the second Greenland expedition. His courage and strength matched Peary's, and his seven-year seniority provided stability. They were the best of friends. Each had often depended on the other in life-and-death situations. Henson was the first African American to winter in the Arctic.

Peary and Henson explored Greenland as a possible starting point for an attempt to reach the North Pole from 1893 to 1895. Peary brought his wife, Josephine, for the second time. She became the first (non-Eskimo) woman to winter in the Arctic and published a book about each expedition. However, problems arose. The fuel supplies were swamped by a wave from a calving iceberg, the sled dogs became sick, and Josephine had to return home with their new baby. Peary remained a second year and repeated his trip to Independence Bay in the spring. Conditions were harsh, and all but one of the dogs died. They had barely survived by finding musk oxen for food and eating them raw. Though Peary had discovered a half-ton iron meteorite, the trip seemed a complete failure. He was ready to try again.

Arctic Ocean

Peary trudged slowly on. He had never felt so cold as he neared Fort Conger. He had walked 250 miles up the coast of Ellesmere Island in Canada with Henson, Dr. Dedrick, and some Eskimos. They had pushed on in darkness, knowing they were almost there. The sight of the hut encouraged them, but when they arrived, Peary found that his toes were frostbitten. Dr. Dedrick amputated some of the toes but feared to remove them all saying, "If I remove them all, you will not be able to walk." After six weeks of agony and waiting at the hut, they decided to return to the ship. They went quickly through the frigid wastes, recording temperatures as low as -60°F. Dragging Peary on a sled for ten days, they reached the ship, where more amputations on both feet left Peary with only two toes.

His ship, *Windward,* got free of the ice in August 1899, but he was not going home yet, in spite of news of the death of his second daughter. He sent more supplies to Fort Conger and then returned there in March 1900. This time he did discover the northern tip of Greenland and camped there. Three times he set out from camp for the North Pole, only to turn back each time. He returned to Fort Conger for another winter. His wife and surviving daughter had come to meet him but were stuck in the ice to the south. In May of 1901, they were reunited for several months.

Peary, Henson, and four Eskimos went north from the northern tip of Ellesmere Island in April 1902. Deep snow and jumbled ice hindered movement, but they toiled on for three weeks until a storm halted them. Cracks opened in the ice and forced Peary to turn back. When he returned to America, the last of his toes were amputated.

Peary was discouraged. The expedition of 1898-1902, his fourth, had set a record for the farthest northern point reached in the North American Arctic—84°17′ N—but he had not matched the record of Fridtjof Nansen. In January of 1895, Nansen had reached 86°13′ N from the European side. Peary had not reached his goal, his mother had died in his absence, he was not expected to walk again, and he was forty-six years old. He felt failure and hopelessness. What more could he do?

Within months, though, Peary designed a ship to advance farther north in the ice. When the *Roosevelt* was complete, he sailed on his fifth voyage, the 1908-9 polar expedition. Peary and Henson reached northern Ellesmere Island by ship. Nansen's ship, the only one to go farther north, had not sailed but drifted while locked in the floating ice.

Peary sent groups out at intervals to set up supply stations for his dash to the pole, but when he set out himself, he found all the groups camped together. They were at the edge of an open water channel, called a lead, hoping that freezing cold or shifting currents would close it soon. This particular lead was a half-mile wide. Finally, it closed and they crossed. As they continued north for five more days, they had to wait at other leads. Supplies had dwindled, and Peary had to admit defeat.

On the way back, the big lead had shifted forty miles south. Peary's party found an ice bridge, but just before the first man reached the far side, it began to break through. The leader barely scrambled back in time, and the party retreated. After several more days, they found another bridge. As they snowshoed across, Peary's boots broke through the crust, and Peary feared for his life. His boots got soaked, but a slushy layer of ice below held, and he got across with only wet feet. Days later, they found one of their support parties lost and out of food. Hares and musk oxen sustained them on the journey back to their ship.

Peary had set a new record for northern travel—87°6' N. But Peary felt he was a failure. "I was only one in a long list of Arctic explorers, dating back through the centuries, all the way from Henry Hudson to the Duke of the Abruzzi, and including Franklin, Kane, and Melville—a long list of valiant men who had striven and failed. I told myself that I had only succeeded, at the price of the best years of my life, in adding a few links to the chain that led from the parallels of civilization towards the polar center, but that, after all, at the end the only word I had written was failure."

Though unsuccessful in reaching the pole, Peary had come within 174 miles of it and had learned valuable lessons. He had learned that Ellesmere Island surpassed Greenland as a starting point for expeditions. He had not foreseen the frequency of leads. He also now knew that supply stations would not work: leads could render them inaccessible and ice floes could drift, moving them far off course. As his ship sailed home and strength returned, Peary began modifying his tactical plans for another attempt the following year.

North Pole

Repairs on the *Roosevelt* required more time than Peary expected. The sixth expedition of 1908-9 reached the north end of

Ellesmere Island in September. Peary spent the next few months transporting supplies to Cape Columbia, where he would begin his journey on February 28, 1909.

Peary divided his men into four groups. Bob Bartlett led the first group, whose task was to break the trail. A few hours later, George Borup departed with the second group. They would travel three days, set up a supply station, and then return for more supplies. The next day, Peary left with the third group, and Henson led the fourth.

Sleds tilted and toppled among the jumbled ice blocks. Two sleds broke on the first day, and Peary progressed only ten miles from his starting point. He camped at two igloos left by Bartlett and surveyed the damage. The punctured fuel cans posed the most serious problem. Without fuel they could not obtain heat for cooking or drying. He would tell Borup to bring more fuel when he brought the second load of supplies.

Peary ended his second day waiting for a wide lead to close. It closed during the night, and in the morning his party crossed. On the other side, the Eskimos found Borup's tracks. Unfortunately, there were sets of tracks going north and south, which meant that Borup had already established a camp farther north and had begun his return south to get the second load. Peary recognized that they had missed Borup, upon whom he had been depending for more fuel. Peary sent Ross Marvin south as a lightly supplied messenger after Borup.

Peary's party advanced a bit but waited for almost a week at a wide lead. Meanwhile, Marvin had arrived at base while Borup was reloading. They would have to catch up with Peary to deliver the fuel, and they did not know he had been stopped by a lead. Borup and Marvin spent five days at a lead, fretting the whole time about getting farther behind.

The long wait in Peary's camp made the Eskimos restless. Some wanted to return to their families, and Peary permitted two to leave. When Borup and Marvin could finally cross their lead, they met the two Eskimos who put them on Peary's track and assured them that he was only a couple of days ahead. Peary, however, still had no news and decided to press on when the lead closed on March 11.

Peary saw a white cloud in the distance three days later. He sighed with relief because he knew that it was the condensation and snow flung into the air by a dog team. Borup and Marvin finally caught up with him and delivered the important fuel. The same day Peary released a number of men. He released more four days later, and on March 19, Borup himself departed. Borup had reached 85°23′ N on his first Arctic expedition. Marvin went back at 86°30′ N, but on his way back to Cape Columbia, he fell through thin ice and drowned in a lead.

Now, the main party consisted only of Peary and Henson, each with two Eskimos and two sleds. Following Bartlett enabled them to make good time—about fifteen miles a day. They caught up with Bartlett's group on March 28.

Creaking and cracking alerted the combined group to moving ice. Their campsite was breaking up! Peary and Henson quickly mushed their dogs across the growing gap, but Bartlett found himself stranded on a small ice floe. Amazingly, the two floes drifted together for a moment, and Bartlett drove his team across.

On March 31, Bartlett turned south from 88° N. He wanted to continue, but the food and fuel had been planned for his support party to come only this far. Peary and Henson selected forty of the best dogs and mushed northward with the four Eskimos. They passed 89° N on April 5 and camped within two miles of the pole. Peary shared his igloo with Egingwah and Segloo; Henson shared an igloo with Ootah and Ookeah.

Peary, Henson, and the four Eskimos traversed the last two miles on April 6, 1909. They continued beyond the pole until the compasses showed that they were walking south. Then they crisscrossed the area back to their igloos. Peary took thirteen measurements to make sure he had attained the long-sought-for North Pole.

Peary spent thirty hours at the pole. When he had raised the battered American flag that had come on all of his Arctic travels, he shook hands with his five companions. Peary also raised the flags of his college fraternity, the Navy League, the World Ensign, and the Red Cross. He gave the thirty-eight dogs a special dinner and took four different photos facing South: left toward the Bering

On the map:

Taimyr Peninsula

RUSSIA

Siberia

Kara Sea

Novaya Zemlya

Murmansk

FINLAND

Laptev Sea

Sevemaya Zemlya

Summer limit of the ice pack in the sea

NEW SIBERIAN ISLANDS

FRANZ JOSEF LAND

Barents Sea

SWEDEN

NORWAY

April 6, 1909
Peary arrives at North Pole

Svalbard

BEAR ISLAND

February 28, 1909
Peary departs for North Pole

North Pole

Bering Sea

Chukchi Sea

Bering Strait

Arctic Ocean

Greenland Sea

ICELAND

Alert

Reykjavik

Barrow

QUEEN ELIZABETH ISLANDS

ELLESMERE ISLAND

GREENLAND

ALASKA

Beaufort Sea

North Magnetic Pole

Thule

Fairbanks

Arctic Circle

VICTORIA ISLAND

BAFFIN ISLAND

Baffin Bay

CANADA

Iqaluit

North Atlantic Ocean

Strait, right toward Sptisbergen, the main island of Norway's Svalbard island group, back toward Cape Columbia, and ahead toward Cape Chelyuskin, the northernmost tip of Russia's Taimyr Peninsula. Finally, he wrote his wife a post card from 90° N.

My dear Jo, I have won at last. Have been here a day. I start for home and you in an hour. Love to the kidsies. —Bert

On April 7, Peary and Henson began the return trip, making a speed of twenty-three miles per day. When they reached land on April 23, they met two Eskimos who had been with Dr. Frederick Cook, a former teammate of Peary's who was making his own bid for the pole. The Eskimos confessed that Cook had coached them to tell of many days' travel over sea ice but admitted they had not left sight of land. Cook's fraudulent claim, however, captured the mind of the American public.

Peary telegraphed from Labrador, "Stars and Stripes Nailed to the Pole!" but Cook had telegraphed his success five days earlier. Cook claimed to have preceded Peary by a year, but his proofs were unconvincing. Abroad, the fraud was recognized, but most Americans believed Cook for decades. Cook was later sentenced to fourteen years in jail for an oil shares fraud. This finally convinced Americans that they should also question Cook's claims to Mount McKinley and the North Pole.

The grueling trip had taken its toll on both Peary and Henson. Matt Henson, usually a husky 155 pounds, had survived as a 112-pound shadow but soon recovered. Exhausted and embroiled in controversy, Peary grew discouraged. Peary published his story *The North Pole* in 1910. Two years later, Henson published his own account entitled *A Negro at the North Pole.*

Robert Peary died on February 20, 1920, in Washington, D.C., after three years of serious illness. Recognition finally came, and he was buried with full military honors. Henson outlived Peary by thirty-five years and became a member of the Explorer's Club in 1937. His body now rests beside Peary's in Arlington National Cemetery.

ROALD AMUNDSEN
Race to the South Pole

Antarctica's Winter

His hand slipped down the rescue line. The sailors on ship tried to pull in the line, but Carl Wienck floundered in the icy seawater. Fast losing strength in the Antarctic waters, his numbed fingers could not grip the line.

"Lower me down to him!" shouted Lieutenant Lecointe. Lecointe hoped to pass a rope around Wienck's waist so that he could be pulled in even without holding on. Two sailors lowered Lecointe toward the waves, and Lecointe reached for young Wienck.

The storm tossed the boat, and frigid waves engulfed Lecointe. Lecointe himself struggled against the lurching ship. The two sailors began to pull Lecointe back before they lost him too. Meanwhile, others drew Wienck to the side of the ship with the rescue line. They called to him to hold tight, but as they hauled up the line, his strength failed. Wienck slipped into the stormy sea.

Wienck's was the first death of the expedition to Antarctica led by Captain Adrien Victor Joseph de Gerlache of Belgium. The captain had purchased a Norwegian ship, renamed it *Belgica,* and signed on many Belgian countrymen for his crew, including his lieutenants. However, he also hired a Romanian zoologist, a Polish geologist, a Russian lab assistant, an American surgeon, and several Norwegian sailors, including Roald Engelbregt Gravning Amundsen, who had volunteered for the post of ship's mate without pay.

Belgica had sailed from Antwerp, Belgium, on August 16, 1897. The surgeon, Frederick Cook, a veteran polar explorer (see Robert Peary), had met them in Rio de Janeiro, Brazil. On December 1 some crew members had deserted at Punta Arenas in Chile's Tierra del Fuego. The remaining nineteen men had continued on December 14 after performing some scientific tests. They had entered Antarctic waters on January 20, 1898, two days before the storm.

The captain discovered Gerlache Strait along the Antarctic Peninsula the next day in calmer weather. They landed some twenty times, mostly on islands, one of which they named after Wienck. They crossed the Antarctic Circle on February 15. Two weeks later they entered the pack ice of the Bellingshausen Sea. They followed channels through the ice but ground to a halt around 71° S. After two days of trying to escape, on March 2 they knew they must winter in Antarctica—a feat never before attempted.

Very few had entered the Antarctic pack ice before. No one had even seen the continent before 1820. On January 27 of that year, the Russian Thaddeus von Bellingshausen sighted hills, and three days later England's Edward Bransfield sighted land. Neither knew that each had found a continent. Skepticism over the continent remained even after more land sightings and the voyage of American Lieutenant Charles Wilkes, which followed the coast for over twelve hundred miles. James Clark Ross had first penetrated the pack ice in 1841, and the next year he set the record for southern exploration at 78° S. Now *Belgica* drifted helplessly with the ice. The polar darkness came on May 17. There would be no glow of dawn for more than two months in the long winter of the Southern Hemisphere.

Lieutenant Danco's heart gave out on June 5. The crew buried him at sea through a hole cut in the ice. Dr. Cook fought scurvy by providing fresh meat—seal and penguin. No one liked the taste, but the captain set the example under the doctor's orders. He kept the men busy while the scientists took measurements. Spirits lifted with the first faint glow of sunlight on July 23. The ice beside the ship was still seven feet thick.

Amundsen, Cook, and Lecointe left the ship for a week to search for passages but without success. Coal and oil ran low. In October, a few small new channels quickly refroze. Some sailors grew incoherent and violent. Amundsen assisted the captain in restraining them. Dr. Cook treated them for "the onset of insanity." Christmas passed quietly, but on New Year's Eve, a lookout spotted open water seven hundred yards away. Using three saws and explosives, they worked thirty days to cut their way from the channel to the boat. As they freed blocks of ice, they pushed them into the icebound sea. By the end of the month, with only thirty yards to go, they watched in agony as a shift in the wind squeezed the passage out of existence.

"Captain de Gerlache!" The sailor on watch roused the sleeping captain at 2 A.M. on February 15, 1899. "The ice is shifting! Our channel is opening again! Hurry!" The captain started the engines for the first time in more than eleven months. With help from tow ropes, the *Belgica* eased through the channel into the open water. However, the open water was but a "lake" separated from the open sea by seven miles of ice. It was March 14 before they emerged from the pack ice. The net drift came to 17° W.

Of the two men who verged on insanity, Knutsen died shortly after their return home. The other, Tollefsen, eventually recovered with help from his countryman Roald Amundsen. Amundsen had learned valuable lessons about proper eating for battling the elements in Antarctica. He could also now claim to have been in the first party to survive an Antarctic winter.

Arctic Passages

Death . . . not the Black Death of disease but the frozen White Death of the Arctic. Two ships under Hugh Willoughby became trapped in the Northeast Passage, and their entire crews perished in 1553. Two out of three of Martin Frobisher's crews perished in their fruitless quest for the Northwest Passage in 1576. Willem Barents and his ship became frozen in the ice near Spitsbergen. A few of his men found a refuge in Lapland, but Barents and most of the crew died in 1597. Henry Hudson and six loyal men were set adrift in the Northwest Passage after the crew mutinied in 1611. John Franklin's two ships became trapped in the ice, and the crews perished from hunger and scurvy in 1848.

Roald Amundsen set sail in 1903 to achieve what so many others had died trying to do. Roald, born July 16, 1872, in Borge, near Oslo, Norway, entered the Northwest Passage in a small ship, the *Gjöa,* with a crew of six. They battled arctic conditions for three years until they finally reached the Bering Sea in 1906. Amundsen had learned more important polar lessons: the importance of proper clothing and the value of dogsleds.

Amundsen then navigated the Northeast Passage from 1918 to 1920. Nils Nordenskjöld, a Finn banished to Sweden, had preceded him in 1878-79. Though second to navigate this passage, Amundsen was first to navigate both passages along the coasts of the Arctic Ocean.

The Race to the South Pole Begins

Hopes dashed, Amundsen reread the article in the *New York Times:* "Robert Peary reaches the North Pole on April 6, 1909." Amundsen had spent a year raising funds from America and from London's Royal Geographic Society for a North Pole expedition. Help from these sources had shamed his Norwegian government into providing more funds. Amundsen had mortgaged his house for the remaining funds. He had also visited famous Norwegian explorer Fridtjof Nansen (1861-1930) and borrowed his ship, the *Fram.*

Nansen had crossed Greenland in 1888, and in his *Fram* had become the first to drift across the Arctic Ocean while locked in polar ice from 1893 to 1896. Now *Fram* could take Amundsen toward the pole, but the quest had been attained by another.

"If the North Pole is discovered, I will head for the South!" thought Amundsen. Within two weeks he read another news item in London's *Times:* "Robert Falcon Scott is preparing an expedition to conquer the South Pole." Amundsen knew that Scott, born in 1868 in Devonshire, England, had been on a previous expedition to reach the pole from 1901 to 1904. Scott, with Ernest Shackleton and Edward Wilson, had reached 82° S. Scott had set the record for the farthest south, so his next attempt could easily succeed. Amundsen would have to move fast.

Scott's ship, the *Terra Nova*, left London on June 1, 1910. He brought Siberian ponies as he had done on his journey with Shackleton. This time, though, he included some motorized vehicles and dogs.

Meanwhile, Amundsen prepared carefully, not forgetting the lessons of his previous expeditions. He carefully planned for food, clothing, and sleds. He embarked with ninety-seven hardy sled dogs from northern Greenland and a carefully selected crew of nineteen. At Madeira, on September 6, 1910, he finally announced his change of plans to his crew, all of whom agreed to continue. Two weeks later he sent letters to the king of Norway and to Nansen to explain his change of plans and to apologize for taking such liberty. He also telegrammed Scott of *Fram*'s move for the Antarctic.

Scott, after stops in South Africa and Australia, received the telegram at his last stop in Port Chalmers, New Zealand. He took ship again on November 29. He reached the Ross Ice Shelf and landed at Cape Evans on Ross Island on January 4, 1911. Amundsen arrived at the Bay of Whales on January 14, 1911. The next morning, Amundsen's crew began three weeks of shuttling supplies to set up their base camp called Framheim two miles away on the Ross Ice Shelf. Scott's crew finished their supply hut on January 17.

Both parties had come to the Ross Sea because, of the two largest indentations into the Antarctic continent, the Ross Sea permits greater penetration by ship. The names of the sea and ice shelf honor British explorer James Clark Ross, who discovered them and who from 1839 to 1842 became the first man to venture beyond the pack ice. Both expeditions would cross the vast Ross Ice Shelf, though at opposite sides. The shelf rises two hundred feet above the sea and is the largest ice shelf in the world. In summer, the shelf melts along the edges and separates from the continent, making it the largest iceberg in the world.

Amundsen selected the Bay of Whales because it is sixty miles farther south than Ross Island. Scott selected Ross Island, following the route of his previous attempt to the pole with Shackleton. The expedition's scientists also wanted to research a penguin colony at the west end of Ross Island. At the time, Mount Erebus at 12,224 feet on Ross Island was the highest known peak and the most active volcano in Antarctica. Shackleton had first climbed the summit in 1908 and had seen a crater 900 feet deep.

Now both expeditions concentrated on setting up supply camps with the short days remaining before the polar winter. Scott made his first outpost thirty-five miles away, but the ponies struggled in the deep snow. Scott sent part of his group and three exhausted ponies back. He pushed on through the blizzard to establish his final outpost at 78°28.5′ S. When he returned to base on March 14, he learned that one of his scientific teams had found Amundsen's ship at the Bay of Whales. All of Scott's scientific expeditions had returned by May 13.

Meanwhile, Amundsen had used dogsleds to establish supply stations at 80° S and 81° S. He had learned from the Eskimos the value of dogsledding, or mushing. By April 21, at the onset of darkness, Amundsen had returned to base after establishing a final outpost with 1.5 tons of supplies at 82° S—only 480 miles from the pole.

Both groups spent the long winter months doing chores. Amundsen's team spent the months overhauling gear and caring for the dogs. They played darts and other games in their leisure moments. When the sun rose again on August 24, they packed the sleds carefully to keep them as light as possible. Scott's men also spent time with equipment and caring for animals, as well as recording barometer, thermometer, and other readings. Each group spent time wondering about the other group. Would Scott or Amundsen reach the pole first? Would Britain or Norway claim the honor? The stage was set and the race was on.

Victory and Defeat

Amundsen left September 8 on a run to the first camp. After three days of good progress, the temperature plunged to -69°F. Two sled dogs froze to death. Temperatures fell farther and the compass fluid froze. They returned to base after dropping off supplies. On October 20, Amundsen set out a second time with four men: Olav Bjaaland, Svere Hassel, Helmer Hanssen, and Oscar Wisting. They traveled on skis while the dogs pulled the supplies. The four sleds with thirteen dogs apiece made twenty miles a day in just five hours of travel. Finding a snow mound from the previous summer, they decided to build one daily to mark their route. Using an hour or so to build the snow mound, they still had plenty of time to eat and rest. On November 4, they arrived at the last outpost and spent two days preparing for the final run.

Scott set out for the pole on November 1. He sent four men ahead in the motorized vehicles, and he and nine other men followed with the ten ponies. His last two men left later with two sleds and twenty-three dogs. Scott's ponies could not get through the blizzard, so they stopped to wait it out and were surprised when the dogsleds easily caught up with them. By November 21, the combined pony and dog groups caught the initial group at 80°30′ S. When the motorized vehicles became stuck in the snow, the first group began a man haul. The men dragged the sleds using ropes around their waists.

Both groups had to climb from the Ross Ice Shelf onto the continent's mainland. Each would ascend a glacier through the mountains for this purpose. Amundsen camped at the base of the Axel Heiberg Glacier on November 14. He named the range of peaks the Queen Maud Mountains after Norway's queen. With forty-two dogs and 340 miles left, he developed a strategy.

Scott arrived at the Beardmore Glacier, the largest known glacier in the world, on December 1. His party holed up for several days in a blizzard and had to shoot the last of the barely surviving ponies. Scott sent four men back with the dogs, and the team felt relieved of the burden of the animals. From here on it would be manpower alone. Scott had also brought a champion skier, but none of the men had bothered to learn from him. Now, they all struggled on unfamiliar skis through difficult glacial terrain. They set a final supply depot at the top of the glacier on December 21 and sent the support crew back to base camp. At the last minute, Scott asked Henry Bowers to accompany him to the pole along with Edward Wilson, Edgar Evans, and Lawrence Oates. The fifth man left the party returning to base camp short-handed and would soon strain the supplies intended for four.

Amundsen gained the top of the range on November 21. This was as far as the ton of supplies brought by the dogs would go. He shot twenty-four of the dogs, as planned, both to reduce the number

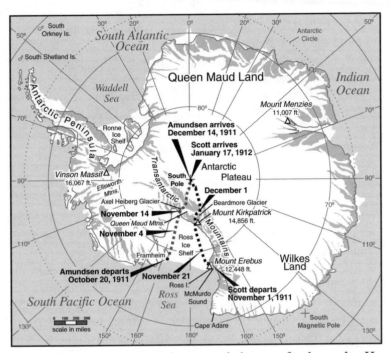

of mouths to feed and to increase their own food supply. He remained four days, hoping that the blizzard would subside, but by November 25, he felt constrained to advance into the driving snow.

Winds bit at Amundsen's face and howled across the snow at thirty-five miles per hour. For ten days, blinding snows and fogs limited visibility. As they struggled to the Antarctic Plateau, they struck out hopefully, only to find that the thin crust of ice hid a maze of crevasses. Each time that man, dog, or sled fell through the crust into a deep crevasse, the party stopped to fish him out with ropes. Their frostbitten faces showed pain and tension on December 8 when they matched Shackleton's southernmost record. Crevasses behind, Amundsen looked ahead over the frozen white waste, wondering if Scott was already at the goal only ninety-five miles away.

On December 14, 1911, Amundsen's group arrived at the pole. It was 3:00 P.M. when their instruments showed that they had arrived. They had come 714 miles in fifty-seven days. They stayed three days for observations to confirm their location. They also sent three men out for twelve miles in different directions to be sure that they had circled it. They looked for signs of Scott but found none. Each man grasped the Norwegian flag as they proudly planted it at the South Pole. One of the men photographed Amundsen on skis with his sled and dogs at the pole. They erected a small tent, left a note for Scott, and shot six more dogs. Amundsen wrote in his diary, "So we arrived and were able to plant our flag at the geographical South Pole. God be thanked!"

As Scott's party approached the pole, Bowers first saw the dark speck of the flag against the white background. They arrived at the pole on January 17, 1912, after seventy-eight days of toil and suffering, crossing 774 miles of snow. Now, disappointment added to their misery, but they spent two days at the pole and photographed themselves with the British flag.

Amundsen's return to Base Camp went very fast. With no supplies to haul and all their needs provided for at supply stations, they returned to Base Camp in only forty days. The five men came into the base camp with eleven dogs on January 25, 1912. They departed immediately for Tasmania.

In Scott's group, the imbalanced diet caused scurvy, and Evans's condition became critical. Wilson, a Christian, helped him, but Scott halted on February 8 for two days to obtain thirty-five pounds of rocks for geologists. The samples increased the heavy burdens each man hauled. At the base of the Beardmore Glacier, Evans had become delirious. He fell asleep on February 17 but did not awaken the next morning. Soon, Oates also began to deteriorate from frostbite. The strained food supply weakened Oates more as the party advanced only twenty-four miles in the next four days. His frostbitten feet turned black and soon became gangrenous. By March 16 at 80° S, Oates had become irrational. That night he went out into the blizzard to stretch and never returned.

Scott, Wilson, and Bowers continued. By March 21, they could not advance through the fierce windstorm. They pitched a camp and settled in. By the next day they had run out of both food and fuel. Scott's diary ends on March 29 with the words "the end cannot be far."

The scientific teams on Scott's expedition also had problems. Ice blocked their ship from reaching the team that explored the coast to Cape Adare on February 18, 1912. The six men spent the Antarctic winter in a small snow cave. One man managed to kill a seal, and they survived on the seal meat and the thirty-six fish from its stomach. They reached base camp November 7, shortly after a search team found the bodies of Scott, Wilson, and Bowers with their diaries. The bodies had been only eleven miles from the supplies at their outpost camp.

Arctic Aloft

Amundsen, with American Lincoln Ellsworth (1880-1951) and Italian Umberto Nobile (1885-1978), crossed the North Pole in the dirigible *Norge* on May 8, 1926. Nobile, the designer, piloted *Norge* for seventy-two hours as they crossed the 3,393 miles from Spitsbergen to Alaska. Their success came two days after American Admiral Richard E. Byrd flew over the pole in an airplane. Thus, Amundsen had not been the first to make the air crossing, but he was the first to do so by balloon. The ballooning feat had been attempted before by the Swede Salomon August Andrée and two friends. They had traveled sixty-six hours on July 11, 1897, but crashed on the ice in a storm, and their bodies and diaries were found thirty-three years later.

Amundsen's life ended in June of 1928. Nobile had been lost ballooning across the Arctic, and Amundsen went out as part of a search party. During the search, Nobile was rescued, but Amundsen disappeared without a trace.

NORBERT CASTERET
The First Cave Diver

Grotto of Montespan

"It's impossible!" affirmed two strong teenage boys. Their father warned Casteret that his younger son had almost drowned attempting to enter the cave. Forcing a way through the river into the cave would be extremely dangerous, but the word *impossible* sparked Norbert Casteret with a challenge.

Two days later, on August 18, 1922, Norbert Casteret of France climbed to a window-sized opening in the mountain from which a powerful stream issued. In swimming trunks, Casteret pushed himself into the hole, keeping his head near the top of the hole above stream level. He grabbed at the rocks around him to hold himself against the force of the stream and then pushed himself forward with arms and legs. In a few minutes, he found himself in a cave with a ten-foot ceiling.

Casteret waded upstream and around bends by candlelight. The cave roof dipped, forcing him to hunker down to pass through. The roof rose again briefly and then plunged right into the river around the next bend. He had hoped to find evidence of human habitation, but Casteret faced a dead end. Or did he?

Casteret wondered where the river came from. Did the water fill an underground tunnel for several miles? Even if the passage were not filled with water everywhere, would it remain large enough for him to pass through? Would there be tangles of branches where a person could get caught? Would it gradually get deeper, or would he get lost in a maze of passages?

Casteret knew he could hold his breath for three minutes relaxing or two minutes swimming. If he went forward underwater, he would have a full minute to find an air pocket before he would have to turn back or risk drowning by pushing on. He carefully set his burning candle on a ledge of rock.

Casteret hunched over and plunged himself into the cold water. The blackness of the cave enclosed him, and he moved hurriedly upstream. He held one hand before him to identify obstructions. The other hand he kept in contact with the roof to guide him and to search for air pockets. Caught up in the darkness, he could not tell how much time had elapsed. Fear flooded over him, but he struggled upstream, knowing that drowning alone in the dark was but seconds away.

Casteret's hand broke the surface, and he immediately stood up straight. He breathed deeply and thrilled with a sense of victory. Though the water lapped at his chin and he could see nothing, to his knowledge never before had anyone entered a cave through a water-filled passage—a sump. He had just dived the first sump in history, thereby inventing a new and dangerous cave-exploring technique.

On the other hand, seeing nothing, he could not know if he was in a room or a junction of passages. If he were not careful, he could easily become disoriented in the blackness and never find his way back. He determined to bring more candles tomorrow and immediately took a deep breath and returned the way he had come. He retrieved his still-burning candle and exited the cave into the light of day.

The next afternoon, having said nothing of his adventure, Casteret returned with more candles, matches in a waterproof box, and a tight rubber bathing cap. Placing a new candle on the ledge, he dove through the sump a second time and returned to his air pocket. Carefully removing a candle and a match from under the bathing cap, he lit the candle and saw that the narrow layer of air between water and ceiling continued around the next bend. Wading chin deep through the river and holding his candle aloft, he headed upstream and soon entered a large room. He crawled up on the bank but shivered as the cold underground air hit his wet body. The water felt warmer than the air.

Casteret moved upstream along the bank, but the narrowing passage soon forced him back into the water. Soon the roof descended to another sump. He left another candle lit on the bank and plunged in again. Instead of smooth walls, this passage had many projections. He tried to ignore the bumps and scrapes so as not to gasp out his precious breath. He knew he should not be spelunking (cave exploring) without a partner. If he injured himself on the projections, or worse, if he simply got his matches wet, he would probably die. There could be no rescue.

With a deep breath, he entered the sump and surfaced in a smaller room, where he lit another candle and continued upstream. In this small chamber, water dripped from overhead like rain. More than once, droplets extinguished his flame, and he had to relight his candle. Soon the chamber diminished in size, forcing him to crawl, and eventually its narrowness forced him to advance sideways. The passage soon became extremely small and narrow, and he gazed at a hole through which he knew he could not fit. Disappointed, he realized his journey must end here.

He poked his head through the hole and saw a pool clogged with mud and branches. Removing his head from the hole, he inserted his hand and scooped water with his cupped palm. Twigs underground made him suspicious, and indeed he could see tadpoles swimming around in his palm. Twigs and tadpoles meant that the water entered the cave from outside just a few feet beyond. This explained why the water was warmer than the air in the cave. As he retraced his route, he found a bison tooth. The tooth excited him, since bison had not lived in France in recorded history, and no bison could have traversed the cave passages anyway. The tooth proved that humans had once brought the tooth to the cave to fashion it into a tool. By the time Casteret left the cave, it was dark; he had spent five hours there.

Casteret returned to the cave in the fall, but the melting snows had turned the stream into a torrent that completely filled the mouth of the cave. Impatiently, he awaited the summer, when he returned with his friend Henri Godin. This time they explored the side passages in the large room.

Together, they negotiated the constricting passage. First, they had to stoop, then crawl, and finally slide along on their stomachs. They wriggled along the tight passage, being careful not to bump the roof. They could neither turn around nor move in any direction but forward. If they reached a dead end, they would have to squirm out backwards.

After one hundred feet of slithering, they arrived in a large room where they could stand. Casteret began scraping away the clay caked on one of the walls and found a flint tool—further evidence that humans had once used the cave. Excited by the find, Godin began to chip away the clay while Casteret began to inspect the passage by candlelight. Soon he noticed clay statues of bears, horses, and lions. Godin found cave paintings of lions, bears, horses, wild asses, hyenas, stags, ibexes, and chamois. Some of the paintings depicted animals extinct in southern France: reindeer, bison, and even mammoths. After several days of visiting, they uncovered bones of horses, bisons, bears, snakes, and reindeer, together with bone spatulas, various flint tools, thirty clay statues, and fifty paintings.

Ice Caves of the Pyrenees

After his first successful sump dives and findings of cave paintings, Casteret went seeking caves with his mother, brother, and wife, Elisabeth, whom he had married in 1924. They climbed high into the Pyrenees Mountains to the Cirque de Gavarnie, where a natural amphitheater sports France's highest waterfall. From here, they crossed into Spain and spotted an opening up on the ice. Wielding axes, they cut steps into the ice to ascend to the opening, which indeed turned out to be a cave. Standing in the opening, they looked down at a frozen underground lake. They walked out on the lake by candlelight but were forced to a stop by a wall of ice.

Two months after that first visit of July 28, 1926, Casteret and Elisabeth returned and climbed over the wall and into hallways of ice through small ice passages. They marveled as they viewed the subterranean glacier—the river of ice beyond the lake—and eventually came out at an opening on the other side of the mountain. They had made a complete trip through the world's highest ice caves.

Casteret returned to Casteret Grotto again in 1950, though he had now been a widower for ten years. This time he brought his daughters, Maud and Gilberte.

Maud felt herself slipping. She had begun crawling to explore under a low ledge. Only her feet remained under the ledge when her head poked through the small hole into a room. The ice tilted downward, and she felt herself slipping. She jerked abruptly trying to stop her slide, but the glassy ice offered no handhold. She was face first and could not see the bottom.

Her father, seeing her speed and struggle, grabbed her feet just before they disappeared from sight. He called to her, and she described the icefall below her. Still held by her father, she grabbed a loose chunk of ice and threw it down the icefall. The chunk fell seventy feet and set off the echoes of a large cavern. Maud had discovered a new room in Casteret Grotto. Using ladders, they descended to admire the 170-foot-wide "Frozen Niagara" from below, over which Maud had almost plummeted with no barrel. They enjoyed the tall columns and intricate draperies reminiscent of ice castle fairylands, but the icy winds limited their time in the cavern. They also discovered some new caverns higher up the mountain, where two bats and an ermine had become frozen in icy death.

Casteret visited over one thousand caves in his lifetime. Many of these caves were in the Pyrenees Mountains of Spain and France. Casteret was born on August 19, 1897, in the department (county) of France called Haute-Garonne. His home was only two miles from Hyena's Lair in the Cavern of Montsaunes. Early in 1947 he visited Lascaux Cave, which had been discovered by teenagers and contains the world's most famous cave paintings.

Seven months later, he spent six nights in the Cave of the Dead Woman (La Henne Morte). Many descents on suspended aluminum ladders took him 1,463 feet deep into the earth. One descent was beside a splashing waterfall, which sprayed everywhere and frequently extinguished the lantern. He had to carefully relight the lantern while dangling precariously from the slippery ladders.

Expedition finds included a bat colony one thousand feet down as well as human footprints.

In 1953, Casteret descended into the Cavern of Pierre Saint-Martin. The entrance to this cave is a vertical pit about 1,050 feet deep. Marcel Loubens had fallen to his death in this pit in 1952, and Casteret could see the entombed body at the bottom of the pit. (The body was finally retrieved in 1954.) From the bottom of the pit, he descended more steep passages into what was then considered the deepest cave in the world. At a depth of 2,230 feet, he discovered the La Verna chamber, which is the largest cave room in Europe. The vast room is 660 feet long, 390 feet wide, and 330 feet high; each dimension exceeds the length of a football field.

Between 1956 and 1960 Casteret discovered four more caves near the Cave of the Dead Woman. As he explored these caves, he found passages connecting them with the Cave of the Dead Woman. The complex cave system came to be known as the *système de la Coumo d'Hyouernèdo*. Today over thirty entrances are known to this system, which descends about thirty-three hundred feet below the surface. Casteret died in 1987.

A. F. TSCHIFFELY
Horseback Across Two Continents

South America

"Que loco!" muttered the photographer for the Buenos Aires newspaper. The phrase was Spanish for "how crazy" and expressed the opinion that a man planning to ride a horse all the way to New York City must certainly be a lunatic. He added, "You will never survive Santiago del Estero, but even if you get out of Argentina, you will die in the mountains of Bolivia and never see La Paz."

A. F. Tschiffely ignored the insult and finished adjusting the packsaddle on Mancha. He had heard it all before from experienced horsemen, but he was about to begin the adventure of his dreams, and he had not ignored the dangers. He had been a British school-teacher before moving to Argentina, and now he wanted a break from teaching. Mounting Gato and leading Mancha, he left the capital and its critics behind on April 23, 1925.

Tschiffely saw the white ground fade into the distance ahead. The white was the salt flats of the dreaded desert Santiago del Estero. He was thirsty and so were his horses. He depended on finding water because carrying enough water would weigh too much. It had taken several days to reach Rosario, where he had spent twelve days waiting for heavy rains to end. Now amidst the cacti and scrubby bushes, he wished for those rains again. Thirst was constant during the long rides from dawn to dusk for ten straight days across the desert.

At Tucumán, with the desert behind, the horses rested. Both horses' names derived from their colors. The name for Mancha, a sixteen-year-old pinto, was short for *manchado* meaning "stained" because of his white color with red splotches. Gato, meaning "cat," was short for *gateado,* which means "cat colored" because of the fifteen-year-old buckskin's dark brown coffee color.

Tschiffely had told Dr. Solanet, a breeder of Argentine Creole horses, about his plans. Dr. Solanet had bought thirty horses from Chief Liempichun, a Tehuelche Indian of Patagonia. The Creole horses were wild descendants of horses brought from Spain in 1535 at the founding of Buenos Aires. The horses had learned survival in Patagonia and could withstand frost and scorching sands without coverings. Dr. Solanet had convinced Tschiffely that the small horses (only fourteen hands high) were the toughest horses anywhere.

For several years Tschiffely had spent all his school vacations breaking the wild horses and getting used to long rides. The horses had been fearful when they saw the cars and buildings of Buenos Aires. At first, they had even ignored the alfafa and barley provided in the stables and had eaten their straw bedding instead. Mancha especially, never let anyone saddle him except Tschiffely. Gato and Mancha almost seemed to prefer the wild desert to the busy city. But soon they were back in the country.

Splash! Gato slipped as he forded a river. Both horse and rider fell into the water and slid down the shallow rapids into a pool. Fortunately, no injuries resulted, and Mancha waited on the far side until the drenched pair regained dry ground.

Another day, a thorn pierced Tschiffely's right hand, and by the next day he recognized signs of a serious case of blood poisoning. Soon both hands were in pain. His right leg became so swollen that he could not wear his boot. His nose began bleeding. It took six days of travel to reach Tres Cruzes, where he spent four weeks without improving. The cramped horses could not be released to graze because of the deadly poisonous *mio mio* weed in the region. The only doctor in town told him to return to Buenos Aires, but Tschiffely rode on in misery.

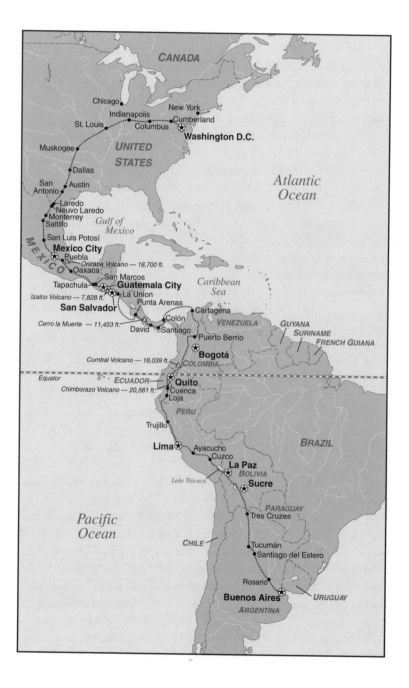

CANADA

Chicago
New York
Indianapolis
St. Louis
Cumberland
Columbus
Washington D.C.

UNITED
STATES

Muskogee

*Atlantic
Ocean*

Dallas

San
Antonio
Austin

Laredo
Neuvo Laredo
Monterrey
Saltillo

*Gulf of
Mexico*

San Luis Potosí

Mexico City
Puebla
Orizaba Volcano — 18,700 ft.
Oaxaca
San Marcos
*Caribbean
Sea*

Tapachula
Guatemala City
Izalco Volcano — 7,828 ft.
La Union
San Salvador
Punta Arenas
Cartagena

Cerro la Muerte — 11,453 ft.
Colón
David
Santiago
VENEZUELA
GUYANA
SURINAME
FRENCH GUIANA

Puerto Berrio
Bogotá

Cumbal Volcano — 16,039 ft.
COLOMBIA

Equator
ECUADOR
Quito
Chimborazo Volcano — 20,561 ft.
Cuenca
Loja

PERU

Trujillo

BRAZIL

Lima
Ayacucho
Cuzco
La Paz
BOLIVIA
Lake Titicaca
Sucre

*Pacific
Ocean*

PARAGUAY
Tres Cruzes

CHILE
Tucumán
Santiago del Estero

Rosario
Buenos Aires
URUGUAY
ARGENTINA

M E X I C O

Among the Aymara Indians of Bolivia, Tschiffely heard of an Indian herb doctor. In five days, the doctor's herbs had cured both his fever and the swelling. Tschiffely showed his appreciation by paying five times the tiny fee charged by the doctor. After several weeks among the Aymara on Bolivia's high plains, he rode on to La Paz, where he visited the Argentine ambassador and rested a few days.

Tschiffely stared at a huge stone idol. Had he been suddenly transported to the Orient? No, two days beyond La Paz he had arrived at Lake Titicaca, the largest lake in South America, requiring twelve hours to cross by steamer. The lake is also the highest navigable lake in the world—11,400 feet in elevation. The idols and ruins of the city of Tiahuanaco, older than the Inca Empire, lay crumbling near the shore.

The ruins consisted of huge stone blocks carefully fitted together, much like the stonework of the pyramids of Egypt. Strange carvings adorned the Gate of the Sun, and rows of pillars lined the ancient temple platform. As he followed the lakeshore north into Peru, Tschiffely watched Aymara Indians ply the lake in reed boats like those shown on the ruins.

Once Gato refused to cross a shallow creek. Tschiffely hit the stubborn horse, but Gato just reared and snorted. Soon an Indian came and said the horse was right. The pool looked safe, only four inches deep, but the bottom was quicksand. Gato's instincts had saved their lives.

After visiting the great Inca capital, Cuzco, and the nearby Inca ruins of Ollantaytambo and Pisacc, Tschiffely began to cross the Andes. He climbed the high passes on steep, tortuous trails and descended the switchbacks into deep canyons. He traveled through winding gorges and across narrow windswept ledges. On one such ledge Gato slipped and fell down the scree; he was stopped at the edge of a steep cliff by a lone tree. Poor Gato's fearful neighing continued the entire time it took to attach ropes and haul him to safety.

In the deep tropical valleys, vampire bats abounded. Tschiffely rubbed his horses with crushed garlic or sprinkled them with Indian pepper to keep the bats away. Occasionally, however, in the morning after he had failed to apply these remedies the night before, he would find big blood clots on the horses' backs and necks where the bats had feasted. Bats often trick the horses by fanning them with their wings in the tropical heat, which offsets the pinprick bite. They fan with their wings the entire time they suck blood and then fly off bloated.

Tschiffely entered the third and last range of the Andes, and he was glad that he had hired an Indian guide at Ayacucho. The rainy season had brought landslides, which necessitated rerouting through the maze of Indian trails. The flash floods had swollen the streams, some of which could be crossed on rope bridges hanging high over the gorges, but others had to be avoided. After the guide left him, Tschiffely found his way into several small towns, and eventually, passing near several American mining installations and the highest railway station in the world, he arrived at Lima.

Tschiffely stayed at Lima for three weeks, both to rest and to readjust to the hot lowland climate. While in Lima, he watched several bullfights but did not enjoy seeing the horses being injured. He also visited the tomb of Pizarro, whose body may be viewed through glass in one of the most magnificent cathedrals in South America.

He reached the Pacific Ocean at Ancón, where skeletons from Peru's final clash with Chile litter the sands. From here to the border of Ecuador, Tschiffely followed the coast through the Peruvian deserts. Where possible, to protect against sinking in the hot, sandy dunes, he led the horses along the wet beach. In spite of a local bubonic plague outbreak, he waited at the edge of a ninety-six-mile desert called Matacaballo (horse killer) for four days until there was a full moon. After the horses drank deeply, they crossed the river, entering the desert at 6:00 P.M. They galloped along the shore at times, rested during fogs, and detoured inland at rocky coasts, guided by the full moon. At sunrise, the heat increased, and by noon it had become a scorcher. An hour later the horses sniffed the air and quickened their pace. After another hour, they came to the river at the end of the Matacaballo. The horses had smelled the water an hour before. They had crossed the desert in twenty hours.

Near Trujillo, Tschiffely visited the ruins of Chan Chan. This adobe city spreads over six square miles. It served as the capital of the mysterious Chimu Empire of the twelfth century, which once controlled six hundred miles of the coast. The people of Chan Chan must have been good engineers to provide enough fresh water for such a large city in the dry coastal desert. Their city had been decorated with carvings and gold panels. Ruins of two other nearby temples built by the Mochica people are even older.

When Tschiffely soon came to the Rio Santa, it was in flood stage. Everyone told him the horses would die crossing and that he should wait for lower water. A local official forbade him from crossing on the grounds that suicide is illegal. He asked advice from the best river runner in the area and learned that there was only one safe landing place on the far side if they wanted to avoid being swept out to sea. For a large fee, the man swam across with the horses and arrived at the far bank a half-mile downstream. Meanwhile, Tschiffely crossed the river with his gear in a small basket on a line strung across the river.

When Tschiffely reached Ecuador's swampy coast, he took to the mountains. As he traveled the muddy paths near Loja, Victor, a sixteen-year-old Indian orphan, began watching him and helping around camp. The governor supplied papers and encouraged Tschiffely to take the boy with him. After Victor had walked several days alongside the horses without complaint, Tschiffely bought him a pony and some clothing.

Victor's excitement at the new sights refreshed Tschiffely. The boy marveled at trains and tunnels. They shared awe at the huge condors circling overhead near the majestic snowy volcanic peaks of Chimborazo and Cotopaxi. Victor's amazement at the big town of Cuenca was far surpassed when they entered his first big city, Quito, where they spent three weeks. Two days after leaving Quito, they celebrated crossing the equator, a concept none too clear in Victor's mind.

Tschiffely and Victor crossed Rumichaca, or Stone Bridge in the Quechua tongue, a natural bridge over the river that divides Ecuador from Colombia. On the bridge a customs officer checked their papers. Food was scarce in Colombia's dry season, and several times they fed the horses sugar cane, bamboo, or even yucca.

As Tschiffely proceeded north, he learned that huge swamps spanned the border with Panama. General Jaramillo, who had explored the swamps for twenty-five years, had been unable to cross with his troops in the war with Panama. He had found no dry land at all there, and much of the area had still never been seen by human eyes. Further progress would have to be by ship, and they booked river passage from Puerto Berrio to Calamar near Barranquilla, and then ocean passage from nearby Cartagena to Colón on the Panama Canal. Though disappointed, Tschiffely saw no other alternatives.

North America

Arriving in Colón in November, Victor was immediately hospitalized for malaria. Released by January but too weak to continue north, he obtained a job in a mechanical workshop. When Tschiffely crossed the canal in early January to proceed north, Mancha suffered a cut that rendered him lame.

Tschiffely had waited for the dry season in January to tackle the jungles, but he had to wait until the end of the month for Mancha to heal. Following good roads to Santiago and jungle trails to David, he hired a native to accompany him through the trackless jungles into Costa Rica. They saw monkeys, wild turkeys, alligators, tapirs, and tiger tracks as they cut their way with machetes through the thick underbrush. The rains made their gear perpetually wet, and they had to use jungle creepers to repair rotted straps and ropes. They crossed the Continental Divide to Palmares, and from the top of Cerro de la Muerte (Death Mountain), 11,500 feet high, they could see both the Atlantic and Pacific Oceans. Descending, they arrived several days later in San José and stayed for three weeks.

Tschiffely, after paying his guide a handsome sum and sending him home by boat to Panama, found it necessary to travel by ship himself. The easy ride across Nicaragua would have to be bypassed because of revolution. This was another disappointment, but he could not justify risking his horses in the midst of guerrilla fighting.

He sailed with his horses from the nearby port of Punta Arenas to La Unión in El Salvador.

At the Rio Lempa, Tschiffely took advantage of the first ferry-boat service they had found at any large river crossing. After seeing San Salvador, the capital, and the Lagoon of Coatepeque, a lake in a volcanic crater, he crossed the border into Guatemala.

Tschiffely followed a road from the border to Guatemala City. He visited the ruins of Guatemala Antigua (Old Guatemala), which had been destroyed by volcanic eruptions long ago. From there he followed a road to San Marcos and then descended to the bridge at the Mexican border. He spent an entire month at the first major town, Tapachula, waiting for Gato to recover from an injury received from a mule kick, but he ended up sending Gato to a veterinarian in Mexico City.

Tschiffely rode Mancha alone to Mexico City. First, he hired a guide to traverse the swampy regions of the coast of the state of Chiapas. In this area, a delicacy, boiled iguana, was a welcome change to the steady diet of frijoles (beans) and tortillas, the staples throughout Central America. Next, a military escort rode with him to Oaxaca as protection from revolutionaries. During his week in Oaxaca, he took a side trip to see the ancient ruins of Mitla with snowcapped Orizaba rising in the background. Finally, a good road speeded him along from Puebla to Mexico City in just three days.

Mexico City gave Tschiffely the grandest reception of the entire trip. They brought Gato, fully recuperated, out to meet him and entertained the adventurer for three weeks. This nation of horsemen, called *charros,* appreciated Tschiffely's feat more than did the people anywhere else he visited. They even had him ride Mancha in the role of honor in the opening ceremonies to the bullfight. Later, the press held a banquet for him at nearby Xochimilco, "the Venice of Mexico."

Of course, his many new friends brought him to visit the huge pyramid and Olmec ruins at nearby Teotihuacán. Teotihuacán means "City of the Gods" in the Aztec language, and its ruins date from before the time of Christ. In fact, by A.D. 500 the city of a hundred thousand people was larger than imperial Rome and certainly the largest in Middle America. The Pyramid of the Sun rises to 240 feet in five terraces, and has the largest base of any pyramid in the world (720 by 760 ft.).

As a finale, they brought Tschiffely to the summit of Cerro de la Estrella (Mountain of the Stars) in the wee hours before dawn. From here he enjoyed a grand view of the lights of the city below, the stars above, and a dramatic sunrise. When he departed, the city officials mounted on horses and accompanied him for the first ten miles north.

Many other Mexican cities, such as San Juan del Rio and Querétaro, gave warm receptions too. In fact, San Luis Potosí held a week of festivities in his honor. As Tschiffely entered his third major desert, the continuous celebration even at small towns finally ended. He had to limit himself to one meal a day, and he was spending Christmas in a desert, but he was able to travel quickly by paralleling the railway to Saltillo. Two days later he arrived in Monterey and then continued to Nuevo Laredo.

Tschiffely crossed the Rio Grande into Laredo, Texas. It was his first visit to the United States of America. Laredo, San Antonio, Austin, and Dallas each welcomed him, and he enjoyed seeing his first cowboy rodeo during his three weeks in San Antonio. Now he could compare the tough frontier riders of the Americas: Argentine gauchos, Mexican *charros,* and American cowboys. Each had interesting skills, but the *charro's Paso de la Muerte* (Death Transfer) had impressed him most, for it combined the breaking of wild broncos, for which all three groups are famous, with the perfect training displayed in horse shows. The *charro* jumped from his own horse onto a wild mare, endured her bucking, spurred her to a gallop, and then jumped back onto his own horse, which had been perfectly trained to gallop riderless alongside.

America amazed and impressed Tschiffely, but it was not because of the nice receptions or the interesting cowboy shows, both of which had been surpassed in Mexico. Instead, the buildings breathed the spirit and drive of America. Skyscrapers, concrete highways, and clean rooms without insect pests were all firsts on his journey, things for which America could rightfully take pride. The young nation showed a determination for excellence.

From Muskogee to St. Louis, the horses enjoyed the clover in the Ozarks, but near the city Tschiffely became concerned about the horses in heavy traffic. He decided to leave Gato with a friend in St. Louis. He moved faster onto Indianapolis and Columbus. In Maryland, a cruel driver crossed the yellow line on purpose just to sideswipe Mancha, who fell to the ground bleeding. Fortunately, Mancha was able to get up and limp to safety. After an accident in Washington, D.C., he decided to finish his ride in Washington instead of New York.

In Washington, Tschiffely's favorite sights were the Lincoln Memorial and Arlington National Cemetery. President Coolidge received him at the White House, and there were numerous other receptions. He also addressed the National Geographic Society.

Tschiffely shipped Mancha to New York and brought Gato there by train. A Buenos Aires antique dealer had mailed him traditional gaucho garb, so he and Mancha appeared appropriately attired when the mayor presented him with a medal. As they paraded down Broadway and Fifth Avenue, he marveled at the skyscrapers, but Tschiffley could not help contrasting New York to the rolling Pampas of Argentina. It was time to go home. After ten days of showing the horses in the International Horse Show at Madison Square Gardens, they took ship on December 1, 1927, for Buenos Aires.

Of course, Tschiffely had a great homecoming reception after twenty days at sea with stops in Rio de Janeiro and Montevideo. He had ridden ten thousand miles across eleven nations on two continents. He had been gone almost nine hundred days, two and a half years, and even excluding rest days, he had traveled 504 days. He had proved that the Creole horses are the toughest horses for enduring harsh conditions for long periods. He had done the impossible.

Aime Felix Tschiffely, born in Switzerland in 1897, died at the age of fifty-eight in London on January 5, 1954, after an unsuccessful surgery.

HAROLD WILLIAM TILMAN
Explorer of Remote Ranges

Bill Tilman, called by one writer "the Last Hero," entered Britain's Royal Artillery as a second lieutenant in World War I for adventure. Born on February 14, 1898, in Liverpool, he was sixteen when he enlisted in 1914, and he spent the war in the trenches. He survived the Battle of the Somme in 1916, the greatest loss of British soldiers ever (nineteen thousand dead on the first day alone). Tilman, after being wounded in 1918, led his company on a forced march through the Ardennes to Bonn near the end of the war.

After several years of living in Africa, Tilman itched for adventure. On September 14, 1933, after a train ride from Nairobi to Kampala, Tilman bicycled sixty miles to Lake Victoria. He slept out in the open in a mosquito net throughout his trip. A week later he reached the border of the Belgian Congo (Zaire) near Lake Kivu. A month after that, at the border of Cameroon, the French detained him a week for importing his bike. He reached the Atlantic at Edea, having covered three thousand miles in fifty-six days.

Nanda Devi

"Will you join me for a climb of Nanda Devi?" Shipton asked Tilman in 1934. Shipton budgeted only 150 British pounds apiece for a five-month climb in the Himalayas.

Nanda Devi rises in a physical and sanctuary. Physically it stands inside a ring of peaks seventy miles around. The surrounding barrier forms a wall twenty-one thousand feet high in places and is breached only once by the extremely rugged Rishi Gorge. The terrain inside this ring is so rough and remote that no man had ever entered this ring of peaks, and only two had ever reached the rim to look in. Nanda Devi, the highest of all, is the most remote of all at the center of this sanctuary at 25,643 feet high, it towers almost one thousand feet higher than the highest peak yet climbed.

Spiritually, the greater region is sacred to the Hindus. It is the source of all four of the great rivers of India. The Brahmaputra, the Indus, and its main tributary, the Suttej, all flow from Mount Kailas just across the border in Tibet. The fourth and most important of the great rivers is the Ganges. Most of the headwater streams flow from Gangotri glacier about thirty miles to the northwest, but some consider the Pindar, which flows from Nanda Devi itself, to be the main source.

Tilman agreed instantly to accompany Shipton, his favorite climbing partner. Eric Earle Shipton (1907-77) was nine years younger than Tilman but an experienced climber. Tilman had met Shipton in Africa and had learned climbing from him on many African peaks. Together they had climbed the difficult Mawenzi Peak of Kilimanjaro in 1930. Six months later they had made the first traverse between the two main peaks of Mount Kenya, Bation (17,040 ft.) and Nelion (17,000 ft.), making first ascents of the rock pillars called Dutton and Peter on the way. In 1932, the year after Shipton had set a record for the highest peak yet climbed (Kamet in the Himalayas), he and Tilman had climbed four peaks in the remote and mysterious Mountains of the Moon (or Ruwenzori): Mount Margherita peak (16,763 ft.) and Alexandra (16,750 ft.) on Mount Stanley, the Vittorio Emmanuel peak of Mount Speke (16,043 ft.), and Edward peak on Mount Baker (15,889 ft.). The following year Tilman had returned to Kilimanjaro and climbed the main peak, Kibo (19,340 ft.), alone.

Tilman and Shipton tackled Nanda Devi but failed to reach the summit. The expedition, however, succeeded in several ways. First, they stayed within their budget, proving that low-budget climbing trips with limited gear were possible. Second, they hired very few Sherpas and hired them as partners rather than coolies. Third, they successfully climbed one of the twenty-one-thousand-foot peaks, and they became the first to enter and explore inside the Nanda Devi sanctuary. Most importantly, it inspired them to return.

Tilman and Shipton made a trip to Mount Everest in 1935. Though they did not reach the summit, they did some exploring and also succeeded in climbing Khartaphu (23,640 ft.), Kellas Rock (23,190 ft.), and several others. It was one of the most successful climbing expeditions ever. Among themselves, the party of six Europeans climbed twenty-six peaks over twenty thousand feet. They also surveyed some new areas and remained within their low budget.

After he returned from Asia, four Americans approached Tilman. "We hope to climb Kanchenjunga," they explained. Kanchenjunga is the third highest mountain in the world. The four young climbers were Charles Houston, W. F. Loomis, Arthur Emmons, and H. Adams Carter.

Tilman was interested but not excited. He was interested because he had no plans, since his partner Shipton had been accepted by the 1936 Everest expedition. His lack of excitement, however, was easily explained by his knowledge that both sides of Kanchenjunga were closed countries for climbers.

Elevation	Peak	Location	Year Climbed	Team
23,359 (7120 m)	Trisul	India	1907	British
23,386 (7128 m)	Pauhunri	Sikkim	1910	British
24,550 (7483 m)	Jongsong	Sikkim	1930	Germany (Dyhrenfurth)
25,446 (7756 m)	Kamet	India	1931	British (Shipton)

The young Americans were obviously hoping to set a climbing record. Tilman reviewed the records of the century. The first seven-thousand-meter (roughly 23,000 feet) peaks ever climbed had been climbed in this century almost thirty years ago. So far, four such records had been set. Although mountaineers had gone higher on Everest, no higher peaks had been reached.

"How about climbing Nanda Devi instead, if your requests are refused for Kanchenjunga?" Nanda Devi, at 25,643 feet (7816 m), though not so high as Kanchenjunga, would still set a new record. Moreover, Tilman had substantial knowledge of the peak and a good chance for success. They agreed, and permission for Kanchenjunga was indeed denied. They also invited three more British climbers: Peter Lloyd, T. Graham Brown, and Noel Odell.

The prospects looked bleak. Rain pelted the camp, and the raging waters of Rishi Gorge drowned out conversation. The Dotial porters were already on strike. Tilman had arrived in April and had begun transporting supplies to save time later. Tilman had hired four Sherpas who had been overlooked by the huge Everest expedition. These included Pasang Kikuli, who had experience attempting Nanga Parbat.

Now, July 26, they had barely begun the trek through the ring of peaks guarding Nanda Devi. The thirty-two Dotial porters departed with their pay in the morning. Only the sixteen Bhotia porters and four Sherpas remained to cross the river with the help of ropes. Tilman suggested that the eight climbers carry sixty-pound loads to get more gear to Base Camp. The Americans agreed readily; they were used to carrying their own supplies, since there are no porters around peaks such as Mount McKinley. Still, the food supplies had to be cut back by a third.

Climbing in earnest began on August 9 when they climbed to nineteen thousand feet and established Camp 1. They had pitched Base Camp at seventeen thousand feet and paid off the Bhotias two days before. The next day had been spent with preparations. After a day of blizzard, Tilman and Odell pushed on to establish Camp 2 at 20,400 feet. Houston and Brown established Camp 3 at 21,400 feet a couple of days later.

Morale sagged again when they spent a week without establishing a higher camp. During the week, each member of the party made at least one climb to Camp 3 with supplies. However, everyone had also become ill. The Westerners had altitude sickness, Pasang was snow-blind, and the other Sherpas had dysentery. By the end of the week, their spirits reached their lowest ebb when they mourned the death of Sherpa Kitar at Base Camp.

A couple of climbers fought snows on August 22 to establish Camp 4 at 21,900 feet. They had gained only five hundred feet, but this small victory broke the depression. Two days later the blizzard lessened, and they brought enough food to Camp 4 to last two weeks.

Houston and Odell took off from Camp 4 on August 25. Tilman had been chosen leader for organizing the summit bid. He had selected Houston and Odell for the first attempt but had not yet decided who would make the second attempt. Houston and Odell bivouacked that night at 23,500 feet. Tilman, Lloyd, and Loomis had accompanied them with supplies before returning to Camp 4.

Two days later, even after a day of rest, the first attempt failed when Houston fell sick. Loomis remained below, nursing his frostbite, but Tilman and Lloyd went up to help, followed by Brown and Carter. Three of them accompanied the sick Houston down to Camp 4, leaving Tilman to replace Houston on the first attempt with Odell. The next morning, August 28, they climbed to twenty-four thousand feet for a higher bivouac.

Tilman and Odell awoke at 5:00 A.M. on August 29. After an hour and a quarter, they were ready to climb. Climbing would help warm up their cold bodies. They spent an hour ascending an arete (rough ridge) and then several hours struggling through deep snow. Weary, they could keep going only by taking turns in the lead. From one to two in the afternoon, they ascended a steep snow gully.

Swoosh! A forty-foot block of snow broke off and slid down the gully. The snow beneath them gave way, and a foot of snow coursed down the mountains. Both men lost their footing and gripped their ice axes, which were embedded in the snow. Only the axes could prevent a plunge of thousands of feet to the glaciers below. Fortunately, their ice axes were more than a foot long, and the snow deeper than a foot did not give way. They regained their feet, having escaped an avalanche.

Tilman and Odell shook hands. After another hour of trudging up the final ridge, they had reached the summit. Their nailed boots, ice axes, crampons, and ropes had served them admirably. They had used neither oxygen nor other high-tech contrivances. Tilman's fame catapulted. Headlines in England announced his victory on the highest mountain ever climbed. Tilman's book *The Ascent of Nanda Devi* (1937) recorded his greatest triumph.

Karakoram

The Himalayas extend twelve hundred miles along China's southern border. To the west, separated from the Himalayas by the Indus River, the Karakoram range stretches only three hundred miles. But in this small area lie of the world's fourteen highest mountains, all over 8000 meters (26,246 ft.), including the second highest in the world—K2. In contrast, the Himalayas boast ten such peaks, but they are spread over a range four times longer.

RANGES WITH PEAKS OVER 7000 METERS

range	length (mi.)	number over 7000 m	highest peak	elev. (ft.)	number over 8000 m
Himalayas	1200	150	Mount Everest	29,028	9
Karakoram	300	113	K2	28,250	5
Kunlun	1675	6	Kongur	25,325	0
Hindu Kush	1000	34	Tirich Mir	25,282	0
Pamirs	150	3	Communism Pk.	24,457	0
Tian Shan	1800	2	Peak Pobeda	24,406	0
Trans-Himalaya	600	3	Nyenchen Tangla	23,497	0
isolated	—	3	Minya Konka	24,901	0

The Karakoram! Asia contains all of the world's 314 peaks over 7000 meters. The Himalayas spot the most, but the Karakoram contains almost as many. This gives the Karakoram the greatest concentration of 7000- and 8000-meter peaks anywhere. It is the most rugged range in the world.

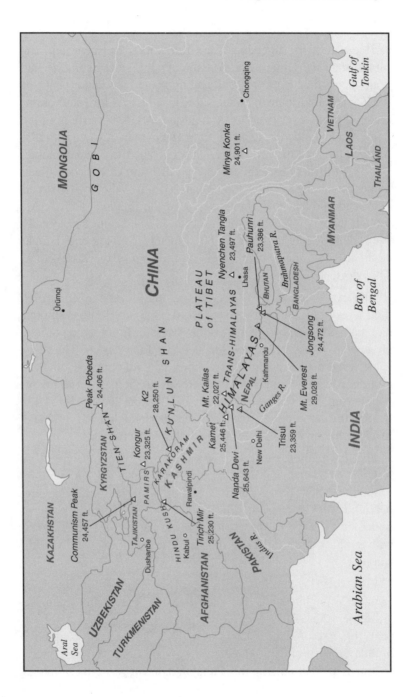

Because of its ruggedness, the Karakoram had been less explored than the Himalayas. British captain T. Montgomerie had done the earliest exploring and had numbered the major peaks of the Karakoram Range in 1856. K2, K4, and K5 (*K* for Karakoram) were all peaks over twenty-six thousand feet. K2 briefly bore the name Mount Godwin-Austen after H. H. Godwin-Austen, who first mapped the area in 1861, but K2 has become the accepted name. In 1897, a British expedition reached the base of K2 and coined names for nearby K4 and K5. The names given by the British, Broad Peak and Hidden Peak, have displaced the previous names. Although these three peaks and a fourth, Gasherbrum, had already been identified as higher than 8000 meters, Shipton and Tilman could still find many blank areas on the map of the Karakoram. They decided to explore.

The expedition of 1937 was the second greatest adventure of their lives (after their respective record-breaking climbs). Shipton had made the plans while on his unsuccessful Everest expedition. He invited Tilman, Michael Spender, and John Auden. The foursome arrived in Rawalpindi on April 27 with supplies for four months. Meeting them here also were seven Sherpas: Angtharkay, Angtensing, Sen Tenzing, Lobsang, Ila, Lhakpa, and Nukku. After buying further supplies, they crossed the Indus on May 24 and reached the town of Askole. The Karakoram at last!

Shipton exulted. He had paid off dozens of porters hired in Askole at the end of May, and only four remained. On June 3, Tilman and Sen Tenzing had caught up with them after staying behind a week because of illness. The party of fifteen was now united on the edge of the great unknown parts of the Karakoram with food for three and a half months. The campfire crackled with warmth.

First, they located the pass crossed by Victorian explorer Sir Francis Younghusband. The pass had not been seen again by Westerners these fifty years. After climbing a twenty-thousand-foot peak, they explored the glaciers around K2. On August 1, Shipton's birthday, they broke into three groups. Auden and the four porters returned to Askole via the Panmah Glacier system. Shipton,

Spender, and five Sherpas went northeast, exploring a range as far as Shimshal Pass.

Tilman, Sen Tenzing, and Ila went west to find Snow Lake. In 1892 Sir Martin Conway had reported a snow basin with mountainous islands rising out of it. Hunter and Fanny Workman reported seeing it ten years later but thought it was a snowcap. Tillman's group not only found it but crossed it and became the first to do so. The "lake" turned out to be seven adjoining glaciers. They also explored the Cornice Glacier and found the outlet (the Workmans had thought that it had no outlet). On the way out, they found tracks in the snow about seven inches in diameter and sixteen inches apart. The Sherpas attributed them to the yeti (abominable snowman), which they described as red and hairy. Tilman saw real tracks, but he never saw whatever made them.

*   *   *

Tilman led the unsuccessful 1938 British expedition to Mount Everest and set his personal altitude record at 27,400 feet (without oxygen). A twenty-four-year-old Sherpa named Tenzing Norgay, who would later become famous, accompanied him. Shipton also climbed on that expedition, but they had few other climbs together because Tilman spent 1940 to 1946 in World War II. He had reenlisted and served in the retreat at Dunkirk as a gunnery officer, helped push the Axis out of North Africa in Tunisia as a major, and parachuted with the special forces behind enemy lines in Albania and the Italian Alps (Dolomites) to help the Resistance and keep German troops away from the Low Countries. Superbly fit, resourceful, experienced in mountainous terrain, and accustomed to independent action during long, tense periods with minimal provisions, he was an ideal choice for these missions. During lulls in the war, he even found time for a few climbs in the Dolomites, Iran, and Tunisia.

After the war, Tillman caught malaria trying to reach Gori Chen (21,450 ft.) in East India, broke an arm on Ben Nevis (4,406 ft.) in Scotland, and failed on Rakaposhi (25,550 ft.) in the Karakoram. He and Shipton made their last three climbs together in 1947 and 1948 in China. All three attempts were unsuccessful (Muztag Ata at 24,388 ft. in the Kunlun Shan, Bogdo Ola at 18,000 ft. in the Tian Shan, and Chaka Aghil near the Mongolian border).

Tilman made two more remarkable discoveries in the Himalayas. In 1949, he explored the Langtang Himalaya and made the first ascent of the minor peak Paldor (19,451 ft.). The more astounding outcome of this trip, however, was the discovery of Shisha Pangma. This peak, now reckoned one of the fourteen highest peaks in the world and exceeding 8000 meters, had remained unknown until then. Its elevation was still not known, so Tilman's discovery was not yet appreciated. The following year, Tilman became the first Westerner ever to receive permission to enter Nepal. He greatly enjoyed visiting the now-famous climbing centers of Namche Bazaar and Thyangboche Monastery. Tilman discovered the Western Cwm and recognized its potential for scaling Everest. After this trek, he wrote his seventh book, *Nepal Himalaya* (1952), while working three years at a British consulate in Burma.

Baffin Island

Tilman steered his yacht *Mischief* between icebergs. A great slab of ice peeled off the edge of a glacier that descended into the sea nearby. The splash sent a great wave toward *Mischief*. Tilman had been yachting in polar regions for nine years and enjoyed the scene passively. *Mischief* rode the swell easily. The turquoise ice slab bobbed back to the surface, a freshly calved iceberg.

Bylot Island! Tilman had succeeded in navigating to this island off the northeast tip of Baffin Island. Four years before he had reached the Crozet Islands in the Southern Indian Ocean on his second attempt. Since he did not always reach his yachting goals, he felt satisfied to have reached Bylot Island.

The real adventure had not yet begun, though. Tilman and a partner from his crew of six proposed to make the first crossing of Baffin Island, located in the Canadian Arctic, on foot. Tilman felt he had well prepared for this. The year before, 1962, he had disembarked on Baffin Island to climb Mount Raleigh and Mount Mischief (named after the yacht). In 1961, he had ascended a 6,370-foot peak on Upernivik Island off the west coast of Greenland. However, crossing Baffin Island would be harder than stopping to climb a peak.

Tilman set out across the icy wastes of Baffin Island with one member of his crew, while the rest of the crew sailed around the island. Tilman had made only one other trek from his yacht. On that 1955 trip he had sailed to the tip of South America to explore the ice channels and fjords. There, after discovering beautiful Waterfall Bay, he and two crew members had explored on foot the glaciers of Patagonia for over a month before returning to the yacht, which they had left in the keeping of the other half of the crew. Returning home via the Panama Canal in mid-1956, he wrote his book *Mischief in Patagonia* (1957), the first and most famous of his eight books on his seafaring days. Crossing Baffin Island, though, would be much more complicated because they would not return to their starting point.

Tilman and his partner trudged through snow a foot and a half deep as they climbed away from the Pond Inlet of Baffin Bay on the northeast side of the island. After about a week, they crossed a pass in the mountain range that forms the backbone of Baffin Island. The elevation of this pass, fifty-seven hundred feet, may not sound very high, but unlike climbs in the Rockies or Alps, this climb had to begin at sea level. Furthermore, this far north, the conditions remain as harsh as the Himalayas all year round.

Beyond the pass, they began the descent toward Steensby Inlet, the northern end of the Foxe Basin. The distance across Baffin Island of only fifty-three miles would take a good hiker only two days on a good trail in the Appalachians. To trek across the island with no trail in harsh conditions, Tilman had prepared for at least a week. In the end it took fifteen days before they arrived on the west coast of Baffin Island.

At the far shore, Tilman tried for several days to send signal fires across the strait to the town where their yacht should now be waiting. With no success, Tilman began to wonder if they would die within sight of safety. Eventually Inuits (sometimes called Eskimos) investigated the smoke signals and brought Tilman and his group across the strait to the yacht, and they returned home to Lymington, England.

Tilman made fourteen more voyages, including a 1965 winter voyage to Heard Island in the Indian Ocean, a 1966-67 voyage to the Antarctic Peninsula, and eight summer voyages to Greenland. Four trips attempted to reach the largest fjord in the world, Scoresby Sound on the east coast of Greenland. *Mischief* hit an iceberg and sank on the first attempt in 1968. The ice pack thwarted the 1969 and 1971 attempts. His 1972 voyage succeeded, but pack ice later trapped and claimed his second yacht, *Sea Breeze.* In his third yacht, *Baroque,* he made his last voyage to Greenland in 1973 and spent the next three summers sailing to Norway's Spitsbergen and making two unsuccessful attempts to reach Canada's Ellesmere Island. In 1978, a former crew member invited him for another Antarctic Peninsula voyage on *En Avante.* They were never heard from again.

THOR HEYERDAHL
Sailing Across Oceans

Pacific Ocean

A shark fin sliced the waves. A blue shark ten feet long made a beeline for the balsa-wood raft. Thor and five friends had been sailing across the Pacific Ocean for months on their raft. They used the many bonitos, squids, and flying fish that landed on deck as bait to catch tunny and the good-tasting dolphin (a fish called *dorado* by the Spanish and not the porpoiselike mammal of the same name). Heyerdahl dangled a dolphin over the water by the raft. The shark approached.

The shark came within inches of the raft, and Heyerdahl looked into its ugly face as its snout broke the surface. In an instant six rows of teeth had severed the fish in half. Heyerdahl, left holding only a tail, thrilled at the shark's power. Cutting up dolphins for food took substantial strength and time. The shark had sliced it so cleanly and effortlessly that Heyerdahl had not felt even a vibration.

As the shark nosed down to dive, its tail broke the surface. Heyerdahl grabbed the notch in the shark's tail with his bare hands and held fast. The skin felt like sandpaper, but it was not hard to maintain his hold. The shark jerked but was paralyzed because its swimming strength was in its tail. When it became calm, Heyerdahl pulled it over the low rim of the raft onto the deck and leaped into the cabin. The freed shark flailed about wildly on deck in its death struggle. It was their ninth shark catch of the day.

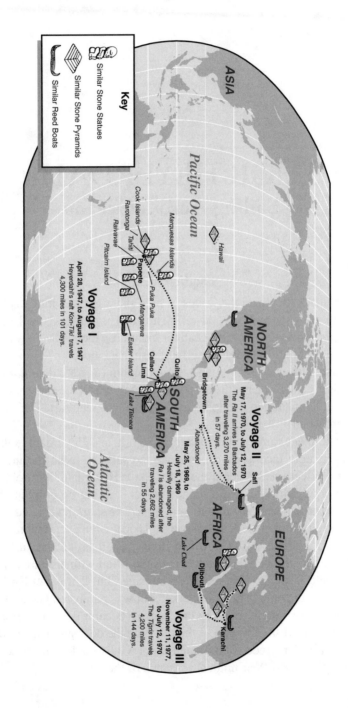

Key

Similar Stone Statues

Similar Stone Pyramids

Similar Reed Boats

ASIA

Pacific Ocean

Hawaii

Cook Islands
Rarotonga
Raivavae
Tahiti
Pitcairn Island
Mangareva
Easter Island

Marquesas Islands

Papeete

Puka Puka

Voyage I

April 28, 1947, to August 7, 1947
Heyerdahl's raft *Kon-Tiki* travels
4,300 miles in 101 days.

Callao
Quito
Lima
Lake Titicaca

SOUTH AMERICA

NORTH AMERICA

Bridgetown

Abandoned

Voyage II

May 17, 1970, to July 12, 1970
The *Ra II* arrives in Barbados
after traveling 3,270 miles
in 57 days.

Safi

May 25, 1969, to
July 18, 1969
Heavily damaged, the
Ra I is abandoned after
traveling 2,662 miles
in 55 days.

Atlantic Ocean

AFRICA

Lake Chad

Djibouti

EUROPE

Voyage III

November 11, 1977,
to July 12, 1970
The *Tigris* travels
4,200 miles
in 144 days.

Karachi

Thor Heyerdahl, born in Larvik, Norway, in 1914, had traveled in the Americas and Polynesia. He knew the accounts of the Spanish conquistadors, the traditions of native Polynesians, and the legends of the American Indians. The Quechua Indians of Peru say that their Inca ancestors drove out a tribe that lived at Tiahuanaco on Lake Titicaca (see Tschiffely). The conquered tribe fled from the Incas on balsa-wood rafts. The rafts headed west on the Humboldt Current in the Pacific and settled on Polynesian islands. Natives on Fatu Hiva and Easter Island have similar legends, which say that their people came from a land of mountains to the east.

Most interestingly, the stories from far-flung islands and the mainland agree in amazing details about the fleeing ruler. Incas say that the leader of those who fled was named Kon-Tiki, the sun king. On Fatu Hiva, the Polynesians say that their leader was Tiki. Is the similarity coincidental? The Easter Islanders claim descent from a leader named Hotu Matua, which means the "Son of the Sun." The natives of Rapa Iti, who went west from Easter Island during its ancient civil war, also agree on key points such as westward travel initiated by a South American sun king.

Archaeologists had laughed at the idea that Indians crossed the Pacific Ocean on balsa-wood rafts. To silence the critics, Heyerdahl and five friends had decided to raft across the Pacific on their own. They had cut nine huge balsa logs from the forests of Ecuador and floated them down the coast to Peru, where they had lashed the logs together with simple hemp ropes. A bamboo deck and cabin and a mangrove mast completed the raft. Heyerdahl had copied the design of the ancient Indians at Lake Titicaca. He named the raft *Kon-Tiki* after the fleeing ruler and painted the ruler's face on the square sail.

Waves washed across the raft. Heyerdahl and his friends had set sail on April 28, 1947. They had learned by trial and error how to navigate the raft because no ancient Indian sailors remained to teach them. They soon found that the Indians had built wisely—even without nails or metal. Water drained between the balsa logs since there was no hull to fill with water, and its short length enabled it to take waves one at a time. The low deck made fishing easy.

Knut Haugland yelled, "Shark!" Shark encounters had become so commonplace that the rafters wondered why Haugland was so concerned. When they gathered at the back of the raft, they understood. The shark was so huge that it stuck out on both ends when it went under the raft—almost sixty feet long. White spots speckled the whale shark's brownish skin. It followed them for an hour until they could not stand the tension. Erik Hesselberg, the biggest and strongest man on the raft, plunged a harpoon into the monster's head. The shark paused and then dove into the depths, snapping the thick harpoon line like thread.

One morning Torstein Raaby woke up with a live eel-like fish, a snake mackerel, in his sleeping bag. The crew also saw whales, which sometimes cruised toward the raft quickly and dove under it at the last second.

On July 30, they caught their first sight of land. The current took them past Puka Puka, however, and they could not land. Finally, on August 7, after 101 days at sea, they ran aground at Raroia in the middle of Polynesia—over forty-three hundred nautical miles across the Pacific Ocean from Peru. The reef damaged the ship, and the mast fell, giving Bengt Danielsson a mild concussion. While they camped near the wreck, Hesselberg and Herman Watzinger went scouting, but eight large poisonous eels attacked them. They slashed at the eels with machetes, drawing sharks to the bloody waters. Hesselberg and Watzinger escaped back to camp by hopping across corals.

The raft excited the local natives from across the lagoon. They called it *pae-pae* and compared it to the ships their ancestors had used. Led by Tiki and his relative Maui, their ancestors had come from Pura, the east. White men usually told them not to believe their legends, but Heyerdahl had proved that rafting to Polynesia was indeed possible. They welcomed the rafters to live with them until a ship could tow the wreck to Tahiti.

The Tahitians showed the same excitement over the *pae-pae*. They too claimed Tiki as an ancestor. Heyerdahl visited Tahiti's life-sized stone statues of Tiki and its small ancient pyramids.

When Heyerdahl returned home, scholars argued that Heyerdahl's trip across the Pacific did not prove that Indians had also crossed. Heyerdahl was disgusted. Was it coincidence, he asked, that a New World crop, the sweet potato, grows throughout Polynesia from Easter Island to Hawaii and New Zealand? Or that pyramids and statues remain on at least nine Polynesian islands with masonry similar to that at Lake Titicaca?

Heyerdahl visited forty-five-square-mile Easter Island for more evidence. Europeans named the island in 1722 because they sighted its coast lined with the great heads on Easter Sunday, but the natives call it *Rapa Nui* or *Te Pito o Te Henua,* "The Navel of the World," a fitting name for the most isolated island in the world. The nearest lands are the Pitcairn Islands, twelve hundred miles west, and Chile, twenty-six hundred miles east. No wonder the natives think of the heavens before they think of other earthly lands. They say that "Easter Island lies east of the sun and west of the moon."

If Heyerdahl was right, Easter Island was the first Polynesian island inhabited, since it contains the largest and most numerous South American–style stone structures. If his critics were right, the first people in Polynesia arrived from the west about A.D. 500 but did not reach Easter Island in the east until 1300. The archaeologists foretold that Heyerdahl would find nothing because habitation was too recent for remains to become buried.

Heyerdahl arrived and surveyed the six hundred stone heads (or *moai*). Most heads stood ten to twenty feet high with long ears but were toppled sometime after the first European sighting. The largest finished head is thirty-two feet high and weighs one hundred tons, but one unfinished head exceeds sixty-six feet and weighs three hundred tons. Red stones called topknots, about six feet in diameter, once sat on top of the statues to depict the Long Ears' red hair tied in a bun. The statues once stood on platforms, called *ahus,* with an approach ramp covering a burial vault. The largest ahu stood fifteen feet high with a three-hundred-foot-long ramp. The neatly cut stones fit together perfectly—just as the stones in the temples at Lake Titicaca.

Heyerdahl visited the red stone topknot quarry on the volcano Puna Pau. Then he spent the night in the crater of Rano Raraku, the quarry for the statue stones. He hoped the ancient quarry would provide him inspiration for solving the puzzle of how the statues were made and moved. Instead, he remembered other strange places he had slept: the altar stone at Stonehenge, a snowdrift on Norway's highest mountain, and the Isle of the Sun in Lake Titicaca.

Heyerdahl's excavations showed that the first inhabitants, the Long Ears, had come about A.D. 380. Easter Island was indeed the first inhabited island in Polynesia. He uncovered statues of a style previously unknown on the island. The new statues, rongo-rongo tablets, reed boats, and the pictures at a ruined village all suggested that the Long Ears had come from Lake Titicaca, led by the son of the sun as the legends told. The oldest excavations contained the best stonework, and the unique style of stone heads developed next. The third period began when the Short Ears arrived a millennium later, possibly from the Gambier Islands twelve hundred miles west, where a legend tells of a defeated chieftain who went east to a solitary island. It was the Short Ears who toppled the heads and killed the Long Ears. Heyerdahl also investigated many caves where people had hidden during the long civil war. The caves contained secret ceremonial places for taboo images (called *aku-akus*) carved from stone.

A twelve-man team, the only surviving Long Ears, unraveled the mystery of construction for Heyerdahl. He had already seen how they cut statues from the rock and then how 180 men pulled a statue overland to its ahu. Prying with long poles, the twelve men slid rocks underneath the statue, and after eighteen days the pile was high enough to tilt the statue upright.

Atlantic Ocean

As he continued his research, Heyerdahl read an intriguing article in an archaeology magazine. It gave sixty points of similarity between Egyptian and Peruvian ruins. Both peoples built huge stone statues and pyramids. Some Peruvian pyramids contained interior passages to royal burial vaults and were oriented according to astronomical observations much as the Egyptian pyramids. The oldest Egyptian pyramids rose in tiers of steps much like the Peruvian pyramids. Ruins on both continents include pictures of bird-headed men and reed boats. Written tablets and sun worship characterized both regions.

Heyerdahl remembered these same features from Easter Island: the fine stonework of the ahus; huge statues; drawings of bird men at Orongo, the ruined village of the bird men with its astronomical observatory, reed boats, and rongo-rongo tablets. In fact, the sun is called Ra throughout Polynesia just as it is in Egypt. He knew Easter Island's people could be traced to Peru, but did Peru's first Indian civilization trace back to Egypt? Heyerdahl decided to make another expedition to find out.

Heyerdahl knew that reed boats had traveled from Egypt throughout the Nile to Ethiopia and Chad as well as across the Mediterranean to Corsica and Morocco. In the Americas, such boats were known as far north as Mexico. Heyerdahl had already seen reed boats demonstrated on Easter Island, and now he visited the other remaining places where they were in use. He visited the Seris Indians of Mexico just in time to see their last reed boat, but he reached Morocco one generation too late. The Ethiopian and Corsican craft were too small, and although some craft on Lake Titicaca were large, the reed used was *totora,* the South American reed instead of the Egyptian papyrus.

The papyrus boats of Lake Chad carried heavy loads, and Heyerdahl also found there three willing boat builders. In February, he imported twelve tons of papyrus from Ethiopia to Egypt. The boat was constructed in the shadow of the Great Pyramid according to ancient Egyptian design and based on counsel from the foremost Egyptologist on papyrus vessels.

Heyerdahl gathered his crew: Italian Carlo Mauri as film photographer and Mexican Santiago Genoves as the ship's quartermaster. After the boat was finished on April 28, he invited Abdullah Djibrine, one of the boat builders from Chad, as the papyrus expert. Then Georges Sourial, an oceanographer from Egypt, signed on board. Finally, Russian doctor Yuri Senkevitch and American navigator Norman Baker, the only experienced sailor on the expedition, completed the crew.

Sourial found a local sail maker who made a big square sail by hand. The orange sun in the center of the red field symbolized their papyrus vessel, *Ra*. Sourial also found a basket maker to hand-weave the cabin, potters to make storage vessels like those in the Cairo Museum, and a baker to fill the jars with Egyptian bread made according to the recipe in the museum. Heyerdahl transported the ship overland to Alexandria, by freighter to Tangier, and overland to Safi in Morocco. He had selected the ancient Atlantic port Safi because reed ships had been used there. The boat was put into the water on May 17, but winds and other problems delayed departure until May 25, 1969.

After two days at sea, a storm broke the oars, but the North Equatorial Current carried the raft steadily west. Senkevitch, who had spent a year in Antarctica but had never sailed, noticed a blue bubble floating on the water one morning as he adjusted ropes. He grabbed the bubble, and long stinging tentacles entangled him. Pain shot through him, and his hand became paralyzed. He had learned about the Portuguese man-of-war the hard way.

On June 18, they passed the Cape Verde Islands, but the ship was slowly coming apart. The reeds remained seaworthy, but the ropes chafed. Heyerdahl and his crew lacked the experience of the ancient Egyptians and had not realized the importance of a few features of the ancient ships. On July 9, the boat split down the middle, but Sourial—a six-foot-five judo champ, engineer, and frogman—swam under the boat to lash the halves together.

Storms racked the boat for three days at the beginning of hurricane season. On July 16, the yacht *Shenandoah* met them, and they cut off the now useless mast from *Ra*. For two days the yacht and the raft sailed together as important cargo was transferred to the yacht. Finally, with a hurricane brewing behind them at sea, Heyerdahl decided to play safe and abandon the raft, even though all six men would have preferred to continue. Unable to steer, they had zigzagged over 3,000 miles across the Atlantic for eight weeks but were now only 2,662 miles west of Safi. Though their destination was still a week away, the distance they had come showed that the reed boat could have reached the West Indies. The first people in the New World could have come from Africa.

Not content, Heyerdahl built another reed boat. He shipped the papyrus from Ethiopia to Morocco this time. Sourial, Mauri,

Genoves, Senkevitch, and Baker joined him again. Since Djibrine could not come, Aymara Indians from Bolivia supervised construction, and two new sailors were found: Kei Ohara of Japan and Madanni Ait Ouhanni of Morocco. *Ra II* set sail on May 6, 1970, and fifty-seven days later on July 12, they arrived at Barbados. They had sailed 3,270 miles across the Atlantic.

Indian Ocean

Next, Heyerdahl studied Sumerian reed boats. In Iraq, he found the Madan people who lived on boats made of their local berdi reeds. The Madan knew that reeds cut in August retained buoyancy longest and would last for many months without waterlogging. Heyerdahl obtained reeds cut in August and hired the Madan to weave berdi reeds into sixty-foot-long bundles. Four Aymara Indians from Lake Titicaca supervised the construction of a reed boat from the bundles, and three men from India made the sail.

The eleven-man crew of the new reed boat, *Tigris,* included Heyerdahl and three of his friends from the *Ra* expeditions: Senkevitch, Mauri, and Baker. Heyerdahl also enlisted three other friends: Detlef Soitzek from Germany; Gherman Carrasco, a filmmaker from Mexico; and Toru Suzuki, an underwater photographer from Japan who lived in Australia. He also took three young men on recommendations: math student Asbjörn Damhus of Denmark, medical student Hans Peter Böhn from Norway, and art student Rashad Nazir Salim of Iraq. Finally, American Norris Brock came to film for *National Geographic.*

Tigris launched from Qurna in Iraq on November 11, 1977. Without major currents to depend on, Heyerdahl and his friends learned ancient navigation techniques. They launched from Qurna, where the Tigris and Euphrates Rivers meet to form the Shatt-al-Arab. The outgoing tide beached them in the river, but after a few days, they entered the Persian Gulf. Strong winds trapped them in shallows around Kuwait's Failaka Island.

Snap! They had thrown out their anchor to wait out the night, but violent waves broke the line. They threw out the other anchor, but its line also snapped, and the wind speeded them along. Mauri heard the crash of breakers and surf. Shipwreck on the reef must be imminent. Lacking anchors, they put on the brakes—a bag dropped behind the boat to create drag. The brake bag filled with mud in the churning shallows and acted as an anchor.

In the morning, the *Tigris* began drifting again because the high tide raised the brake bag off the bottom. The wind carried them into more extensive shallows in spite of hard rowing. They saw a boat approaching and hoped for help.

"If you won't pay us now, we will get your money when the reef smashes you to bits," the pirates threatened. Instead of helping, the pirates demanded a ransom in Kuwaiti dinars equivalent to two thousand dollars. The pirates laughed at Heyerdahl's bargaining.

Far beyond the pirates, Heyerdahl saw a large Russian ship. Heyerdahl said he would not pay so much yet; maybe the Russians would help. The Russian ship sent a motor launch, but it did not have enough power to pull the *Tigris* against the wind. The mother ship could not get within seven miles. After an entire day of fighting to stay clear of the reefs, they heard the breakers again as dusk approached. Heyerdahl gave up and agreed to pay the pirates.

Salim boarded the motorized pirate boat, called a dhow. The dhow and motor launch combined their power and towed the *Tigris* out to deeper waters. Heyerdahl passed the ransom money across, and all watched in suspense as the head pirate counted it. Satisfied, he nodded to his henchmen. Released, Salim jumped back onto the *Tigris*. The pirate dhow extinguished its lantern and disappeared into the night.

Heyerdahl wanted to know how far Sumerians could have traveled. Scholars said that Sumerians traveled only on the Tigris and Euphrates because the type of reed they used could not withstand seawater. Yet the Sumerian ruins show reed ships in the ocean. Their cuneiform inscriptions mention trade with sea powers called Dilmun, Magan, and Meluhha. Also, stone, scarabs, and other goods known only from Egypt have been found at Falaika Island, proving a vast sea trade. Which was right—the scholars or the Sumerian paintings and cuneiform records?

Sumerians knew that a great flood had destroyed the world, but they mixed up some of the details. Instead of Noah, they believed their king Ziusudra built the ark and later settled at Dilmun, from which colonies departed to build Sumer, the first city of Mesopotamia. Archaeological evidence suggests that Dilmun is modern-day Bahrain. The four-thousand-year-old ruins of a port contained not only stone from nearby Jiddah but also copper from Oman, ivory from Africa or India, and flint weights from the Indus Valley of Pakistan.

Heyerdahl landed at Bahrain to see the ruins—ancient Dilmun. They saw the many freshwater springs that had made the island important, the ancient stone pyramids covered by burial mounds, the buried port city recently excavated, and an ancient temple in ziggurat style. The large stone blocks fit together perfectly without mortar, but there was no stone on the island. The government granted permission for Heyerdahl to see Jiddah, a nearby island containing the ancient stone quarry but now a penal colony closed to tourists. The islanders also repaired Heyerdahl's sail and ship from damage caused by towing and insufficient navigation skills.

With the repaired sail, the crew learned to navigate the ship. They steered through the narrow strait into the Indian Ocean. They avoided high cliffs, supertankers, and offshore oil platforms. On New Year's Eve they celebrated their successful navigation and entrance into the Indian Ocean. Landing in Oman, they visited ruins and copper mines along the north coast. The ancients spoke of a place called Magan that had a copper mountain. This explained the ruined city and the step pyramid (ziggurat) with a temple on top. It also explained why the people of this region had been called Macas in the time of Pliny the Elder.

Next, they sailed across to Karachi in Pakistan, arriving on January 27. They toured ruins upstream in the Indus Valley. The original name of the ruin is lost, but the famed civilization now called Mohenjo-Daro must have been Meluhha. Here, they saw soapstone seals like those at Bahrain. The seals depicted reed ships identical to those in Sumerian records. Now they knew that the Sumerian accounts of sea trade with Dilmun, Magan, and Meluhha were correct.

Heyerdahl sailed from Karachi toward the African coast. He and his crew watched hammerhead sharks swallow a dolphin (dorado) whole. They passed the ancient nation of Punt, now Somalia.

Finally, they landed at Djibouti. Wars in Somalia and Eritrea limited their movement, and Yemen and Ethiopia refused them entry. They had sailed for 144 days and forty-two hundred miles. The reed vessel showed no sign of rotting after five months at sea. Since they were not allowed to enter the Red Sea, they burned *Tigris* on April 3, 1978, as a political statement.

EARL SHAFFER
Hiking the Appalachian Trail

The Appalachian Mountains, named for the Apalachee Indians of Florida, extend fifteen hundred miles from Birmingham, Alabama, to the Gaspé Peninsula of Quebec, Canada. The mountains seem endless, and many ranges within them have separate names. The highest peak of each of the major ranges is shown below. The Adirondack Mountains of New York are not considered part of the Appalachians .

The South

A shrill scream broke the steady patter of raindrops. Earl Shaffer dropped his ax and listened through the gloomy twilight. He turned slowly, peering through the gloom. Was a mountain lion stalking him, or was a lady in distress? He shivered and drew near the fire. As he grew calmer, he recognized the scream of a wildcat. Wildcats, called bobcats in some regions, do not attack adults unless cornered—unlike mountain lions.

Shaffer crossed the wide summit of Blood Mountain (4,461 ft.) the next day. The view surpassed the previous sights of his trip, which included the start of the trail on Mount Oglethorpe, the tallest waterfall in the Appalachians, Amicalola Falls, Springer Mountain, and Long Creek Falls. He enjoyed the view but not the rain, which had drenched him daily these first few days of his hike. He had started on April 4, 1948, having decided to hike the entire Appalachian Trail.

Although trail planners had laid out and hiked most of the route, no one had yet journeyed from end to end in one trip. Shaffer, born on November 8, 1918, in York, Pennsylvania, had recently returned from World War II at the age of twenty-nine. He had decided to combine the solace of the wilderness with the challenge of the first through-hike.

Shaffer flopped onto the ground. He felt dizzy, and his legs were sore and wobbly. He had walked twenty-five miles, and the last few miles of steep climbing had brought him close to collapse. He had found his challenge but still hoped to reach the rustic shelter on Tray Mountain (4,430 ft.) for the evening. Rising, he hauled himself up the last steep grade to the summit. He was so weary, he hardly noticed the spectacular panoramic view, but he instantly noted that no shelter could fit on this craggy pinnacle. His last reserves were exhausted. Cold from the chilly mountain night, he removed his backpack, put on all his clothes, and slept on the ground.

Shaffer had not covered even one hundred miles yet, and he must travel more than two thousand total. He was still in Georgia, only the first of fourteen states on the route. Nevertheless, by morning he felt refreshed. He found the missing shelter only half a mile farther on a ridge below the summit crags. This experience taught him not to give up too quickly. He had been on the trail one week when he crossed the state line into North Carolina.

North Carolina, however, turned out to be rugged country. The Nantahala Mountains stretch all the way to the Great Smoky Mountains. Several of the summits—Standing Indian, Mount Albert, Wayah Bald, and Cheoah Bald—offered beautiful views across the wilderness. Standing Indian was Shaffer's first five-thousand-foot peak, of which there are 195 in the South. The view from Standing Indian has earned it the nickname "Grandstand of the Southern Appalachians."

Shaffer hummed "On Top of Old Smoky" as he climbed Parsons Bald (4,948 ft.), where the Cherokees say the bears gather to hibernate, into the Great Smoky Mountains. He had beautiful weather all four of his days in the Smokies. The "Old Smoky" of the song refers to Clingmans Dome, the highest peak in the range and formerly called Smoky Dome. In fact, Clingmans Dome is the

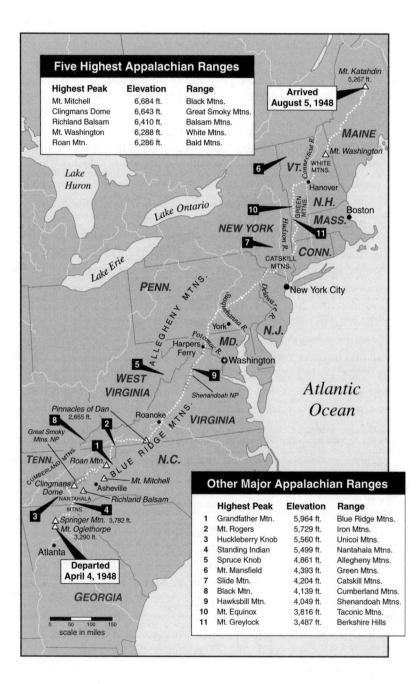

Five Highest Appalachian Ranges

Highest Peak	Elevation	Range
Mt. Mitchell	6,684 ft.	Black Mtns.
Clingmans Dome	6,643 ft.	Great Smoky Mtns.
Richland Balsam	6,410 ft.	Balsam Mtns.
Mt. Washington	6,288 ft.	White Mtns.
Roan Mtn.	6,286 ft.	Bald Mtns.

Mt. Katahdin
5,267 ft.

**Arrived
August 5, 1948**

MAINE

Lake
Huron

Mt. Washington

WHITE
MTNS.

Connecticut R.

VT.

6

Hanover

Lake Ontario

N.H.

GREEN
MTNS.

Hudson R.

10

MASS.

Boston

NEW YORK

11

7

CONN.

Lake Erie

CATSKILL
MTNS.

PENN.

ALLEGHENY MTNS.

New York City

Delaware R.

Susquehanna R.

York

N.J.

Potomac R.

Harpers
Ferry

MD.

5

Washington

WEST
VIRGINIA

9

Shenandoah NP

*Atlantic
Ocean*

Pinnacles of Dan
2,655 ft.

8

Roanoke

2

BLUE RIDGE MTNS.

VIRGINIA

Great Smoky
Mtns. NP

1

TENN.

CUMBERLAND MTNS.

Roan Mtn.

N.C.

Clingmans
Dome

Mt. Mitchell

Asheville

NANTAHALA
MTNS.

Richland Balsam

3

4

Springer Mtn. 3,782 ft.

Mt. Oglethorpe
3,290 ft.

Atlanta

**Departed
April 4, 1948**

GEORGIA

0   50   100   150
scale in miles

Other Major Appalachian Ranges

	Highest Peak	Elevation	Range
1	Grandfather Mtn.	5,964 ft.	Blue Ridge Mtns.
2	Mt. Rogers	5,729 ft.	Iron Mtns.
3	Huckleberry Knob	5,560 ft.	Unicoi Mtns.
4	Standing Indian	5,499 ft.	Nantahala Mtns.
5	Spruce Knob	4,861 ft.	Allegheny Mtns.
6	Mt. Mansfield	4,393 ft.	Green Mtns.
7	Slide Mtn.	4,204 ft.	Catskill Mtns.
8	Black Mtn.	4,139 ft.	Cumberland Mtns.
9	Hawksbill Mtn.	4,049 ft.	Shenandoah Mtns.
10	Mt. Equinox	3,816 ft.	Taconic Mtns.
11	Mt. Greylock	3,487 ft.	Berkshire Hills

highest peak on the entire Appalachian Trail and third highest east of the Mississippi.

The Smokies contain the greatest remaining deciduous forest in the world. the ruggedness of the range provided natural protection to the virgin forest on its slopes. Of the forty-one peaks that exceed six thousand feet in elevation east of the Mississippi, the Smokies contain a dozen, making this the most rugged of the Eastern ranges. The Appalachian Trail passes in sight of all twelve of these Sixers, including Mount Le Conte, the highest from its base, and remote Mount Guyot. The trail follows the North Carolina–Tennessee state line along this chain of high peaks.

Beyond the Smokies, Shaffer followed the trail along the state line through Hot Springs into the Bald Mountains. Balds are mountains with no trees. The grassy balds have great views, and the heath balds, such as Roan Mountain, have beautiful displays of rhododendron. Soon Shaffer crossed the Nolichucky River, where he listened to the whippoorwills most of the night.

Shaffer spent a month hiking across Virginia, which boasts five hundred miles of trail. Fully a quarter of the entire trail lies in this one state. Following the trail, he climbed Virginia's highest mountain, Mount Rogers, and crossed its farmlands and valleys. Before he got very far through the farmlands, he bought mosquito netting. Later, he enjoyed the rugged Pinnacles of Dan and the Peaks of Otter in the famous Blue Ridge Mountains.

Shaffer stared at a sign pointing north into the brush. The trail had become faint, but now he realized that there would be no trail at all for the next seven miles. The trail was being relocated, and the new route was not completed. Shaffer got out his compass and began pushing through the dense tangles of brush.

Rattle! Rattle, rattle, rattle! Shaffer froze in his tracks. He could barely see through the brush. As soon as he heard its warning, he knew he had disturbed a rattlesnake. Memories of the wildcat crowded back into his mind as his eyes searched the ground for this new threat. He spotted the viper just two feet ahead. The rattler shook its ten rattles and coiled its sinuous three-and-a-half-foot body. Shaffer retreated and picked up some long sticks before pushing forward again.

The Blue Ridge soon became a long spine of peaks across Shenandoah National Park. Shaffer took a few side trips in the park to see its highlights: Hawksbill Mountain, Dark Hollow Falls, the six waterfalls of White Oak Canyon, and Old Rag Mountain.

Soon after Shenandoah, Shaffer hiked into Harpers Ferry, West Virginia, the site of a famous Civil War battle. The Shenandoah River joins the Potomac River here as well, and when he had crossed the bridge over the Potomac, he found himself in Maryland. Soon, he had finished the twenty-three-mile walk across Maryland to the Mason-Dixon Line. He had completed his trek across Dixie.

The North

Shaffer felt at home crossing the hills and low mountains of the mid-Atlantic states. He made good time on the familiar rocky trails of his home state of Pennsylvania. He passed through Pilger Ruh, a spring where the Moravian missionary Count Zinzendorf stopped in 1742 on his way to preach to the Shawnee Indians. Shaffer even enjoyed a day with his family before crossing the Poconos.

At the Delaware Water Gap, Shaffer crossed the Delaware River on a bridge and entered New Jersey. Soon he came to the first natural lake of his trip, Sunfish Pond. From here to the end of the trail, Shaffer would see at least one lake or pond every day. He also hiked along Kittatinny Ridge (1,803), the highest mountain in New Jersey, with its peak at High Point State Park.

In New York, Shaffer climbed Bear Mountain (1,305 ft.), where a raccoon got into his water supply. The next day, he paid a five-cent toll to cross the Bear Mountain Bridge over the Hudson River, the lowest point on the entire trail.

Shaffer's first night in Connecticut he built a small fire, which spluttered and crackled in the light rain. He thought "about most everything under Creation" as the fire seemed to speak to him. The next day, he hiked through Dark Entry in Connecticut, with its cascading brook. It was one of his favorite places on the entire trail.

In Massachusetts, Shaffer crossed both Mount Everett and Mount Greylock in the Berkshire Mountains. Mount Greylock is the highest mountain in the state and has an observation tower on its top.

Vermont's Long Trail extends north to south across the state through the beautiful Green Mountains. It had already been built when planners decided that its southern third would also become part of the Appalachian Trail, and so it became the first part completed of the Appalachian Trail. Shaffer followed the trail over Stratton Mountain, into Clarendon Gorge, and across Killington Peak to Sherburne Pass. Little Rocky Pond was another of his favorite spots. However, he would now have to head east to New Hampshire, and he had heard that the connecting trail had been destroyed by hurricanes.

Shaffer waded waist deep across a flooded meadow. No work had been done on the trail in the ten years since the hurricane, and hiking was very difficult. Often he had to improvise a shelter for the night in the devastated area. He made a tepee from branches and covered it with his rain poncho.

Shaffer crossed the Connecticut River and entered Hanover, New Hampshire, on the campus of Dartmouth College. Soon Shaffer met Jimmy Calloway and Paul Yambert, who had started from the north end of the Appalachian Trail on June 1. They hoped to hike the whole trail, and Shaffer figured these two big college boys from Tennessee would be able to make it. He was glad he had started almost two months before them.

The trees got shorter and shorter as Shaffer climbed the White Mountains. Soon there was nothing taller than bushes, and suddenly he found himself in another world on Mount Moosilauke (4,802 ft.). Nothing lived but scattered flowers and ground cover on the bare rocks scoured by howling winds. Shaffer had climbed above the timberline into the tundra, or alpine zone, for his first time. Even the southern balds do not reach the tree line, and the highest southern peaks have forested summits. Shaffer found this alpine zone awe inspiring.

After hiking through Lost River, where a river disappears in huge boulder caves, Shaffer took a wrong turn in a poorly marked area and ended up climbing Mount Cannon and Mount Lafayette before he returned to the main trail. He did not mind because the peaks offered him more time above the timberline. The trail above the timberline was well marked. Since there were no trees to blaze, the planners had built cairns, small mounds of rocks, to mark the way.

Soon glacial lakes were added to the alpine scenery as he climbed Mount Pleasant (now renamed Mount Eisenhower) into the Presidential Range. The Northeast has only one Sixer and nine other peaks exceeding five thousand feet in elevation. The Presidential Range contains the five highest of these ten peaks. Shaffer crossed four of them: Mount Monroe, Mount Washington, Mount Adams, and Mount Madison.

Mount Washington is the highest mountain in the northeastern states and boasts the worst weather in the world. The world-record wind speed of 241 miles per hour was recorded at the summit, and snow can fall during any month—not to mention the rain and storms. The harsh beauty mesmerized Shaffer, and he could have stayed forever, but he knew that a ten-foot snowfall would strand him indefinitely, so he hurried across the peaks. Entering his last shelter in New Hampshire, he surprised a porcupine that was chewing on the floorboards.

Shaffer followed the trail over several of Maine's major peaks: Old Speck, Baldpate, and Sugarloaf. While hiking, he saw deer many times. He found beaver dams and listened to owls and loons. He glimpsed mink and fox as they crossed the trail. The trail passed near two moose, and he barely avoided being charged by the cow moose, which snorted at him when he neared her yearling. He also crossed several canyons, including Gulf Hagas, sometimes called the "Grand Canyon of the East."

Shaffer reflected on the beauty of Maine as he neared the end of the trail on Mount Katahdin. Until Maine, he had not found any wilderness as remote as North Carolina's. Maine did not have North Carolina's rugged Smokies, but he found many proofs of how remote this wilderness had been. Its remoteness was suggested by the many wild animals but proved by the loons on the lakes. Loons, with their haunting cries, will not remain around places that people frequent. He also remembered a sign that read, "Trail closed, in bad condition to Bigelow. Travel at your own risk." After that, there had been a hundred-mile wilderness where no shelters had yet been built. He recalled, too, the summit register on Sugarloaf. In the last five years, only five people had signed it—and two of those five had been Calloway and Yambert only a month before.

At 1:30 P.M. on August 5, 1948, Shaffer reached the summit of Mount Katahdin. He had hiked for four months—124 days—and covered 2,050 miles. He was the first to complete the trek, since Calloway and Yambert were still in central Virginia (and then quit hiking to return to college). It would be three years until a second hiker completed the entire trail. In 1951, Gene Espy became that second hiker, shortly before Chester Dziengielewski and Martin Papendick became the first party to hike the entire trail heading south.

In 1965, Shaffer repeated his adventure but in the opposite direction. Shaffer departed from Mount Katahdin on July 20 and hiked ninety-nine days to the new southern terminus on Springer Mountain. The now well-developed trail had been rerouted in many places. For instance, the trail now visits Roan Mountain but misses the Pinnacles of Dan.

Shaffer has worked on maintaining and rerouting the trail. His hikes helped focus public attention on the trail, and in 1968 the Appalachian Trail became the first complete National Scenic Trail. Still single and an antique collector, he gives occasional slide presentations about his hike emphasizing the continuing encroachment of civilization on the trail.

EDMUND HILLARY
On Mount Everest

Tom Bourdillon watched Charles Evans fall. Could he save Evans with the rope connecting them? Or would the rope pull him into oblivion with Evans? Immediately, he dug his ice axe into the ground as an anchor and began wrapping the rope around his axe. His precarious perch on the steep icy slope made it difficult in his hurry. Evans reached the end of the rope, and his weight jerked the axe free. Bourdillon struggled to hold their combined weight from his awkward position. His feet slid, and he fell on his back down the mountain.

Bourdillon rolled to his stomach and pushed his ice axe into the snow as a brake. He and Evans kept falling, but as he pushed harder they began to slow. Though his attempted belay had failed, it had slowed his partner's fall, giving him time to brake. When they stopped, both men sat for a long time.

Edmund Hillary listened to Bourdillon's report of yesterday's climb. Bourdillon and Evans had camped at Camp 8 on the South Col (*col* is French for "a pass" and is common in Europe and Asia). They had climbed to the South Peak of Mount Everest, 28,700 feet, surpassing the previous altitude record set by Mallory, but had not reached the main summit. Tired, they had almost died in the fall while descending, but they finally returned to the South Col. They were glad they had not pushed for the main summit because the fall would probably have killed them if they had been any more exhausted. Besides their new record, they had two other contributions that were essential to Hillary. They had cached supplies at the South Peak and provided a report of conditions there. Since no one else had ever reached that point, they alone could supply information critical to Hillary's climb in the days ahead.

Hillary reviewed the expedition's progress. From Kathmandu on March 10, 1953, they had walked 175 miles with fifteen tons of equipment to the Buddhist monastery at Thyangboche (13,500 ft. elevation), where yaks grazed and the abbots told stories about the abominable snowman. Thirteen miles farther they had set up base camp at 17,900 feet, where they had paid and released most of the 450 porters. They grew accustomed to the altitude and trained the remaining porters in ice climbing. On April 13, the fifty-man party had begun transporting equipment up the Khumbu Icefall at the base of the Khumbu Glacier. They stayed away from the snowy cliffs at the sides of the valley to avoid being hit by avalanches, but they eventually abandoned Camp 2 due to dangerous shifting ice. After rescuing porters who had fallen through thin ice into crevasses, they established Camp 3 on top of the glacier at 20,200 feet, and by May 18 they had transported three tons of equipment to Camp 4, the forward camp, or tent village.

The face of Mount Everest being too steep, the expedition had climbed upward on neighboring Lhotse. George Lowe had worked eleven days straight establishing a route halfway up the face of Lhotse with Camps 5, 6, and 7 spaced every thousand vertical feet. From there, on May 21, Wilfrid Noyce and Annullu had pioneered the horizontal traverse, gradually ascending to the South Col for Camp 8, on the flanks of Everest itself. The next day Hillary, Tenzing Norgay, and Charles Wylie had led fourteen Sherpa porters across. On May 24, John Hunt and several others had arrived, and the following day they had all rested. On May 26, John Hunt and Da Namgyal had trail blazed to an altitude of 27,350 feet. Bourdillon and Evans had followed behind and gone on to reach the South Peak later that day.

"Come back safely. Remember that. But get up if you can," John Hunt, leader of the British expedition, admonished Hillary in parting. He hoped Hillary and Norgay could get to the top—but not

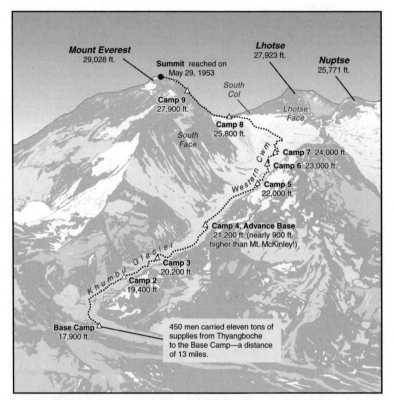

Mount Everest
29,028 ft.

Summit reached on
May 29, 1953

Lhotse
27,923 ft.

Nuptse
25,771 ft.

South
Col

Camp 9
27,900 ft.

Lhotse
Face

South
Face

Camp 8
25,800 ft.

Western Cwm

Camp 7 24,000 ft.

Camp 6 23,000 ft.

Camp 5
22,000 ft.

Camp 4, Advance Base
21,200 ft. (nearly 900 ft.
higher than Mt. McKinley!)

Glacier

Camp 3
20,200 ft.

Camp 2
19,400 ft.

Khumbu Glacier

Base Camp
17,900 ft.

450 men carried eleven tons of
supplies from Thyangboche
to the Base Camp—a distance
of 13 miles.

at risk of their lives. Hunt and most of the other climbers descended to conserve supplies at Camp 8.

Hillary and his five remaining companions now prepared for the last attempt. The six men dozed fitfully in the two tents pitched at Camp 8 in the South Col, a snowy saddle between Lhotse and Mount Everest, the fourth highest and the highest mountain in the world, respectively.

Pemba's dry heaves awakened Hillary. The thin air at 25,800 feet caused altitude sickness and made them all lose their appetite and feel lightheaded. Pemba had been included among the six because he had held up so well at twice the altitude that usually caused altitude sickness, but this sudden case would end his climb. The only cure is descent, and Pemba had to go down.

George Lowe, at thirty-nine the oldest man on the team but the strongest at cutting snow steps, started blazing the icy trail with Alfred Gregory and Ang Nyima. Two hours later, Edmund Hillary and Tenzing Norgay came after them on the fresh-cut ice trail and caught up by noon. The three trailblazers rested near a battered tent that Tenzing recognized as his last camp with Lambert on the unsuccessful Swiss expedition of the year before.

Hillary recalled his own part in the Swiss expedition last year, but he had not come this far himself. It was this previous experience that had caused Hunt to include Hillary on the present expedition. Hillary, born on July 20, 1919, in Auckland, New Zealand, was the only New Zealander on the British expedition.

In fact, few people had ever been this far. The Dalai Lama of Tibet in 1920 had signed the first climbing permits for Mount Everest but then prohibited climbing again in the late 1940s. In 1949, Nepal had permitted the first climbs from the south. All the attempts during those years had failed, seven from the north and one from the south. Of these, Mallory and Irvine in 1924 had come closest to reaching the summit. Mallory once called the mountain a great "white fang," but he answered those who asked why anyone would climb Mount Everest with the famous words, "Because it's there." Though Mallory and Irvine had attained twenty-eight thousand feet, they had not lived to tell it and were last seen climbing into the mists. In fact, this "white fang" had claimed sixteen lives so far.

Furthermore, there are only fourteen mountains greater than twenty-six thousand feet in elevation in the whole world. All defied climbing until 1950. Many people died on these peaks. In 1950, Herzog and Lachenal, two Frenchmen, had succeeded in scaling Annapurna. None of the other high peaks had been conquered, and even Annapurna's elevation of 26,504 feet had not surpassed the altitude record of Mallory and Irvine.

Hillary's thoughts returned to Everest as he and his four friends began climbing up its steep slopes. They soon found the supplies placed by John Hunt two days before and rested again briefly. Everest filled Hillary's thoughts. He recalled that the mountain had been named after Sir George Everest, who had retired as head of the geographical survey of India in 1843. Sir Everest had simply numbered the world's highest peak as Peak 15, but his successor, as head of the survey, decided to name it in Sir Everest's honor. Of course, the mountain already had local names. The Tibetans call it Chomolungma, meaning Goddess Mother of the World. In Nepal, it is called Sagarmatha, which has a similar meaning (and which eventually became the name for Sagarmatha National Park).

Hillary hoped to find room for a tent, but the steep ridge rarely offered room even to sit. Finally, his party found a small icy area, barely large enough for two people to stretch out. It tilted down at a thirty-degree angle toward an ice cliff of several thousand feet, but it would serve as Camp 9. After the three trailblazers left, Hillary and Norgay bedded down at 6:30 P.M. at 27,900 feet—the highest camp in history.

Hillary and Norgay awoke at 4:00 A.M. The first rays breaking on the peaks of treacherous Ama Dablam and distant Makalu inspired them to climb. Norgay pointed to Thyangboche Monastery in the distance, fifteen thousand feet below. By 9:00 A.M., they reached the South Peak and found the supplies left by Bourdillon and Evans three days before. Pushing on, they came to a forty-foot-high boulder. To the left they looked down eight thousand feet into the icy, glacier-filled valley, called the Western Cwm, that they had spent well over a month climbing. To the right, a snowy cornice that could easily break off and trigger an avalanche projected over a valley ten thousand feet below. Before them a sheer rock face rose forty feet.

Their only chance was to shimmy up a narrow gap, or chimney, between the rock face and the snow cornice. Hoping that the snow would hold their weight, Hillary and then Norgay wedged their way between rock and ice, inching their way up for a half-hour. The boulder overcome, they continued climbing.

Edmund Hillary and Tenzing Norgay reached the top of the world. Their handshake turned into a hug as they shared the joy of victory. At 11:30 A.M. on May 29, 1953, for the first time, they had an unrestricted view of the vast range of unconquered peaks spreading in all directions. Hillary shot photos in every direction as proof of their success, including one of Norgay waving his ice axe from which fluttered four flags: Great Britain as the source of the expedition, Nepal and India for the location and porters, and the United Nations for the international effort.

Hillary took off his oxygen mask for a while to feel the thin, chilly air at 29,028 feet above sea level and to conserve oxygen for the descent. It was very hard to breathe. His legs became heavy, and each task became slow and laborious. Lack of oxygen also affects the mind and causes climbers to make poor decisions, so Hillary made sure to put the mask back on before descending.

Hillary and Norgay descended quickly, except in the treacherous area below the South Peak where Evans had fallen. The winds had erased their trail. Though very tired, they had to cut steps all over again. At the South Col, a lone figure came out from Camp 8 to meet them with hot soup—George Lowe. Hillary sipped the steaming soup. With his New Zealand accent, he quietly informed Lowe of their success: "Well, we knocked the blighter off."

The next morning, they descended to Camp 7, where Charles Wylie and his Sherpa porters met them. Some of these Sherpas had worked with many expeditions trying to reach the summit. Norgay himself had been on five previous expeditions. The Indian and Nepalese Sherpas shouted the victory, *"Everest katm ho gya"*—"Everest has had it."

Descending to Camp 4, the group shared the victory with leader John Hunt, who had worked so hard preparing clothes and food, transporting gear and ropes, guiding practices in the Swiss Alps, coordinating schedules, planning routes and camps, and caching supplies as high as 27,350 feet. After two months of hardships, the entire team shared the joy of victory. Even though only two had reached the summit, the entire team had contributed to the expedition. The expedition had succeeded because of teamwork.

A few days later at Thyangboche, they informed the abbots that they had not seen the yeti. The yeti, or abominable snowman, is supposedly a creature five feet high and covered with reddish hair, whose exploits are legendary throughout the Himalayas. In fact, none of the expeditions had ever spotted the yeti—except perhaps Mallory and Irvine.

Mount Everest is surpassed in certain characteristics elsewhere in the world. Although Mount Everest rises steeply (12,000 ft. above the Tibetan Plateau), Mount McKinley rises 19,000 feet from its lowland base. Mount Everest presents technical difficulties for climbers, but such difficulties are matched by famous ascents in the Alps. The cold temperatures of -40°F can freeze the perspiration on a climber's feet, causing frostbite, but Greenland's icecap reaches even colder temperatures. The icefalls and crevasses of Mount Everest's glaciers pose many threats to climbers, but Antarctica has even larger glaciers. Mount Everest has severe weather and biting winds, but the Atlantic gales buffeting the Scottish Highlands are equally strong. However, none of these other places combine all these factors at once: steepness, technical difficulty, cold, glaciers, and winds. In summer, the powder snows threaten climbers with avalanches; and in winter the gales blow away the snow, but they blow too hard for humans to endure.

Besides all these harsh conditions, Mount Everest has yet another harsh condition—one that is unmatched anywhere else. Mount Everest has the world's highest altitudes, and it is the only mountain in the world that is high enough to puncture the jet stream. Such high altitudes provide only one third as much oxygen as necessary. Even a physically fit professional football or basketball star, if deposited at the top of Mount Everest by helicopter, would become delirious within fifteen minutes without oxygen equipment. Because of Hillary's willingness to endure such harsh conditions, Queen Elizabeth II of Britain knighted the beekeeper from New Zealand. The conqueror of Everest became Sir Edmund Hillary.

These harsh conditions combined with the highest altitude have earned Mount Everest the nickname, the "Third Pole." Certainly, it is the pinnacle of all climbing achievements in history. Its ascent is the culmination of the altitude records of the century (see also Harold Tilman) as shown in the following chart.

HIGHEST PEAK EVER CLIMBED

Elevation					
ft.	m	Peak	Place	Date	Team
23,359	7120	Trisul	India	6-12-07	British
23,386	7128	Pauhunri	Sikkim	1910	British
24,550	7483	Jongsong	Sikkim	1930	German Dyhrenfurth
25,446	7756	Kamet	India	6-21-31	British Shipton
25,643	7816	Nanda Devi	India	8-29-36	U.S.-British Tilman
26,504	8079	Annapurna	Nepal	6-3-50	French Herzog
29,028	8848	Everest	Nepal	5-29-53	British Hillary

PETE SCHOENING
To Antarctica's Highest Peaks

Rescue on K2

Pete Schoening watched George Bell slip on the ice and lose control. Bell, a physics professor from Cornell University, was roped to Tony Streather, an English army officer who had already climbed Tirich Mir. Since Streather was leading, he had not seen Bell slip and was not prepared to arrest Bell's fall. Bell's wild plunge jerked Streather off balance, and they tumbled together down the face of K2, the second highest mountain in the world.

Schoening gasped as Bell and Streather snagged the rope of the next two climbers below them. Charlie Houston was one of America's Himalayan climbing experts at the time, but because he and Bob Bates had been traversing the same steep icy slope just below Bell and Streather, they did not see the fall above and behind them. The ropes tangled and the momentum ripped Houston and Bates into the same headlong plunge. Now four men hurtled toward death in free fall down the glacier.

Schoening looked across at the campsite ridge. The team of eight had been so close to camp. Schoening could see Bob Craig, the Aspen ski instructor, already unroped at the campsite. Schoening had belayed Craig down the steep gully only a few minutes earlier, and Craig was already at camp and out of danger.

After Craig, Schoening had also belayed the two geologists: Dee Molenaar first and then Art Gilkey of Iowa. Actually, Gilkey was strapped to a stretcher. Schoening, the strongest man on the team, had remained last to belay the stretcher down the gully. The stretcher, resting on an ice ledge in the gully below, was tied to Schoening above and also to Molenaar, who was moving toward the campsite. Schoening suddenly realized that the four falling men were on a collision course with Molenaar's rope. If the collision dislodged Molenaar, it would pull the stretcher and then Schoening into the free fall as well.

Schoening and his team had arrived in Karachi on May 28, 1953, and had set up Base Camp at the foot of K2 on June 19. They had toiled up K2's Abruzzi Ridge, establishing seven camps, until he and Art Gilkey had fought the fierce winds and frigid foul weather to establish Camp 8 at 25,400 feet on August 1. The team had spent a miserable week at Camp 8; a tent had collapsed the first night. The blizzard never gave opportunity for a summit attempt. Gilkey had developed blood clots and thrombosis in the veins of his legs, and Dr. Charles Houston, the leader, had decided to evacuate. They waited for better weather, but Gilkey grew worse. On August 10, it had taken all day to lower the stretcher the five hundred vertical feet to Camp 7, and now the fall had occurred. Summit hopes were dashed, but could they even hope for life?

Streather crashed into Molenaar's rope and tumbled over it. With the ropes thus tangled, the weight of four men yanked Molenaar off his feet. Schoening's mind raced as he braced himself for the impact of five bodies reaching the end of their ropes. All their weight would hang on Schoening via Gilkey's stretcher. Had Schoening any chance of breaking the fall of five men and then supporting the weight of all six? If not, Bob Craig would have to attempt a descent from Camp 7 alone. Schoening recoiled at the prospect of joining the human avalanche that was about to claim seven lives on K2. Schoening was staring death in the face.

Schoening felt the jerk on his rope, which he gripped with all his might. How long could he hold it? He reminded himself that six men depended on him for life. The pull eased. He saw a jumble of limbs as Bates, Molenaar, and Streather came to rest. Houston slid farther. He was slumped unconscious on a ledge above a high ice cliff, but his rope to Bates had held. Bell also remained roped, though he wandered in a daze on his tether to Streather, having fallen the farthest of all.

Bates descended and roused Houston, who asked, "Where are we?" The concussion had left him confused, but Bates ordered him to climb, and he did.

Exhausted and with evening fast approaching, the party set up camp. It was hard to get it pitched in the driving snow. Schoening was weak with the tension and had begun coughing. Bates and Streather went to fetch the stretcher. It was gone! As they looked around, they noticed the ice-swept signs of an avalanche. Gilkey had been swept away, and K2 had claimed another life.

The climbers spent another full day descending to Camp 6, but by the following day they reached Camp 4 at dusk. After belaying the rest of the team, Houston prayed the Lord's Prayer before descending the final chimney with no one to belay him.

The team reached Base Camp two days later. They were heavy-hearted, numb, and completely exhausted. The porters helped them pile rocks as a memorial for Art Gilkey. Bates read from the Bible and prayed to complete the funeral service. George Bell had frost-bitten feet and had to be carried over one hundred miles to Skardu. One-and-a-half toes had to be amputated.

All the climbers thanked Schoening for holding out and saving their lives. Schoening was twenty-nine years old and already known for his strength. He often continued to climb when everyone else needed rest. However, his ability to check the fall of five men at once for those critical seconds amazed them all.

No glory came to this expedition, but there had been teamwork. The exciting evacuation story was completely lost in the news of Hillary's success on Everest, which had occurred the day after the K2 team had arrived in Karachi. However, the American expedition had been just as heroic in its own way. This epic retreat has been called "the finest moment in the history of American mountaineering." Back home in Seattle, Schoening regretted only their failure to save Gilkey.

Hidden Peak

Nick Clinch, a law student from Pasadena, reviewed the climbers on the expedition. He had a permit to climb Hidden Peak in Pakistan but not enough climbers. Hidden Peak is one of the 8000-meter peaks and twelfth highest in the world. By the fall of 1957, years after Hillary had climbed Everest, it was one of only three that still had never been climbed four.

So far three other friends from California had agreed to go: Tom McCormack (a rancher from Rio Vista), Bob Swift, and Andy Kaufman. Clinch had also finally found a climber/medical student in Tom Nevison. He decided to invite Pakistani climbers. This would make it a joint expedition of America and Pakistan. As far as he knew, no foreign climbing teams had ever included Pakistanis, and it would be a nice gesture. While he awaited the selection of Tas Rizvi and Mohd Akram, he polled his team on who else to invite. The first choice on every ballot was Pete Schoening.

When Schoening finally obtained leave from his chemical engineering job, the team consulted on who would be leader. Clinch wanted the leader to be the most experienced climber, and Schoening became the leader by consensus. Schoening, however, was glad for Clinch to complete the arrangements. There remained only a few months until the new team would be in the snows on Hidden Peak.

"That mountain is huge," thought Clinch. He got his first view of Hidden Peak as they pitched and stocked Base Camp on the upper Baltoro Glacier June 5-9. Clinch had arrived in Karachi on April 29, finished preparations, and gone on to Rawalpindi. By May 15, the team had assembled at Skardu, where the long approach march began. Their Balti porters had insisted on remaining barefoot, even on the ice of the glacier. Now, after taking their pay, they departed. Their team retained only six special high-altitude porters.

Schoening, Kaufman, and Clinch went up for a couple of days to look over the Roch Ridge route, which had been recommended by climbers from a previous attempt. As they returned, sinking waist deep in the snow, Schoening kept a steady relentless pace. Clinch grew weary but did not understand why. Looking at Kaufman's weary face, he suddenly realized that they were both tired because they were tied to a man who did not know his own strength.

Meanwhile, the others had explored the northwest ridge. They compared notes on the two routes, and after some debate, Schoening called for a vote. The team would climb the Roch Ridge. By June 13, they had established Camp 1. The next day Schoening and Nevison began attaching ropes on the steep ridge above, which would enable the six porters to help carry supplies up. Within a few more days, they attached the rest of the ropes and made Camp 2.

"Hey, look! A snow leopard!" Akram called to Schoening at dusk on June 19. Schoening saw nothing and returned to writing. When Akram called again, they looked around camp and found paw prints two-and-a-half inches long. Akram was right; there were snow leopards around their camp.

Schoening and Akram rose early the next day and hauled another load of supplies to Camp 1. When Schoening said they had kept a steady pace, Clinch noted Akram's weariness. Clinch reassured him, "Don't worry . . . no one can keep up with Pete." Akram felt relieved, and Schoening continued to Camp 2. On June 22, Schoening opened the route to Camp 3 but broke his ice axe as he was chopping ice for a tent platform. When Clinch heard about the broken axe, he looked doubtful. No one had ever broken a new Bhend axe on ice. Nevison confirmed it, though, saying "He was chopping ice. I saw him do it."

The following day, Schoening and Kaufman carried loads to Camp 3 and descended again to Camp 2. As Clinch trudged in from Camp 1, Schoening saw him and came down to carry his pack up the last seventy yards. On June 25, a larger group made a similar roundtrip. This way they could stockpile supplies at higher elevations without using them up. Climbing to higher elevations and sleeping at lower ones also helped them grow acclimated to the elevation.

Qasim, the strongest of the porters, followed Schoening's earlier example. Qasim, Clinch, and Swift had arrived at Camp 3 first, and when he saw Rizvi climbing wearily , Qasim went down to carry his pack the last stretch. When they returned to Camp 2, they heard that Kaufman and another porter had climbed from Camp 1 to

Camp 2 with supplies and then returned to Camp 1. This proved that Kaufman was now acclimated and in good shape. No one had made a roundtrip on the steep, long, and difficult stretch between those two camps since the first haul on June 15. It had been Qasim who did that first one.

Clinch, Rizvi, Qasim, and another porter climbed to Camp 3 on June 26. A blizzard trapped them the next day, but it finally stopped two days later. Before they got moving, Schoening, Kaufman, and a porter arrived.

"How did you get here so early?" asked Clinch.

"We bivouacked on the ridge."

Clinch's mouth dropped open. "In the blizzard?"

Schoening explained that they had begun in the snow, but as it got worse the porter would not use his goggles to improve visibility. This resulted in snow blindness, which had slowed them further, and they had been forced to pitch the tent for the night.

The rest of the team arrived at Camp 3 later that afternoon. All agreed that they should establish Camps 4 and 5 and reach the summit as fast as possible. Schoening called for a written vote for summit teams. They counted the scraps of paper. Although no one had voted for himself, it was otherwise unanimous: Schoening and Kaufman would make the first attempt. A second vote decided that Swift, Nevison, and Rizvi would support them and make a second attempt. That would leave Clinch and McCormack to support the second group and make a third attempt if possible.

Camp 4 was established on June 29. They had finally reached the plateau on top, and the steep ridge was behind them. The plateau connected the summit of Hidden Peak several miles away with South Hidden Peak and Urdok Peak. However, the last stretch of ridge had been difficult, and the carry from Camp 3 was short. They had been forced to cut through a cornice, then rappel into an ice cave below, and then crampon out onto the plateau. With fixed ropes, porters could pass supplies to the ice cave, but they absolutely refused to rappel. Meanwhile, Rizvi and McCormack had not felt well, so they remained in the third group, and Clinch took Rizvi's place in the second summit bid.

Snows halted them for four days. They got two deliveries from porters. The porters would yell from the top of the rappel; climbers would cross the plateau to meet them and then receive the packs that they lowered on the ropes. The entire team was glad for the brave Baltis who had climbed this high and made runs between camps unescorted. During this time, Kaufman's face, sunburnt and blistered from exposure, began cracking and bleeding. They put salve on it, but it just grew worse.

On July 4, they set out again, hoping to establish Camp 5. They were roped together, each carrying fifty pounds. The man in front, though, would have to break trail. They would take turns doing this while carrying a light pack and using oxygen masks. Schoening went first, sinking up to his knees with each step. They were surprised that such a strong man was going so slowly. It took a half-hour to cover about a half mile. As each man's turn came, he realized how difficult it was. Carrying heavier loads over a broken trail without oxygen masks was easier than breaking trail even with the benefit of an oxygen mask and no load. As each man's turn ended, he collapsed in the snow for the rest time and rearranging of packs. After the first round of half-hour stints, the oxygen regulator jammed.

For the second round, the lead man would not have oxygen. They decided on ten-minute turns. Each man achieved about one hundred feet distance and thirty feet elevation. Swift was last and did a bit better. Schoening took a third shift and got them to Camp 5. It was 3:00 P.M., and it had taken a whole day to climb fifteen hundred feet and cross a stretch of about three miles. Hidden Peak still taunted them, being twice as far ahead.

Everyone dumped the supplies, and Schoening and Kaufman thanked them and prepared for the night. With words of encouragement, the others returned to Camp 4. Going downhill on a broken trail without loads was much easier, but they still required rests every half-hour.

The wristwatch alarm borrowed from Nevison sounded at 3:00 A.M. Everything moved slowly, though. Cooking breakfast and dressing, including coats and crampons, required two hours. They had slept all right using the oxygen tanks, and now it was time.

Again, they sank knee-deep with every step, but there was less to carry. Twice they crossed snow bridges over crevasses and another time crossed a cornice where it had recently broken. Five hours later they reached a col a mile from Camp 5 and five hundred feet above it. As they progressed, it got icier. They no longer sank in with each step, but they had to spend time belaying one another on some icy ridges. When they realized the oxygen bottles were empty, they discarded them and started the second ones. After a wearisome climb of a chimney with crumbling ice and snow, they ascended the final ridge and reached the summit!

The view of K2 was spectacular. Schoening pointed out the site of Camp 8, used in 1953. Thoughts of that disastrous climb reminded him that he was no longer single. Schoening, born July 30, 1927, in Seattle, had married Mell Deuter after returning from K2.

Flashes interrupted Schoening's reminescence. Camp 3 far below was sending mirror signals. They flashed back using a metal can. His party photographed themselves and the flags. By 4:00 P.M., after spending an hour on the summit, they started down. By 7:30 P.M., they were back at the high col, where their last oxygen ran out. Soon it was dark, but they made it to Camp 5 by 9:00 P.M. They boiled a pot of snow—it was the only water they had had to drink all day. Too tired to boil more, they fell asleep.

Meanwhile, Nevison and Swift had descended to Camp 3 for more supplies. It was they who had signaled with mirrors. When they returned that evening to Camp 4, they told Clinch about the signals. Through binoculars, they had watched Schoening and Kaufman descending slowly, but they had lost sight of the pair at dusk. They also shared news from Base Camp that Alaska had become the forty-ninth state and that the monsoon was due at K2 within a week.

The next morning, Schoening and Kaufman continued down, while the three men at Camp 4 started up. When they met, Schoening and Kaufman immediately collapsed. Kaufman volunteered, "Pete Schoening climbed this mountain. Pete broke trail over two-thirds of the way." The other three considered. They would have a third man to take turns, but it would obviously be exhausting. At length, they decided that the expedition had already succeeded and that the potential danger of the coming monsoon was not worth the risk to extra climbers on the summit. The three continued to Camp 5, but only to bring down gear.

As they descended, the team rejoiced over the victory of July 5, 1958, for America and Pakistan on Hidden Peak. This was the only 8000-meter peak on which these nations gained a first ascent.

Vinson Massif

Eighty-mile-per-hour winds ripped through tent fabric. The chill winds bent poles as they whipped across the Antarctic Plateau. The famed gusts of Antarctica lifted stored boxes and crashed them onto the glacial ice. Sleeping bags, pots, and food rations spilled from the broken boxes and were strewn by the winds across the ice in a two-mile radius.

The six men at the base scurried after the gear. They wondered how the four men were doing at Camp 1 on the slopes of Vinson Massif, the highest mountain in Antarctica. They could not think much because they had to focus on chasing gear. The team would not survive the bitter cold unless they could regather most of the essential gear. The closest outside help was Byrd Station, 450 miles away.

After sacrificing their sleep, the men at Base Camp had regained most of their gear. At noon the next day, they finally established radio contact with Camp 1. Expedition leader Nick Clinch at Camp 1 listened to the report that "Base Camp is flattened!" and decided to descend to help with repairs. If the expedition were to succeed in climbing Antarctica's highest peak, Clinch would have to act as organizer and leave the climbing glory to others. Clinch sent Barry Corbet up to Camp 1 as his replacement. Corbet, of Jackson, Wyoming, had been on the first American ascent of Mount Everest in 1963 and would be a good replacement. Corbet would climb with Bill Long of Anchorage, who had climbed on three continents.

Schoening remained at Camp 1. He had been in the other tent at Camp 1 with his partner John Evans. Though their tent had bent poles, the high camp had fared better than Base Camp. John Evans of Minneapolis, though younger, had pioneered a difficult new route on Canada's highest peak, Mount Logan, and was likely the most muscular man on the team.

Schoening, Evans, Long, and Corbet had been selected as the climbers most likely to summit. On December 17, they had established Camp 3 and spent another windy and sleepless night. They all knew that not only was this mountain the highest on the seventh continent, but this continent was the only one on which the highest peak had not already been climbed.

The peak was not well known. Standing in the Sentinel Range of the Ellsworth Mountains, it stood in mountains that had not even been discovered until American Lincoln Ellsworth spotted them from a plane in 1935. It was not until 1957 that a land survey located Vinson Massif (named after Representative Carl Vinson of Georgia) as the highest summit at 16,860 feet (corrected in 1972 to 16,067 ft.). Rising high on the coldest continent, Vinson's extreme cold easily surpasses Mount Everest's harsh conditions, which result primarily from oxygen deficiency. Vinson also has a good chance at exceeding the cold of Mount McKinley, which is usually considered the coldest mountain on earth because it is so high and so far north.

The next morning, December 18, 1966, the four climbers rose early and trudged up the windblown summit of Vinson Massif. By December 20, the rest of the team had also reached the summit:

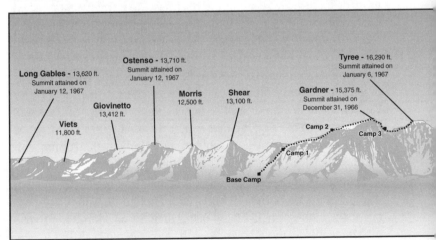

Nick Clinch, Sam Silverstein of New York City, Charley Hollister of Massachusetts, and three men from the Seattle area—Brian Marts, Eiichi Fukushima, and Dick Wahlstrom. The next day, December 21, the entire team climbed neighboring Mount Shinn, the third highest peak on the continent, from Camp 1. The ten climbers celebrated their two successes with a very white Christmas on the Antarctic Plateau at eighty-five hundred feet.

Evans and Marts made the first ascent of Mount Gardner from a new base camp on New Year's Eve. After the New Year's Day blizzard, most of the team climbed Mount Gardner and descended to Base Camp. They had pitched Camps 1 and 2 on a route up Mount Gardner because they were hoping to find a route up rugged Mount Tyree, the second highest peak on the continent.

Evans and Corbet descended the sheer ice from Mount Gardner to reach a narrow windswept ridge toward Mount Tyree. They pitched Camp 3 on the ridge and camped alone on January 4. They hoped they could cross the pinnacles between them and Tyree's summit.

The next morning, they scaled the first tower with pitons and carabiners but could not descend the far side. Defeated, they returned to Camp 2, where only two men remained to greet them. Since ten men had given over a week of effort, Evans and Corbet

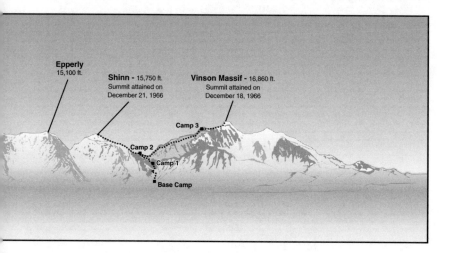

wanted to try one more time to succeed for the team. Tomorrow would be their last chance.

Using their fixed ropes, they quickly descended Mount Gardner early on January 6. At the base of the tower that had defeated them, they descended a snowy cliff and ascended a couloir (steep gully). They traversed the rocky pinnacles along the remainder of the ridge and stopped for lunch after seven hours of climbing. Temperatures of 25° below zero kept the stop short. Alternating leads for another five and a half hours of steep climbing, they pulled themselves over the last icy ledge to the summit.

During their final week in Antarctica, Clinch and Corbet provided Base Camp support for two simultaneous climbs. Schoening, Marts, Fukushima, and Long struggled up Long Gables, which had been named after Long and his brother, both of whom had been on the first surveying team in 1957. They succeeded in climbing this second most difficult peak of the trip on January 12, 1967. Meanwhile, Evans, Silverstein, Hollister, and Wahlstrom ascended Mount Ostenso, giving the American expedition its sixth Antarctic summit, including more than half of the major peaks in the Sentinel Range.

Peter K. Schoening returned home to the Seattle area, where he and his wife live with their six children. Schoening continues to climb. During the 1980s, he climbed in remote areas of China.

JACQUES PICCARD
The Bottom of the Ocean

Stratosphere by Balloon

Jacques Piccard's father, Auguste (1884-1962), invented the stratosphere balloon using principles that would later be applied to bathyscaphs. Manned balloons could not rise into the stratosphere because the low oxygen level suffocated the pilots. Pilots swiftly grew dizzy, blacked out, and died. Auguste Piccard's new balloon carried an airtight gondola. He named it *FNRS* for *Fonds National de la Recherche Scientifique,* the organization that had financed him. On May 27, 1931, Auguste Piccard and his partner Paul Kipfer lifted off from Augsburg, Germany. They ascended to a record height of 51,775 feet in about a half-hour. Since the hydrogen-release rope tangled, they waited for sunset when cooler air would naturally stretch the rope and open the valve. When the balloon did not return on schedule, the media reported that the balloon was floating "out of control and occupied only by the dead." The balloonists landed safely on the Gurgl Glacier (now Piccard Glacier) in the Tyrollean Alps of Austria. However, the record did not stand long.

Jacques Piccard watched his father and Max Cosyns rise to 53,152 feet on August 18, 1932. Jacques, born on July 28, 1922, was only ten years old. His father had launched from Zurich and eventually landed in northern Italy. Two years later, Jacques's uncle, Jean Felix Piccard (1884-1963), rose to 57,579 feet with his wife on October 27, 1934, at Dearborn, Michigan. Mrs. Piccard set a long-standing altitude record for women and became the first woman in the stratosphere. Later, Jean helped design *Skyhook,* which reached over one hundred thousand feet.

High-altitude balloons rise because they are filled with helium, which is lighter than air. Releasing some gas partially empties the balloon to make it descend. Throwing ballast (lead pellets) overboard lightens the balloon to make it rise again. Pilots control the vertical heights of balloons, but winds control the direction, much like a sailboat. Balloons drift, having no engines.

Bathyscaphs

In 1840, oceanographers believed that life would be crushed by the water pressure at any depth below 1700 feet. However, from 1869 to the turn of the century, trawlers brought fish and starfish to the surface from depths as low as of twenty thousand feet. In 1951, a Danish ship obtained sea cucumbers and anemones from a depth of 33,400 feet.

During World War I, Mindanao Trench was the deepest known spot in the world, but during World War II a nearby spot was found to be deeper at 34,440 feet. Later, the Tonga Trench was sounded at 34,880 feet deep. In 1951, three ships of various nations sounded the Challenger Deep in the Mariana Trench, finding and confirming the current record depth of 35,800 feet.

There are three types of underwater vessels. *Submarines* are similar to airplanes in providing engine power and steering. Subs are not designed to withstand sea bottom pressures, have no portholes for observations, and are crowded with weapons. *Bathyspheres* are similar to kites in that they are always a engineless, watertight sphere used for the first deep-ocean descents. A barge lowers the two-and-a-half-ton steel sphere on a cable and then draws it back up. William Beebe and Otis Barton made such descents to depths of half a mile in the early 1930s. *Bathyscaphs,* however, are similar to balloons. They are self-contained vessels not linked to the surface. Lacking an engine, they are driven by the currents. Auguste Piccard invented the bathyscaph.

The many-ton bathyscaph dives when the air compartments at each end are flooded. To return to the surface, tons of iron pellets are jettisoned. For safety, the ballast is mounted on the outside and held by huge electromagnets. Any power failure disables the magnets, thus dropping the ballast and sending the vessel back to the surface. Piccard's vessel also contained twenty-eight thousand gallons of gasoline. Since gasoline floats on water, it serves much like helium in a balloon. A valve permitted gasoline to be released into the sea, reducing buoyancy for the descent. Bathyscaph operators control vertical motion, but ocean currents determine horizontal motion.

Process	Balloon	Bathyscaph
leaving the surface of the earth	helium (lighter than air)	vessel weight (heavier than water)
returning to the surface	release helium (to descend)	drop ballast (to ascend)
adjusting vertical position or speed	drop ballast or release some helium	drop ballast or release some gasoline

The first bathyscaph, *FNRS-2,* made an unmanned dive to 4,500 feet in the Atlantic Ocean near the Cape Verde Islands on November 3, 1948. The French obtained the bathyscaph and remodeled it as the *FNRS-3.* They sent Houot and Willm to a depth of 1,150 feet off the coast near Toulon for a record depth in a manned vessel.

Mediterranean

Stuck in the mud at the bottom of the sea! Mud covered the front porthole of the *Trieste.* Jacques Piccard and his father, Auguste, moved to the back porthole. They had hoped to make great ocean bottom discoveries on this deepest manned dive, but all they could see was a vast featureless plain. Now, almost two miles deep at 10,390 feet, they were embedded in sea floor muck. The physicists had been warned to expect suction, but Piccard's calculations had shown that there should be nothing to fear.

Piccard threw the switch to drop the ballast. They could see the iron pellets dropping into the sea from the rear porthole, but the bathyscaph was not moving! With Swiss funding and Italian engineering, they had built the bathyscaph *Trieste*. They had descended in the new vessel to 3,750 feet near the island of Capri on August 1, 1953, to beat the French record. Now, they had achieved a much better record, but would they survive?

Finally, a lurch signaled that they were rising. The bathyscaph broke the surface at 10:35 A.M. on September 29, 1953, more than two hours after their dive began at 8:19. The Piccards had succeeded in making the first dive to the sea floor. The Italian navy, which had towed the bathyscaph to the dive site near the Isle of Ponza in the Tyrrhenian Sea, immediately honored both men as admirals. Jacques's father decided that would be his last dive and gave Jacques complete command of the vessel.

In the spring of 1954, the French took the *FNRS-3* to the Atlantic near the Cape Verde Islands for a record-setting dive to a depth of 13,284 feet. This record was deeper than the entire Mediterranean, so Piccard's scientific dives could not beat the French record. He needed a new location, although once he had descended with his wife, Marie Claude Piccard, who thereby set a long-standing depth record for women and became the first woman on the sea floor.

Piccard invited American oceanographers to visit the Mediterranean for demonstration dives in the summer of 1957. On one exploration off the island of Capri on July 26, 1957, they triggered an undersea landslide. One ballast mechanism clogged, but the other functioned and returned *Trieste* to the surface. After the demonstrations, the U.S. Navy purchased the *Trieste,* moved it to San Diego, and hired Piccard as pilot. The navy prepared the *Trieste* for dives in the Mariana Trench by moving it to Guam after installing a stronger sphere forged by a steel contractor in Essen, Germany.

Pacific

Jacques Piccard inventoried the damages from the two-day and 220-mile tow from Guam to the Challenger Deep. The surface telephone had been ripped away by the waves. Surface contact would be limited to the acoustic phone. The tachometer, which measured the speed of descent, was inoperative. Descent speed would have to be calculated using the depth gauge and a watch. The current meter hung by just a few wires. Waves tossed the bobbing vessel as Jacques struggled with canceling the last dive of the season, the dive he had been waiting for all his life. He could not bring himself to cancel his last chance to visit the Mariana Trench on this January 23 of 1960.

"We will dive!" Piccard decided. By 8:23 A.M., he and Lieutenant Don Walsh began sinking into the Pacific Ocean, hoping to be the first to reach the deepest place on earth. It took forty minutes to sink the first eight hundred feet because warm gas and water in the bathyscaph tended to rise in the cold layer of water called the thermocline. They then plunged into the zone of twilight at one thousand feet. As they fell through seas of plankton, they enjoyed the view, which looked like an upward-falling snowstorm. They were glad to be in the peacefulness of the depths instead of the squall on the surface. Once Walsh noted a fluorescent deep-sea fish, which left a trail of light visible through the porthole of the sinking bathyscaph.

Piccard could only glance at the view because he had to monitor all the dials. Outside water temperature, pressure due to depth, and gasoline temperature all affect the speed of descent. He maintained safe speeds to avoid crashes with the side of the trench. For a safe descent, he had to know the amounts of ballast and gasoline released and still available. He also monitored the cabin conditions—temperature, humidity, and percentage of carbon dioxide. With the tachometer broken, he had additional calculations to make as well. By 9:20, at twenty-four hundred feet down, the sea beyond their headlights was pitch-black. Trickling leaks appeared ten minutes later. As the descent continued and pressure increased, the leaks sealed themselves.

By 11:15, Piccard and Walsh had surpassed all depth records. Piccard recalled his previous dives in the Pacific. With Andreas Richnitzer in *Trieste,* he had descended two hours to the sea floor of the Pacific Ocean at 18,150 feet at 1:10 P.M. on November 15, 1959. They had observed phosphorescent deep-sea fish, annelid worms, pteropods (mollusks with undulating winglike membranes attached to the foot), and holes and humps on the sea floor made by burrowing sea creatures. With Walsh on January 8, 1960, he had descended twenty-three thousand feet into the Nero Deep of the Mariana Trench—though not quite to the bottom because of an inoperative gasoline-release valve. Now, two weeks later, they were already three thousand feet deeper than most of the Pacific.

At 11:44, Piccard slowed their descent from three feet per second to one foot per second. They were 29,150 feet below sea level. Piccard noted that they were as far below the sea as Mount Everest is above it.

Piccard and Walsh felt an explosion at 12:06. The bathyscaph shook. They had experienced such shocks before. The various tanks were designed to withstand the enormous water pressure, and everything else had holes so that water could freely enter. However, if someone had neglected to make a hole in a small exterior tube, it imploded when the water pressure became great enough. Usually, though, implosions were high-pitched.

They turned off everything they could and listened in silence. What had caused the shock? As they listened, they began to hear more strange sounds. Crackling sounds came from all directions. It sounded like rice showering a wedding car. Were they passing through a cloud of shrimp? Were the cracklings and the crash related? Seeing no threat to life, they descended.

Finally, the sonar depth meter registered the bottom. Walsh counted down their distance to the bottom. It took ten minutes to descend that last 250 feet, and they touched down at 1:06 P.M. The depth gauge showed a depth of 37,800 feet, but it had been calibrated for fresh water, and a later correction for salinity reduced the measurement to 35,800 feet—consistent with the soundings taken by American, British, and Russian ships.

A sole, motionless and half-buried in the ooze of the ocean floor, peered at the bathyscaph lights intruding into its dark, murky world. The fish moved slowly away, but Piccard and Walsh rejoiced. Not only had they been the first to reach the deepest spot on earth, but they had also proved that life could withstand the pressure on the ocean floor. Previous dives had shown that brittle stars and certain other forms of life could live at extreme depths, but now they had spotted the first fish at the bottom, even at the deepest spot on earth.

In their twenty minutes on the bottom, Piccard took notes on the conditions. The bottom was flat, covered by ooze, and almost featureless. The water temperature was 36°F, and there was no current. Besides the sole, they also saw a red shrimp. With the back light, Walsh saw a crack in the antechamber. This explained the big noise earlier and would complicate their exit from the bathyscaph when they returned to the surface. They decided to forgo some time on the bottom to leave extra time at the surface for any search and rescue. In the worst case, they would surface in rough seas and be towed back to Guam before exiting the bathyscaph. With only a few candy bars for food, a tow of up to five days would be quite uncomfortable.

Piccard dropped all the ballast and began floating toward the surface. By 4:02, at a depth of thirteen thousand feet, they had almost reached a speed of four feet per second. After rising another ten thousand feet, they sped upwards at five feet per second.

The bathyscaph surfaced at 4:56 P.M., and they felt the rocking of the waves. Walsh slowly leaked compressed air into the antechamber, hoping not to put too much pressure on the crack. It took fifteen minutes, but they successfully drained the antechamber. They would not need a special rescue. As a dinghy transported them to the mother ship, they noticed that the bathyscaph had lost all its paint. In the great cold depths, the metal had contracted, causing the paint to buckle and peel. This explained the crackling noises. The noises had been caused by peeling paint—not clouds of shrimp.

In Washington, President Eisenhower presented Don Walsh with the Legion of Merit. He also awarded Jacques Piccard with the navy's Distinguished Public Service Award. Eisenhower later wrote to him the following: "As a citizen of Switzerland, a country admired by all the free world for its love of freedom and independence, you have the gratitude of all of the people of the United States for helping to further open the doors of this important scientific field [oceanography]." Though born in Brussels, Belgium, Piccard was a citizen of Switzerland because of his parents.

Atlantic

Jacques Piccard designed a new type of vessel, a *mesoscaph,* for drifting in middle ocean depths. He launched the mesoscaph *Ben Franklin* from Florida on December 11, 1968. The rest of the six-man crew included Don Kazimir, Erwin Aebersold, Harold Dorr, John Greve, and Ray Davis. The three-day test dive proved the vessel sea worthy and provided opportunities for observing soles, rays, jacks, and barracudas.

*　　*　　*　　*

Frank Busby saw a flash of silver through the porthole and scrambled across the cabin for a closer look. A swordfish, fully as long as a prone man, waved his sword menacingly at the strange vessel. Frank noted their depth habitually for the logbook: they were 827 feet deep at 6:09 A.M. on July 17.

Suddenly, the swordfish lunged. It struck the hull with the point of its sword. Busby and Ken Haigh both heard the impact and wondered what would have happened if it had struck the porthole, which it had missed by only six inches. Busby ran for a camera while a second swordfish arrived on the scene. He returned too late; the fish were gone.

The mesoscaph had been launched in the Gulf Stream near Palm Beach, Florida, at 8:54 P.M. on July 14, 1969. The crew included Jacques Piccard; Captain Don Kazimir; Swiss pilot Erwin Aebersold; NASA engineer Chet May; and two naval oceanographers, Frank Busby of the U.S. Navy, and Ken Haigh of the British Royal Navy. In less than an hour, they had landed on the bottom at a depth of almost seventeen hundred feet. They had watched for two days but saw only crabs, plankton, sea urchins, anemones, and small fish in burrows.

After the bottom observations, the mesoscaph drifted in midocean, where they saw much more sea life. Besides the swordfish attack on July 17, they watched a barracuda and a hammerhead shark on July 26. On August 5, they saw a school of tuna playing in the bubbles from their vessel. On August 12, they watched a jellyfish and a blue shark. They were excited to be able to make the first such recordings of many of these ocean fish in their natural habitat.

The evening of August 13 marked one month since the dive began. Only two news items had reached them by ham radio: on July 24 they heard of the *Apollo 11* success, and on August 3 of Heyerdahl's voyage on *Ra*. With the month of drifting complete, though, they surfaced at 8 A.M. and opened the hatch. The tow to Portland, Maine, required another day, and a week later, they reached New York harbor, where a fireboat spurted jets of water to honor their success.

ERIC RYBACK
Treks Out West

The Pacific Crest

A deer stood surrounded by snapping coyotes on the frozen lake. Weary and dying from loss of blood, the deer soon collapsed and expired. Eric Ryback watched the scene in horror from across the lake. He, too, was weary. He had trudged twenty miles through deep snow. He wanted to pitch camp, but the pack of coyotes made him fearful.

Ryback faced a steep climb up an icy ridge, but he preferred that to the coyotes. After shouldering his eighty-pound backpack, he began kicking steps in the ice. Slowly, he began to climb away from the grisly scene. As he reached the top, he stepped hastily. He fell and began to slide on his backpack down the icy ridge.

"I'm going to die," Ryback thought as he remembered the rocks at the bottom on which he would surely be smashed. As his speed increased, his hands sought to slow his descent. There was nothing to grasp, and the friction with the ice burned his hands. Suddenly, his speed slowed. He felt the frame of the backpack cutting into the ice. Instantly, he shifted all his weight onto the frame. As he slowed more, he dug his heels into the ice.

Ryback reclimbed the ridge slowly and cautiously. He had slid the length of a football field and did not want to repeat the performance. At the top he took a final glance at the deserted but

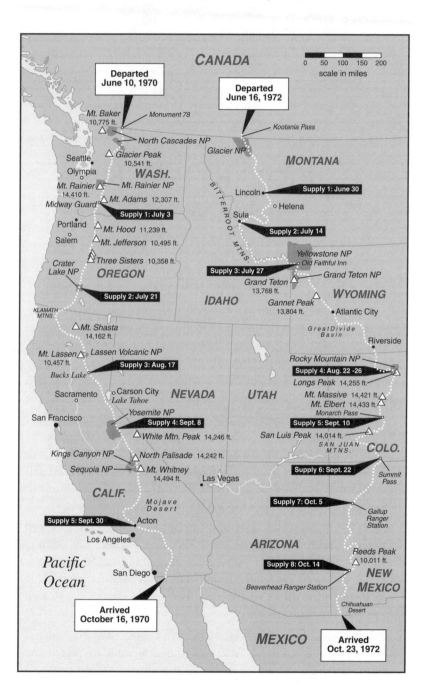

Departed
June 10, 1970

Departed
June 16, 1972

CANADA

0   50   100   150   200
scale in miles

Mt. Baker
10,775 ft.   Monument 78

Kootania Pass

North Cascades NP

Glacier NP

Seattle   Glacier Peak
Olympia   10,541 ft.
            WASH.   MONTANA

Mt. Rainier   Mt. Rainier NP   Lincoln   Supply 1: June 30
14,410 ft.
Midway Guard   Mt. Adams   12,307 ft.   Helena
            Supply 1: July 3

Portland   Mt. Hood   11,239 ft.   Sula
Salem   Mt. Jefferson 10,495 ft.   Supply 2: July 14

Crater   Yellowstone NP
Lake NP   Three Sisters 10,358 ft.   Old Faithful Inn

            OREGON   Supply 3: July 27   Grand Teton NP
      Supply 2: July 21   Grand Teton   Grand Teton NP
                    13,768 ft.   WYOMING
            IDAHO   Gannet Peak
KLAMATH   13,804 ft.   Atlantic City
MTNS.

            Mt. Shasta   Great Divide
            14,162 ft.   Basin
                                Riverside
Mt. Lassen   Lassen Volcanic NP   Rocky Mountain NP
10,457 ft.   Supply 3: Aug. 17   Supply 4: Aug. 22 -26
Bucks Lake   Longs Peak 14,255 ft.

Sacramento   Carson City   NEVADA   UTAH   Mt. Massive 14,421 ft.
            Lake Tahoe   Mt. Elbert 14,433 ft.
            Yosemite NP   Monarch Pass
San Francisco   Supply 4: Sept. 8   Supply 5: Sept. 10
            White Mtn. Peak 14,246 ft.   San Luis Peak 14,014 ft.
Kings Canyon NP   North Palisade 14,242 ft.   SAN JUAN
Sequoia NP   Mt. Whitney   MTNS.   COLO.
            14,494 ft.   Las Vegas   Supply 6: Sept. 22
      CALIF.   Summit
            Mojave   Pass
            Desert   Supply 7: Oct. 5
Supply 5: Sept. 30   Acton   Gallup
                                Ranger
Los Angeles   Station
                    ARIZONA   Reeds Peak
Pacific   10,011 ft.
                Supply 8: Oct. 14   NEW
Ocean   San Diego   MEXICO
                    Beaverhead Ranger Station
            Arrived   Chihuahuan
            October 16, 1970   Desert

                        MEXICO   Arrived
                            Oct. 23, 1972

bloodstained frozen lake. He found a flat spot away from the steep drops and crawled into his sleeping bag for the night.

Ryback, inspired by the stories of *Kon-Tiki* and Sir Edmund Hillary, had craved his own adventures. After his junior year in a Michigan high school, he had hiked the entire Appalachian Trail. Now, a year later at age eighteen, he had set out to hike the Pacific Crest from Canada to Mexico. He had arrived the day before at Manning Provincial Park in Canada after a flight to Vancouver. This morning he had crossed back into the United States at Monument 78, and now his first day on the trail, June 10, 1970, had ended.

The treacherous icy ridge had already taught Ryback that this mountain range would not be like the rolling mountains of the Appalachians. On his previous trek, he stayed in shelters along the trail and resupplied weekly at communities where he crossed roads. In contrast, this wilderness stretched for hundreds of miles, and there was rarely a sign of civilization within an hour's drive of the infrequent roads. He had picked five locations along his route for obtaining supplies. These locations were 375 miles apart, and he hoped to travel that distance in twenty-two days. His backpack, then, had to accommodate twenty-two days' worth of supplies, which is why the 130-pound trekker found himself carrying 80 pounds, half of which was food.

Snow blanketed the Pasayten Wilderness, and Ryback saw no sign of a trail. He sank in snow up to his knees as he crossed Slate Peak. Could he really cross the majestic Cascade Range of Washington and Oregon and then the rugged High Sierra of California? On his eighth day, he reached the first road at Rainy Pass. The snows in North Cascades National Park made him too tired to enjoy the serene beauty. Weariness fled, though, at his first view of a ten-thousand-foot peak. The great glaciers descending massive Glacier Peak renewed his enthusiasm. His pace quickened to Stevens Pass at the end of the second week.

Mount Rainier eclipsed Ryback's memory of Glacier Peak. From the summit of Red Mountain, he sighted the grand snow-capped peak and knew he had to climb it. At White Pass, he detoured twenty miles west along the road to Mount Rainier National Park.

The climb required two days. Two guides led Ryback to Camp Muir, where they spent a night at high elevation—ten thousand feet. Early in the morning, they roped together for the crossing of glaciers and crevasses. They reached Mount Rainier's main summit, Columbia Crest, in time to enjoy the sunrise of July 1. At 14,410 feet, Mount Rainier is the fifth highest peak in the contiguous states. Since it is only eighty-four feet lower than any of the others and much farther north, it is easily the snowiest and most majestic of them. It is considered the most photographed peak in the world.

Ryback drank in those cold moments at the summit. He could look down at the two lower peaks of Mount Rainier. Liberty Cap, a major peak in its own right, sprawled to the northwest, and Point Success stood as a minor bump to the southwest. He also looked far to the south toward his next goal, Mount Adams. He began the descent to the inn and then to White Pass, where he could get his own photo of Mount Rainier. His detour had cost three days, but it had been worth it.

Steep cliffs dropped away on both sides of the narrow path. Goat Rocks (7,775 ft.), a rocky snow-covered ridge, narrowed at one point to two feet. After his earlier fall, Ryback found the crossing nerve-racking. He crossed the six miles very slowly. At lower elevations, he found his first snowless trails and soon found his first supply point, a ranger station called Midway Guard. He spent July 3 with the rangers and took photos of lofty Mount Adams, the second highest mountain in Washington. Three days later he crossed the bridge over the mighty Columbia River and entered Oregon.

Ryback, on the advice of an old-timer, followed Eagle Creek to see its many waterfalls, including Punch Bowl Falls, Tunnel Falls, and Criss Cross Falls. Mosquitos swarmed him that night at Wahtum Lake, where he rejoined the Pacific Crest Trail. On the slopes of Mount Hood, he found Ramona Falls, of which he wrote, "the most beautiful I had yet seen."

Three more days of easy travel to Paradise Park, Olallie Meadows, and Breitenbush assured Ryback that he had passed south of the snow fields. Even the trail circling snowcapped Mount Hood,

Oregon's highest peak and the most climbed major summit in the world, had been free of snow. He had not reckoned on snowy Mount Jefferson. He spent two days on the snow fields, but after all his practice in Washington, he had no trouble. He was glad for the relief from mosquitos.

Ryback drank the last drops of his water and realized he should have filled both bottles. With snow and streams everywhere, he had not sensed danger. However, after passing distinctive Three Fingered Jack, he had entered the Mount Washington Wilderness. Before him stretched a barren field of jumbled lava—treeless, snowless, and streamless. With parched throat, he glared at Mount Washington (7,794 ft.), the source of the lava. His hopes for water at the McKenzie Pass road were dashed. No oasis greeted him, and the black lava absorbed the summer heat. The devastated region felt like a blast furnace. After a full day without water, he camped and quenched his thirst at Lava Camp Lake.

After a day of enjoying views of Obsidian Falls and the trio of peaks called the Three Sisters, Ryback faced more problems. Mosquitos swarmed him so thickly that he could not open his mouth. It helped to keep moving, but for several days meals and sleeping were torture. He itched constantly as he reached mosquito-free Waldo Lake and Lake Odell, hurried across the Diamond Peak Wilderness, and skirted Mount Thielson (9,182 ft.).

As he entered Crater Lake National Park, he crossed another volcanic desert, but he had learned his lesson and was prepared. He ran out of fuel and ate a half-cooked breakfast, but he reached his second supply point later that day, July 21, at the park headquarters.

The deep blue of America's deepest lake stunned Ryback on his visit the next morning. Wizard Island rose from the waters, a volcanic remnant in the sparkling jewel rimmed by peaks. He decided immediately to hike the twenty-five miles around the lake. He could see snowcapped Mount Shasta, a majestic volcano like Mount Rainier. A Fourteener (14,000-foot peak), it is one of two in California that are not in the High Sierra. By supper, he had not tired of the views and determined to see the sunset over the lake. He raced the setting sun up Mount Scott (8,926 ft.) and reached it just in time. The glorious sunset scene prompted him to acknowledge its Creator: "Oh God, that is beautiful. Thank You." He slept on the summit.

*　　*　　*　　*

Fire! Ryback ran toward the fiery tongues licking the brush. He stomped them out only to see puffs of wind rekindle the smoldering tinder. Soon sparks carried by the breeze lit dry pine needles covering the ground nearby. He despaired of quenching the blaze and futilely called for help. Tense with visions of a blackened forest, he tried one more idea. Running to his pack, he grabbed his plastic rain jacket and began to use it like a blanket to suffocate the flames. After an hour's work, the flames subsided. He covered the smoldering areas with dirt, filled his pots and canteen at the nearby lake, and doused the burned area. Several tedious hours had brought success.

Ryback had saved a forest between Crater Lake and Mount McLaughlin, but he was angry. If something as small as a cigarette can ignite a forest, why would people leave a smoldering campfire? The previous campers might never know that their campfire habits had started a forest fire. Their carelessness had burned one hundred square yards of forest and cost him some time and a raincoat. How many more blazes would those unintentional arsons set?

Ryback entered California on July 30. No trail crossed the next four hundred miles. He would report on this remote region to the U.S. Forest Service in exchange for storage rights at his five supply points. Ryback debated two possible routes for his own trek. The direct route via Mount Shasta would cross volcanic desert. The westward loop into the Siskiyou, Klamath, and Marble Mountains would be longer but offered plenty of water. The Forest Service was not sure either route could be crossed and was interested in his trip as a check on whether a route for the Pacific Crest Trail across northern California was even feasible. Ryback opted for the longer route but still had to contend with temperatures as high as 113°F. With map and compass, he followed exposed ridges. He crossed the Klamath River into the Marble Mountain Wilderness on August 6.

Noises just a few feet away startled Ryback from sleep. He saw a large bear silhouetted against the night. The bear was digging with his back toward Ryback. Ryback, in his sleeping bag, rolled away from the bear. The bear looked at him several times but kept digging. Soon the bear came toward Ryback to investigate. Ryback, trapped in his sleeping bag, knew he would be mauled even if he could get out and run. He had only seconds as the bear crossed the short distance that Ryback had rolled. Ryback jumped out of his sleeping bag, leaping and screaming as loud as he could. The bear reared up on his hind legs, with his claws outstretched, to assess the unfamiliar event. Confused, the bear ambled away. Ryback yelled again. His scare tactic had worked at the expense of shattered nerves.

Ryback rationed his dwindling food supply as he passed Castle Crags and Burney Falls. Fishermen in the Thousand Lakes Wilderness supplemented his diet, but he suffered severe hunger pains by the time he reached Lassen Volcanic National Park. Mount Lassen, a typical Cascade volcano, had erupted in 1914—the most recent eruption in the contiguous states (it would be ten years before the eruption of beautiful Mount St. Helens, which Ryback had seen from the summit of Mount Ranier). Ryback hardly noticed it in his hunger.

For three days, he skipped breakfast, had a few crackers for lunch, and half of a freeze-dried food packet for dinner. At the North Fork of the Feather River, he ran out of crackers. Ryback hiked the next day without food to fuel him. At supper time on August 17, he rejoiced to see his third supply station at Bucks Lake near Quincy in the transition zone between the Cascade Range and the High Sierra. The ranger made Ryback feel at home, and he set off the following morning.

Ryback gripped handholds as he descended from Dick's Peak. He had slept on the summit the previous night to watch the sunset and to see the sunrise over Lake Tahoe. High winds and cold had made his sleep fitful, and now he found the descent difficult with his fingers too cold for normal use. He eased along a narrow ledge, but shadows caused a misstep and he fell. Colors danced before his eyes, and he lost consciousness.

Ryback's throbbing headache roused him. He sat up slowly but felt dizzy. He checked his watch as he collected his wits and realized that he had been unconscious for over two hours. When he finally reached the base of the peak, he rested two days before his aches subsided enough to continue. Beyond Sonora Pass, he joined two hikers for four days to Hetch Hetchy Reservoir in Yosemite National Park. On September 8 he visited Tuolumne Meadows and Yosemite Valley, where he obtained his supplies. He entered the valley between Bridal Veil Falls and the famous cliff called El Capitan. Beyond, he saw Yosemite Falls, the highest waterfall on the continent. When he saw Half Dome, he immediately wanted to climb it.

Ryback hiked the trail past Vernal Falls and Nevada Falls and turned up the route to Half Dome (8,842 ft.). He was glad for the cables, which offered handholds to those climbing the barren, rounded dome side of the mountain. At the top he crawled on his stomach and nosed over the edge to peer down the sheer northern face. He could see climbers ascending the cliff with ropes, and when they joined him at the top, he learned that they had been climbing for three days. Ryback slept on the summit.

The next two hundred miles of the Pacific Crest followed the John Muir Trail, a true wilderness trail. No roads cross the spectacular Sierra Nevada wilderness from Yosemite Valley to Mount Whitney. The trail passes all eleven Fourteeners (14,000-foot peaks) in the High Sierras. As he hiked through Kings Canyon National Park, Ryback had good views of the five peaks in the Palisade group. Though North Palisade is higher, blocklike Thunderbolt Peak was the last of California's Fourteeners to be successfully climbed because of its difficulty.

On September 17 in Sequoia National Park, Ryback glimpsed Mount Whitney, one of the six Fourteeners of the Mount Whitney group and the highest mountain in the contiguous states. He slept on its summit at the end of the John Muir Trail on September 21.

Ryback came to the end of the Sierra three days later. He spent two days in the Domeland Wilderness and then entered the Mojave Desert near Tehachapi. During the two-mile vertical descent in five days, he abruptly switched from bitter cold nights to severe heat. Even the rattlesnakes seemed sluggish in the afternoons. His final supply point was Acton on September 30.

Though hot, hiking was much easier in the flatter terrain. Ryback crossed the Angeles National Forest and climbed Mount Baden-Powell, named for the founder of the Boy Scouts and topped with a monument in his honor. A few more days brought him across the San Bernardino Mountains and eventually to Warner Springs on October 12. A ranger joined Ryback for the last two days of his 129-day journey, and reporters captured the last few steps of the twenty-five hundred miles on film. As Ryback approached the fence at the Mexican border on October 16, his father came running to greet him.

The Continental Divide

Snow shifted beneath Ryback's feet. Eric felt himself sinking. Arms extended and grasping snow, he found himself hanging in a snow hole. He heard the snowmelt in a gurgling stream below him. How far down was it? Chunks of snow broke away and fell into the stream, which whisked them over the brink of the high ridge.

Tim, Eric's brother, grabbed Eric's pack and held him. Himself waist deep in snow, Tim could not get enough leverage to pull him upward. Each movement dislodged more snow, widening the hole. With a great heave, Tim pulled the sixty-five-pound pack toward him and shouted in horror when he saw he had only the pack—not his brother.

"Eric!" he yelled. Tears came as hopelessness overwhelmed him. In an instant, though, he realized that Eric had kicked his boots into the icy sides of the hole and had slipped his arms out of the pack to extend his reach. Soon Eric pulled himself onto the top of the snow field, where Tim stood with the pack, sobbing softly from the released tension of imminent disaster.

It was time to revise their plans. On the day before, June 16, 1972, they had climbed Kootania Pass in Glacier National Park from the Canadian side. Over the winter, the park had received eighty feet of snow, and many thirty-foot drifts still remained. They knew that the trail crossed the sheer face of the Garden Wall on narrow ledges, but as they looked at that famous arete, they could see snow draping the cliffs. After one harrowing experience with the snow, it would be insanity to attempt the Garden Wall—even 。

with the one ice pick in their possession. They took an alternate route through a low valley.

The Rybacks climbed Logan Pass to return to the Continental Divide, the dividing line and backbone of the North American continent. Water that runs off to the west flows into the Pacific Ocean, and water flowing east reaches the Atlantic Ocean (or Gulf of Mexico). When completed, the Continental Divide Trail would follow the divide, crossing and recrossing it many times. Eric proposed to hike the route in its current, unfinished condition. Tim, his younger but taller brother, had decided to join him. The authorities had told them it might be impossible, but Eric had been told the same thing about the Pacific Crest, so he had not been concerned. The deep snow at Logan Pass reminded him once again of the warnings.

The Rybacks followed lower routes to Two Medicine Pass. They looked down on azure lakes nestled in valleys surrounded by snowy peaks. Pitching the tarp beyond the pass high above the timberline, they prepared for the usual evening storm. As they crawled into their sleeping bags under the tarp, a mountain goat wandered by in the fog.

Two days later, with more rain, they found themselves fording rivers waist deep in the Bob Marshall Wilderness. They forded twenty-two rivers. Rain and fords left them cold and wet, so they were glad for their wool clothing which retains warmth even when wet. They reached Lincoln, their first supply stop, on June 30. The U.S. Forest Service had agreed to place their boxes of supplies at strategic points every three hundred miles along their route in exchange for information about the conditions along the Continental Divide. Each supply point had food and supplies for sixteen days.

Occasionally, they took breaks from hiking. One day they visited with gold miners. Another time, in the open range west of Helena, Eric dozed while Tim played classical pieces on his recorder. Eric awoke with a cow munching grass next to his head. Tim insisted the cows liked pieces by Telemann more than those by Byrd. One evening in the Anaconda-Pintlar Wilderness, they watched a gorgeous sunset. Before long they arrived at Sula, the second supply stop, and prepared for the Bitterroot Range along the Idaho and Montana border.

"Jump!" shouted Eric as rocks began to slide beneath Tim's feet. Tim lurched, trying to keep his balance, and careened off a boulder, which joined the slide. Tim staggered toward the edge of the slide, but as he did more rocks and scree joined those crashing down the side of the peak. Tim disappeared from Eric's view. Eric called, "Tim! Where are you? Are you hurt?" Tim called back, "Over here." Eric sensed trouble; his brother hadn't answered the second question. Indeed, Tim had a bloody gash extending the length of his calf. Eric cleaned and bandaged the injury and told Tim to rest. Eric pitched camp at the summit. When he returned, Tim was able to limp up to camp on his own while Eric carried his pack.

Tim limped for a while, but within four days he had already hiked a twenty-six-mile day. Three days later, July 26, they awoke at dawn to see elk splashing one another in Summit Lake. After that first night in Yellowstone National Park, they ceased enjoying the park. Permit-rationed campsites forced them to lodge at Old Faithful Inn, where they resupplied. The next morning, they waited with the mobs for the eruption of Old Faithful. In spite of the 150-foot spectacle, the commercialization and hordes of people disgusted them. They hurried past the thermal pools and geyser fields and entered Grand Teton National Park two days later.

For the first few days in August, they decided to make about forty miles a day by hiking in the light of a full moon. They hiked seventy-two hours with only two hours of sleep each night and twenty-minute breaks every hour during the night. They covered well over one hundred miles this way but became irritable and exhausted. This marathon brought them to Wyoming's spectacular and remote Wind River Range but had strained them mentally and physically. Eric, goal-oriented and experienced with treks, bounced back quickly, but Tim remained depressed. Eric missed Tim's satirical wit and romanticism. Eric realized his happiness depended on Tim's happiness, and he became gloomy too. Even the beauty of Squaretop over Upper Green Lake failed to arouse them. Tim's condition improved some with more nights of normal sleep, and on August 8 at Pipestone Lake, they camped on top of a thirty-foot rock outcropping with cliffs on three sides. The castlelike rock revived Tim's romanticism as he acted out Teutonic legends. The next day at Cross Lake, Eric caught eight trout in ten minutes with a borrowed fishing rod, and the fresh meat restored their strength and spirits.

On August 10, they reached Lizard Head Pass and then spent the night in the Cirque of the Towers, a small alpine valley surrounded by eleven-thousand-foot pinnacles. Three days later they bought some canned goods in the small town of Atlantic City, Wyoming, as preparation for crossing the Great Divide Basin. The Continental Divide splits and rejoins one hundred miles south, thus creating a basin where water flows neither to the Pacific nor to the Atlantic. No rivers flow into or out of the dead basin. Sand dunes cover vast portions, and local ranchers call it the Red Desert. None venture there during the heat of August, but in Atlantic City Eric learned of the only route across that remains free of shifting sands. As they entered the desert, they admired antelope racing across it effortlessly.

Eric and Tim panted, prone on the Red Desert. They had lost the route and consumed the last of their water on the second day. They now sprawled, parched and gasping, in the 120°F heat. In the cooler evening, they trudged zombielike due south toward the interstate. They walked through the twilight into the night, not even speaking in order to conserve moisture. Eric turned to Tim and realized he was alone. His parched throat could not yell, so he retraced his steps for several minutes to a slouched form. Tim did not respond to his name, and Eric shook him until he finally groaned. While removing Tim's pack, Eric became dizzy and fell beside him.

They awoke at the first light and continued south. At noon, as the temperature soared, they came to an abandoned shack. The shack was locked, but after searching the grounds, they found a metal tank of liquid. It smelled of kerosene, but Eric discovered that the surface film of kerosene covered water. By swirling and sipping, they were able to quench their thirst and fill their bottles with the foul-tasting water. The next morning, Tim banged pots together to scare off a wild horse, and the sight of distant mountains encouraged them both. When they arrived at an interstate rest stop, they guzzled water and slept long. At Riverside, a partial supply point, they picked up five days of food to get them to Milner Pass.

The Rybacks entered Colorado the next day. Three days later, after passing Mount Zirkel and Rabbit Ears Pass, they came to Milner Pass in Rocky Mountains National Park. The brothers waited by the Continental Divide sign until their parents and little brother drove up on schedule for the midtrip celebration. They resupplied here and spent four days with the family sightseeing and recuperating. Tim, still exhausted from the night treks and desert adventure, decided to stop. At the end of the four days, on August 26, they dropped Eric at Milner Pass and wished him well. Eric Ryback continued alone.

Ryback climbed Longs Peak, 14,251 feet above sea level. Colorado boasts fifty-four Fourteeners. Longs Peak ranks fifteenth, but it is one of the longer and more challenging climbs. It is also popular since it is the highest peak in the famous Rocky Mountains National Park. Higher than the better-known Pikes Peak, it is also among the six Fourteeners rising high above the Great Plains in the Front Range.

Ryback scrambled through the boulder field and passed through the Keyhole. He then spiraled up the mountain on the narrow ledges that offered tremendous views. Ryback's love for unspoiled wilderness had prompted him to arise early, and he reached the summit before anyone else. At the summit, he thought about how much Tim would have enjoyed the climb, but he did not get depressed. He left when he heard other people coming. He met a dozen hikers on his descent.

Landmarks passed quickly for Ryback, buoyed by the family reunion. He crossed Interstate 80 at Loveland Pass two days beyond Longs Peak. On September 5, he camped on Mount Massive, one of fifteen Fourteeners in the Sawatch Range, others of which he could see to the north and south. He marveled at the high peaks in all directions. On the Pacific Crest the high peaks had formed a majestic backbone. While these were not so snowy and majestic, the rugged expanse in all directions held an awe of its own. He could see the Mosquito Range to the northeast, with its five Fourteeners and the Elk Range to the west with its six Fourteeners.

Among all Colorado's Fourteeners, Mount Massive is surpassed only by Mount Elbert, which Ryback saw the following day. Storms prohibited views of the Fourteeners in the Collegiate Peaks portion of the Sawatch Range, but he reached his supplies at Long Branch Ranger Station near Monarch Pass on September 10.

Views of San Luis Peak, one of thirteen Fourteeners in the San Juan Range, on September 13 spurred him on. He sighted another, Uncompahgre Peak, a couple of days later. The first winter snows greeted him as he looped around the headwaters of the Rio Grande. He was relieved when he crossed the last major summit in the range, South Fork Peak, one of Colorado's 583 Thirteeners. Beyond Wolf Creek Pass at Summit Pass, he reached his supplies at South Fork Guard Station.

Entering New Mexico the next day, Ryback made good time across the high plateau. His trek captured the imagination of the Indians of the Jicarilla Apache Reservation. They dubbed him Chief Crazyfoot, and he appreciated the daily water they brought him. Coyote howls accompanied him beyond the reservation, and one venturesome coyote followed him for a while. On October 5, he arrived at the Gallup Ranger Station, his supply point. Nine days later, he arrived at his final supply point, the Beaverhead Ranger Station, after crossing the Black Range. The summits of Lookout Mountain, Diamond Peak, and Reeds Peak were the last three summits of the trek.

Ryback hiked nine days across the Chihuahan Desert. The parched ground reminded him of Wyoming's Red Desert, but here he saw cacti, which did not grow in Wyoming. His father and Tim greeted him at the Mexican border fence on October 23 after 130 days and twenty-six hundred-miles.

Ryback, born March 19, 1952, in Detroit, Michigan, later finished school. After a year at the University of Denver, he transferred to Idaho State University. He completed his bachelor's degree in 1976.

JOHN WILCOX
The Ultimate Spelunking Trip

Flint Ridge Caves

John Wilcox entered the Austin entrance of the Flint Ridge Cave system. His goal was a boulder pile called Q-87, the most distant-known spot in the world's longest cave. Although the known passages totaled almost eighty-three miles in length, there were enough entrances that the most remote spot was about five miles from the closest entrance. Still, he knew it would require twenty-four hours to make the roundtrip because much of the distance would be covered crawling on hands and knees. Q-87 had been visited only three times before and had not been visited at all in six years.

No one could get beyond it, but Wilcox wanted to see it himself. Wilcox, born on August 18, 1937, in Columbus, Ohio, had been in charge of exploring the cave system for about six months. He now had a team of four that was ready to go. Pat Crowther, her husband Will, Gary Eller, and Wilcox himself entered the Austin entrance at 8:00 A.M. on Memorial Day weekend of 1972 and locked the steel gate behind them.

The four cavers walked for hours over the mud passageways and left the long boulder-filled passage called Swinnerton Avenue at a place called the Duck Under. From there, they crawled on their hands and knees to the spot where someone had written "Best Way Down." After descending, they began wading knee-deep in the

Candlelight River. Soon they came to a junction marking the beginning of two surveys.

Spelunkers had explored many passages over the years, mapping as they went. Each survey, or series of mapping trips, was designated by a letter, and the individual features and openings along the surveyed passage were numbered. Wilcox's team ignored the A-survey passage, which they hoped to visit later. Instead, they entered the passage of the N-survey. This passage had caused much excitement years ago because it was the first survey that found passages that went under the Houchins River Valley that separated the Flint Ridge Cave System from Mammoth Cave. Soon they reached the end of the N-survey and Q-1, the beginning of the Q-survey. It took far less time to crawl through the passages than it had taken the initial explorers to map them.

At Q-17, Wilcox stopped and said, "No one has ever explored this side passage; let's check it out." They crawled thirty feet to a mud embankment that almost touched the ceiling. Eller began scooping out mud from the embankment. Within ten minutes, he had scooped out enough to give him room to squeeze through. Wilcox, being larger, had to scoop out mud for five more minutes before he could get through. The Crowthers fit through easily behind Wilcox. They had entered a part of the cave never before seen by humans.

Soon the passage split three ways. Stone ledges blocked the entrance to the lowest passage with a stream snaking through it. Wilcox was too big for the other two passages. Pat Crowther tried going up the high passage. She squirmed through a right-hand turn, slid a few feet on her belly down a mud bank, and stuck. The passage was so small that she could not turn around, so she began to back up. She stopped herself and kept calm, thinking in detail about how she had gotten there. Soon she backed uphill and into the tightest spot and stuck again. She was sure her feet must be visible around the turn to her friends. She called out, and they responded. Their voices encouraged her, though she could not understand their words. Soon she was out, shaking from the tension. Finally, she decided to check the third passage. It was easier, but she got stuck momentarily because she missed the wide part backing out. This passage held no further options, and they returned to the main passage.

At Q-33, Wilcox stopped at another side passage. When it got tight, Eller tried to continue. Soon he had to remove his sweatshirt to get farther. When he heard dripping water, he hoped for a passage, so he took off his shirt and squeezed between the muddy floor and ceiling. He could not reach the water. As he backed out, sharp rocks tore at his pants. Wilcox scraped as much mud off Eller's back and chest as he could with a putty knife. Pat Crowther was a bit smaller than Eller but too tired to try it. They returned again to the main passage.

The first time they found a place where they could sit up, they called a break. They were at Q-85, and their headlamps showed them the rock pile of Q-87 at the end of the passage fifteen feet away. Wilcox edged himself up the boulder pile. He could stand erect only if he was willing to stare up at the precariously wedged boulders. Wilcox crawled down into a narrow hole along the bottom of the pile. No one had ever been willing to crawl into the pile with such a high risk of falling boulders. Wilcox entered but soon saw that it went nowhere.

Wilcox screwed pipe sections together to make a long hook. They used it as a lever to move boulders, but the size of the passage allowed only one person to pry at a time. As boulders rolled down the pile, the others stacked them out of the way along the cave walls. After four hours of dislodging boulders, they saw that there was no progress. Boulders kept coming. No new holes opened, and the lever began to stick in the mud. They started back. At the wide junction with the A-survey, they slept for a half-hour and ate a little. Six hours later, they arrived at the Austin entrance exhausted.

Back home, Wilcox mapped the two small explorations at Q-17 and Q-33. As an engineer, he carefully noted each detail. He was determined to efficiently check out every option. Why? Q-87 was the passage that came the closest to a known passage in Mammoth Cave. Everyone hoped to find a connection between the two cave systems.

The Flint Ridge Cave system was a combination of many caves and much exploration. Wilcox reviewed the system. Discovered in

1903, Unknown Cave was immediately explored for 1.3 miles. Floyd Collins discovered Crystal Cave in 1917 and explored it for five years before he was trapped in a rock fall that ultimately defeated rescuers and ended in his death. In 1955 Jack Lehrberger and Bill Austin explored miles of new passages in Unknown Cave and exited at Crystal Cave. They were the first to show that Unknown/Crystal formed a single cave system. A year later, the Austin entrance was dug to facilitate exploration.

Colossal Cave had been discovered at its Bedquilt entrance in 1871. By 1897, the Woodson, Main, and Hazen entrances were all known and connected by two-and-a-half miles of passages. Salts Cave was explored by Indians, but modern mapping was begun in 1912 by Floyd Collins. The Pike Chapman entrance helped exploration. In 1960 Dave Deamer, only nineteen years old and eager to explore, was with experienced Jack Lehrberger and leader Spike Werner in Colossal Cave when after they had crawled along a stream and scaled a pit they arrived in Salts Cave. Five hours later they exited Salts Cave; they had proved that Colossal/Salts was a single cave system.

One year later, Deamer and Werner with Bob Keller and Judy Powell investigated a boulder pile in Unknown Cave. When they had almost given up moving boulders, Deamer felt wind. Within an hour, they followed the new passage to the pit at the point of the previous year's connection. They had just connected the passages to form one big system twenty-one miles long under Flint Ridge.

At that time Mammoth Cave had forty-four miles of mapped passages but had been recently surpassed as the longest cave by Hölloch Cave in Switzerland. By 1964, the Q and A surveys leading from Flint Ridge under Houchins Valley to Mammoth Cave Ridge had extended the Flint Ridge Cave system to thirty-three miles. In 1967 Flint Ridge Cave with fifty miles of passages surpassed Mammoth Cave, where exploring was still prohibited. Two years later, Flint Ridge Cave reached sixty-two miles and surpassed Hölloch Cave as longest in the world. In 1969, there had finally been some further exploration in Mammoth Cave. Now, Wilcox knew that Flint Ridge had about eighty-three miles of passages,

Hölloch had seventy-two miles, and Mammoth remained third with fifty-eight miles.

Second Try

On July 15, 1972, Wilcox led a second trip to Q-87. Pat Crowther came along again with two young cavers—Mark Jancin and Eric Hatleburg. They took no detours this time and reached Q-87 in seven-and-a-half hours. After four-and-a-half hours working on the rock pile, they gave up again. This time, they would make some stops on the way back.

Pat Crowther squeezed into the passage at Q-33. She got beyond where Eller had stopped over a month earlier, but she advanced only twelve feet in a quarter-hour. She found herself at the bottom of a high-domed pit. She stood next to a pool of water, but there was no other way out. It was the first new discovery of this trip, but it would not prove fruitful for other explorers. She returned to join the others.

At Q-17, a ledge blocked the side passage. The young cavers chipped at it a while but to no avail. Wilcox stuck a crowbar into a ceiling crack and heaved. The ledges broke away, but a huge rock, weighing 150 pounds, fell from the ceiling and crashed across the opening. The small main passage made it awkward to get to, and only one person could push at a time. No one could move it. Frustrated, Wilcox shoved the crowbar in place and heaved with all the muscle developed from years of gymnastic efforts in caves. The boulder eased out of the way. They all fit in but soon found that they could not progress any farther than before. The tired team crawled back to Q-1 and through the N-survey to the A-survey junction.

"We really should go look to find out what we'll be up against next time." Wilcox explained that the A-survey ended at A-12, so it was not far but would require a belly crawl through six inches of water. As they got to the end, the passage split.

Wilcox looked confused. The maps showed no side passages here. He went left and came abruptly to a slab of rock that he recognized from the survey report by John Bridge. He stuck the crowbar under it, but it just squished in the mud below. This was the dead end. But what was the other passage then?

Wilcox backtracked and crawled into the right fork. He crawled until he could feel the floor on his chest and the ceiling on his back. He could hardly move, but he knew that Pat Crowther must have gone that way. Too tired to continue, he waited in the nine-inch-high chest compressor for her return.

Meanwhile, Pat had gone through the narrow tunnel into the expedition's second new passage of the trip. She squeezed through the low spot and slid along a ledge that dropped into a crack. The passage was shaped like an ice-cream cone. The bottom was a narrow crack that could trap a person, while the top offered hardly a support for a body being dragged by gravity into the crack. She searched for handholds and used her arms to push her body against the ceiling. It was slow and strenuous. She realized that she was crossing the most dangerous place she had ever seen in a cave. No one would be able to pull out a caver who slipped down out of the crack. The top of the passage was hardly big enough for a person, so rescuers would not have much room to work. They would be miles from the entrance, and they would need their strength just to get themselves through. She knew that the tight spot would be the key to any further exploration.

She heard water as the passage curved and opened into a room. A stream entered from the left, dropped eight feet over a waterfall before her, and continued through a crawlway below. She was too tired to climb down the falls, but her compass told her that the water was heading west toward Mammoth Cave! She rested briefly and returned through the Tight Spot to Wilcox. They rejoiced over the potential, but both wondered if Wilcox could fit through the Tight Spot. They also wondered why this passage had not been recorded. Perhaps the explorer had been large and had assumed it ended. They would later learn that three parties had been here, and all had thought it too small. One man, Davidson, had put it on the map but forgot to describe it, and it was soon completely forgotten. No one would have ever found it if Wilcox had not determined to see everything for himself.

Follow-up

Roger Brucker was excited. He had lived and caved in the area longer than anyone currently living there. Although he had not been at the key connections, he had been indirectly involved in all of them. Brucker and Red Watson had explored beyond the farthest depths of Crystal Cave and marked the spot while Lehrberger and Austin explored from Unknown Cave. Brucker had led the exploration of Colossal Cave on which Werner found the passage, which Werner and two others followed the next day to Salts Cave. Brucker had also advised Deamer on the Unknown/Salts connection. Brucker's enthusiasm had inspired many of the cavers.

Brucker entered the cave with his son and young Richard Zopf on August 26. He hoped to connect to Mammoth Cave, but he had gained weight since his youthful explorations in Crystal Cave. His son Tom, on the other hand, was in excellent shape. Zopf, the strongest of the three, dragged a car jack all the way to the end of the A-survey. He then pulled himself through the tight spot. Tom came through next, coached by Zopf. Roger Brucker started through but could not fit. He took dictation from the younger men for the map until they were out of earshot. Roger backed out and took the jack to see if he could move the slab that Wilcox's crowbar had not been able to budge. He spent a half-hour with no success and then settled down to await the "kids."

Meanwhile, Tom and Richard descended the waterfall and entered the upper half of the split-level drain. Eventually, this passage grew too narrow, and they backed out. They started down the water level, but soon Richard got tired and decided to stop and nap. Tom pushed on alone, crawling through the drains. Passing between drains in a small room, he noticed a blind cavefish and a white crayfish. He knew that this was a good sign, and his excitement grew. After more twists and turns, the crawlway became a walkway. Tom began to run.

After one thousand feet, he slowed to a walk, panting. He was alone and farther out in Flint Ridge than anyone else had ever been. Each member of the team was alone, and it could be a long way yet. They still had to return all the way to the Austin entrance. If only his dad could have fit through, they could have explored and mapped to the end together. He stopped at a mud embankment and scraped on it his initials, "T. B." He returned to Zopf, and then both returned to his father.

After hearing their report, Wilcox was ready to try again. He put Pat Crowther in charge in case he could not fit through the Tight Spot. They took Tom Brucker and Richard Zopf, the largest man who had so far made it through. Wilcox was taller than Zopf by four inches and substantially broader and thicker as well. Wilcox, though, had not gained weight like Roger Brucker. He would give it a try, and if he could not squeeze through, Crowther would still have a mapping team. They entered the cave on August 30 and went directly to the Tight Spot. Tom and Pat sailed through and continued the B-survey that had been started four days earlier. Zopf stayed to coach Wilcox.

Wilcox entered the Tight Spot and stuck. He could not fit and had to back out. He removed his shirt to reduce his size and tried again, starting with his left arm first. He inched forward, and the constricted walls scraped bits of skin from his body. Finally, with Zopf's coaching, he emerged. Though Wilcox was the maximum size for the Tight Spot, a man of the same size but less strength would still not be able to get through. For the next seven hours they mapped passages that Tom had explored. It was twelve hundred feet to B-87. They put away the survey equipment and walked a bit farther. Tom's initials were just around the corner. Their time was up, but they all looked longingly at the virgin passages ahead. Crowther decided they could take fifteen minutes.

Tom sprang into the passage. Excited, the four cavers splashed through pools of crayfish and then belly crawled in a small tube. Dropping from the tube into a pool, Tom looked back for Zopf. His light flashed across the muddy walls and suddenly revealed an arrow smudged on the wall. How could there be markings in a passage farther from civilization even than Q-87? The arrow pointed downstream. It must point toward Mammoth Cave. Tom shouted with excitement!

As he showed his find to Zopf, they read the initials "P. H." next to the arrow. Looking around, Zopf found the inscription "Pete H." Now they were both shouting.

Wilcox and Crowther heard the shouting ahead. Now it was their turn to find initials—"L. H."

This confirmed what all of them knew: Pete Hanson and Leo Hunt had been explorers in Mammoth Cave in the 1930s. No one had seen these markers since they were made in 1938. They immediately named the river which Tom had found "Hanson's Lost River."

Too excited to stop, they decided to explore for another hour. They continued a quarter mile through pools, but now they noticed brown fish and crayfish with eyes! Fish with eyes never stray too far from entrances. Another quarter mile, and the exploreres were waist deep with three feet of air space. They knew that in wetter years, this would all be under water. The river became shallower as the passage widened.

It was midnight. They had continued for two hours beyond the arrow, over a mile behind them. Wilcox pondered. Obviously, Hanson and Hunt had known of this river. Yet if it really led to Mammoth Cave, how had it been lost to modern explorers? Where could it emerge? Why had no one else found it and explored it from the Mammoth Cave side? Wilcox began to wonder if Hanson and Hunt had explored in other caves of the region. Maybe they had connected to some other cave.

"We have to turn back," Crowther announced. They all knew it. They left their initials on the wall with the date 8-30-72. They were five-and-a-half miles from the entrance. B-87 was now the farthest mapped point in the cave, farther than Q-87. They had explored a mile beyond B-87. They had penetrated a mile beyond the farthest known spot in any cave in the world. They exited the Austin entrance at 6:15 A.M. as the bats were returning from their night flight.

More Attempts

Two days later, John Wilcox told Joe Davidson and Roger Brucker about "Pete H." These leaders of the Cave Research

Foundation got excited. Davidson had recently stepped down from the presidency and had not been on a remote trip for some time. He did not think he could go. Others had to return to daily work responsibilities. Wilcox, Zopf, and Gary Eller were ready, but they needed a fourth. Davidson reluctantly agreed.

The party moved rapidly to the Tight Spot. Eller, at five foot eight inches and 140 pounds, should have no trouble. Davidson, a bit taller than Wilcox, who was six feet tall, wormed into the hole. Though Davidson was not bigger around the chest, he would have the same struggle as Wilcox. Davidson's arms began quivering, and he feared sliding down into the horrible crevice. He felt rock above and below as Wilcox had, but his strength was ebbing. Wilcox tried to encourage him, but Davidson replied that even if he got through he would not be able to return after more caving. Maybe another time, but he would have to back out today.

The expedition would not get farther. To salvage something of the trip, Davidson offered to wait a few hours for them. Wilcox and Zopf took Eller to see "Pete H." It was a three-hour roundtrip, and they also explored a side passage where Tom had been able to run for five hundred feet. They retraced Tom's dash and crawled into the smaller passage at the end. After continuing another one thousand feet in the passage, they found some pottery fragments. Had they been washed in from elsewhere or had Indians somehow arrived here? They returned to Davidson.

Pat Crowther, Richard Zopf, Ellen Brucker (Tom's sister), and John Bridge entered Mammoth Cave the following day, hoping to go upstream. In wet suits, they swam two hundred feet across Echo River to the boats at the dock where the boat tours had begun in decades past. They crossed Cascade Hall and soon arrived at Roaring River. They floated on inner tubes into a number of side passages, but all of the passages either ended or became siphons, underwater tunnels. After exhausting the possibilities, they returned shivering along the handrails in Cascade Hall and continued out the historic entrance of Mammoth Cave. Another failure.

Flint-Mammoth Connection

Wilcox worried about rumors. Many would accept the names as conclusive. If the press got the story and it was later shown that they had connected to some small neighboring cave, it would create a mess. He really hoped to follow this route to the end before the rumors reached the media, but it was not easy to get a group together—especially when the group had to consist of experienced cavers who could endure the most extreme caving and who also had the strength and appropriate size for the Tight Spot. He also wanted to beat the autumn rains when the river level would rise.

It was September 9 before Wilcox finally got another party together. Eller came up again from Atlanta. Pat Crowther, whose home was in Massachusetts, happened to be in Columbus, Ohio, and was able to come also. Richard Zopf was still in town and only too happy for the privilege. With Steve Wells and a national park ranger, Steve Pinnix, they would have six.

Pinnix, though an experienced caver, had never been in the Flint Ridge Cave system before. Wilcox was glad to have the national park representative along. The others enjoyed giving him the grand tour. His eyes lit up at the gypsum and mirabilite formations on Turner Avenue. He was pleased to see places he had often heard about, such as the Duck Under and Candlelight River. By this time, he knew he would never be able to retrace the route through the maze of crawlways. The vastness of the cave system overwhelmed him.

Relief propelled them after the last member passed safely through the Tight Spot. By 4:00 P.M., they had arrived at B-87. Here, Wilcox split them into two teams for a leapfrog survey. Zopf, Wells, and Eller, the three younger men, continued the B-survey. Crowther and Pinnix went on with Wilcox, the oldest of all at thirty-five. After estimating where the younger guys would finish with thirty survey points, they began a C-survey. Wilcox's group left a signal at their starting point and began surveying a comfortable knee crawl with occasional places to rise to a stoop. Soon the younger guys finished their part and raced ahead, likewise counting thirty stations before starting the D-survey.

Wilcox's group reached the beginning of Eller's D-survey at 8:00 P.M. As they crawled on, they saw that the other group had a difficult stretch with a low ceiling and deeper water. They caught up to the tired advance party at D-23. They rested on a mud bank and told Wilcox that one of the compasses had quit working in the water. All together, four thousand feet had been mapped, and it was 8:15 P.M.

"Enough mapping. Let's spend the last of our time exploring." Wilcox's statement brought new life to the tired mappers. About six hundred feet later, Wilcox, Zopf, and Crowther recognized their own initials where they had left them with those of Tom Brucker. Tom, though a fearless explorer of only nineteen years, had lost interest after the previous trip. He considered the connection history.

"It took guts for you guys to come all the way out here that first time," Wells exclaimed. It was quite a long way from where Tom had earlier left his "T. B." The Tight Spot and the Austin entrance seemed very remote.

The ceiling dropped slightly with every step. After 450 feet, the ceiling came down to only a foot above the water. The group watched as Wilcox inched forward. All prepared for disappointment. Would the ceiling drop into the river, where only scuba divers could continue? Would this be the bitter end? Who could drag scuba gear through all they had come through? Had Hanson and Hunt come from some side passage they had not yet explored?

Wilcox edged along the wall at the shallowest spot. Up to his thighs in water, he bent so that his cheeks grazed the water, keeping his nose up. He waded forward. The ceiling rose slightly. He edged forward again and watched the ceiling disappear into heights that his small lamp could not illuminate. "It's big!" His exclamation echoed so much that it proved the size to the entire party.

Now the party advanced behind Wilcox. The walls widened as Wilcox came waist deep into a large lake. He advanced and his eyes slowly adjusted to the broad expanse. Was that a glint of metal? Water lapped at his chest as he surged ahead. Crowther, just behind, slipped and went in up to her neck. A second compass was ruined; only two remained to get them back.

"A tourist trail!" Wilcox yelled. They had done it. All soon scrambled up the mud bank shivering. After walking around a bend in the trail, they recognized where they were: Cascade Hall, which Crowther had walked through a week before, hoping to find the mouth of Hanson's Lost River. If she had explored Echo Lake instead of Roaring River, they would have found it. Apparently, the one-foot clearance was underwater in all but the driest years. Though obvious and in a famous part of Mammoth Cave, Hanson's Lost River could have remained lost indefinitely from the Mammoth Cave side. No one expected a new passage in the most familiar part of the cave. Their initials five-and-a-half miles deep in Flint Ridge had been only six hundred feet from a tourist trail in Mammoth Cave!

They immediately changed plans. First, they ate a meal since it was 9:00 P.M. They would not have to return to the Austin entrance because Pinnix could let them out the elevator entrance. This would save many hours. They decided to finish the survey. Eller's group returned to D-23 and continued. The third compass malfunctioned in the foot of water in the D-survey. Again, they had to wait for Wilcox's group, this time at D-37.

Wilcox's group worked backwards from the lake and met Eller's crew. They set E-20 with the last working compass and joked about having driven "the golden spike." They left the elevator entrance, over seven miles by cave from the Austin entrance, at 1:00 A.M. after fourteen-and-a-half hours underground.

Wilcox's thoroughness and efficiency had paid off. Later they learned that Hanson's Lost River appeared on the very first maps of the cave made by the great black cave explorer Stephen Bishop (1821-57). Both Hanson's Lost River at one end and the Chest Compressor leading to the Tight Spot at the other end had each been visited at least twice but later became forgotten. It took Wilcox, an engineer who paid attention to details, to find the lost leads.

In the final months they had added 3.5 miles to the 83 miles of Flint Ridge. Now, combined with the fifty-eight miles of Mammoth Cave, the system had grown to 144.5 miles. The Swiss cave would never be a serious rival to the Flint-Mammoth system again. Of course, from now on most people would call the system Mammoth Cave after the most famous portion and the national park.

On the other side of Mammoth Cave Ridge across Doyel Valley lies Joppa Ridge. Proctor Cave in Joppa Ridge was discovered in 1863. Explorations began in earnest in 1972, and within seven years, 10 miles of passages were known. On June 28, 1979, a connection to Mammoth Cave was found. Since explorations had also continued in the Flint Ridge area, the total length of the cave was now 215 miles. By 1982, the system had reached to 236 miles.

Roppel Cave on Toohey Ridge was discovered in 1976. Within five years, 27 miles had been explored. A connection was found on September 10, 1983, to the Mammoth Cave system, bringing the total to 294 miles. By 1989, further explorations increased the total length to 329 miles.

Meanwhile, Hölloch Cave had increased to 83 miles, but had been surpassed by yet another cave. Optimisticeskaja in the Ukraine measures 103 miles. These three, together with 77-mile Jewel Cave in South Dakota, were the world's only caves known to be over 70 miles in length in 1989. Mammoth Cave takes the length record without a contest, being over three times longer than its nearest competitor.

ROBYN DAVIDSON
By Camel Across the Outback

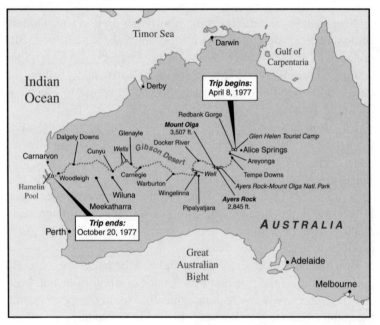

Aborigine children crowded around Rama Rama or "crazy lady." They meant it as an endearing term, for Robyn Davidson had captured their interest. Davidson had arrived at the Pitjantjatjara tribe's settlement in Areyonga on April 11, the fourth day of her trip from Alice Springs. News of her journey had preceded her, and the children had met her on the outskirts of town. They loved petting her black dog, Diggety, and they begged for rides on her four camels, Dookie, Bub, Zeleika, and Goliath. Davidson had spent several years training the camels at Alice Springs, but four days in Australia's Great Sandy Desert had taken its toll.

Alice Springs had been her camel training base. She had become hardened by the wild frontier town and had lost some of her optimistic idealism. Alice Springs was as wild as America's territories of the Old West, and in fact was located in Australia's remote Northern Territory rather than a province. Its dry browns and rusts and livestock towns could pass for west Texas if one did not look too closely at the species of plants and animals. Davidson had taken her camels 150 miles north of Alice Springs to Utopia on a practice run.

Areyonga was a settlement for Aborigines around a missionary station. After resting three days in Areyonga, she headed west. She hoped to cross the Outback and reach the ocean, but the Aborigines warned her of danger. First, it would be difficult to follow the unused old route to Tempe Downs. Second, it would be much too far to the ocean, which they called *uru pulka,* or the big lake.

Davidson faced a dead-end canyon. She had apparently taken the wrong way when the trail faded. She returned the way she had come. Five miles later, another dead end and another backtrack. Was she lost as the Aborigines had warned? She recalled the tear streaked faces of her father, sister, and friends when they had seen her off near Alice Springs. Davidson pored over the maps and made readings with her compass, but in the end she made her best guess and kept moving.

Bub had been skittish all week, and now he began bucking. He bucked off all of the five hundred pounds of supplies he had been carrying. Spread over more than a mile, they took considerable time to regather. Each night, Davidson dreamed she was hopelessly lost, but three days later she arrived at temple Downs. She had finished her first one hundred miles.

Davidson looked out across the rolling dunes of red sand. As she admired the desolate beauty, she saw a black cloud. Soon the swarm of flies engulfed her caravan. She had grown used to the flies and ignored them because they didn't bite, but there had never been so many. They covered any exposed flesh, crawling in and out of eyelids, ears, and nostrils. As dusk settled, clouds of mosquitos replaced the clouds of flies.

Davidson had reached Ayers Rock, Australia's most famous landmark, on April 28. Ayers Rock is the largest monolith in the world, and Davidson spent four days exploring the area, including some caves on its north side. Then she struck out for Docker River, another Aborigine village.

Rain beat down upon Davidson's little caravan a week or two later. The first rain of the trip turned the dusty path into mud, which provides no traction for camels. Dookie's back legs slipped, and he crashed to the ground. When Davidson finally got him to stand, he was limping. It took a few more days to reach Docker River. In the evenings when she hobbled the other camels and let them wander and graze, she had to cut shrubbery to feed Dookie. She hoped he would recover.

Docker River gave Davidson a bigger reception than Areyonga. The whole town turned out to meet her. Dookie recovered after a month, and while she waited, Davidson joined the Aborigines in their food gathering. She learned to enjoy the various plant and insect foods—including witchetty grubs. She found the grubs, larvae of moths, by digging around plant roots. Davidson munched on the squirming grubs, a delicacy to the Aborigines. The grubs were as long as her palm, plump, segmented, and cream colored.

Three wild bull camels faced Davidson's small caravan. She had just left Docker River that morning, June 1, and already she faced a crisis entering the Gibson Desert. Knowing Bub's propensity to run away in danger, she tied him and got him seated. She knew her only female, Zeleika, was in the greatest danger, but so were any other dogs, camels, or humans who got in the way. Heeding the warnings from her friends in Alice Springs and her Aborigine friends, she shot the wild camels when they came too close.

Davidson considered the three weeks from Wingelinna to Warburton the highlight of her trip because of Mr. Eddie. A group of Aborigines who had met her just before Wingelinna decided that one of their wise old men should accompany her for two days to Pipalyatjara. Mr. Eddie was the one who was selected. Davidson and Mr. Eddie enjoyed learning from each other much so that when they arrived at Pipalyatjara, Mr. Eddie decided to continue with her for two hundred miles. They quickly learned to laugh at themselves and their attempts to communicate. They knew very little of each other's languages.

One day, tourists came. They wanted an Aborigine photo. The tourists rudely used a racist term for Aborigine, and Davidson exploded in anger. The Aborigines had suffered slaughter and forced settlement, much as the American Indians had. They had repeatedly been cheated and victimized. Davidson felt embarrassed to be of the same race as the tourists.

In spite of the rudeness, Mr. Eddie had posed for their cameras. After posing, he demanded payment in broken English interspersed with Aborigine phrases and waves of his stick. After the tourists threw money and ran away, he relaxed. Davidson had been crying over the incident, but now she realized that he had been acting. He had played the stereotypical Aborigine in the photos to please them and then insisted on payment for his services. Over the years, he had learned to ignore the mistreatment. He refused to let the injustices depress him, and Davidson's respect for him grew even greater. She considered him to be the perfect gentleman.

Mr. Eddie had seen her tears and anger and knew that she understood his role-playing. They looked at each other and laughed. It was a good lesson for Davidson. Her own frustrations with tourists and journalists seemed very small now. She had learned a valuable lesson: difficulties do not control human reactions. If Mr. Eddie could take such demeaning and humiliating treatment in stride, she determined to follow his good example through her own difficulties.

On July 3, Davidson and Mr. Eddie arrived at Warburton, the last Aborigine settlement on the reserve. Davidson was sorry to part company and showed her appreciation by giving him a rifle like her own. He had often admired her rifle, and he lit up with joy and gratitude at the gift. Her trip across the Aborigine reserve would be the highlight of her journey.

Davidson headed up the Gunbarrel Highway on July 15. Some highway! Only the best four-wheel-drive vehicles could negotiate the two parallel wheel ruts that crossed the nine hundred miles of desert. The Aborigines said that only about six vehicles per year make it across. Davidson followed the Gunbarrel for 350 miles on her way to Carnegie and Glenayle.

Davidson led her camels through the streets of Carnegie on July 27. It was abandoned. The three-year drought had turned it into a ghost town. She had no food but would have to continue to Glenayle. She ate dog food with Diggety and rationed everything. With limited water, she had not bathed in a month. What if Glenayle were deserted too?

As Davidson neared Glenayle, cattle corpses littered the desert. Starving horses and cattle loitered along the way. Many people had moved away, but the Ward family tenaciously struggled against poverty in Glenayle. The Wards nursed Davidson, Diggety, and the other camels back to health for a week.

Diggety died on August 9, and Davidson became depressed. She had left Glenayle two days earlier and had come to a well that marked the Canning Stock Route. She had spent three days at the oasis where Diggety had eaten poisoned bait intended for wild dingos. Davidson could not stand watching him suffer in his death struggles and had to shoot him. The Canning route is famous in Australia and extends one thousand miles. Davidson did not look forward to the 170 difficult miles of it that she would follow—especially without Diggety.

On August 27, Davidson and her camels reached Cunyu, the place where she would leave the Canning Route. After a few days of rest, she continued but soon had to treat Zeleika for internal bleeding. Zeleika had been nursing her calf, baby Goliath, since they had left Alice Springs. Now, Robyn worried about Zeleika. Could she stand the loss of another of her faithful animal escorts?

The camels' eyes bulged at the sight of the Indian Ocean on October 19. They had never seen so much water. Approaching hesitantly, they waded into the cool waves. Davidson laughed as the camels repeatedly spat out water when they tried to drink. They would eventually learn that salt water is not for drinking.

The Burke-Wills expedition had crossed the Australian Outback from south to north in 1860, but only a few men had reached the north coast. The one who survived the return trip was found and fed by Aborigines until his rescue in September of 1861. Davidson's seventeen-hundred-mile and 195-day trip of 1977 had traversed the Outback from east to west. She had been the first person to do so. She had crossed half a continent solo.

After enjoying four days at the beach, she left her camels with friends and got a ride to Carnarvon. She had originally intended to reach the coast at Carnarvon, but had changed her plans in order to visit friends and to avoid the media. From Carnarvon she flew to New York to write her story for National Geographic, which had provided some funding for her. It was her first international trip, and she missed the quiet desert while in the midst of the megalopolis.

Davidson had been born in September of 1950 at Miles about two hundred miles west of Brisbane in the province of Queensland, Australia. In the 1990s, she crossed another desert. This time she lived with the nomadic Raharis for a year in the Thar Desert of India and Pakistan. She has published books on both adventures and currently lives in London.

NAOMI UEMURA
The North Pole Solo

Naomi Uemura instantly became alert as the barking of his sled dogs pierced the polar night. He huddled in his sleeping bag inside his tent. He knew that his sled dogs feared only two things in the Arctic: people and polar bears. Since no people would be walking through the Arctic ice floes before dawn, Uemura listened for the padding and snuffling of an approaching polar bear. He could not reach his unloaded gun.

The yelping dogs broke loose and scattered from where Uemura had staked them for the night. Soon he heard heavy footfalls. The bear nosed through his food supply, eating whatever it wanted. Uemura grew fearful and began to sweat profusely as he listened to the bear's breathing through the tent wall. He wondered if his solo journey to the North Pole would end so soon. He had left only four days previously, on March 6, 1978, from Ellesmere Island, Canada.

Uemura heard the tent ripping as the bear clawed through the fabric. Playing dead, he shrank down deeper into his sleeping bag. The polar bear nudged Uemura's back with his nose but then abruptly departed.

Uemura sighed with relief and immediately arose and collected his remaining gear. At only five feet three inches tall and 135 pounds, he had only his wits to outmatch the massive polar bear. Uemura knew about polar bears after mushing seventy-five-hundred

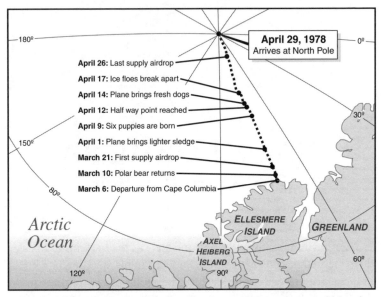

miles from Greenland to Alaska. Such experiences assured him that he had not seen the last of that bear.

The next morning, Uemura was waiting for it. He had oiled his gun with kerosene to be sure that it would fire in the forty below zero cold. At the first dog's bark, Uemura positioned himself for firing. He could see the massive bulk of the bear coming toward him. He waited tensely until it was within range and fired. The bear reared up on its hind legs but then turned to retreat. It did not get far before it slumped to the ground. Uemura shot it several times to be certain it was dead before he relaxed. The crisis was over.

The next morning he continued his sledding toward the North Pole. It was his sixth day on the Arctic Ocean on the first solo attempt for the pole. For a week he battled through pressure ridges of jumbled ice. Finally, he reached flat ice, only to find channels of open water. When the floating sheets of ice split, the deep Arctic Ocean on which they float is exposed. Uemura had to wait a day for the channel to freeze over again before he could cross. After that he moved faster—up to twelve miles a day. On April 1, an airplane brought him fresh supplies and a lighter sledge.

Uemura took sightings at noon on April 13. According to his calculations, he must have crossed the halfway point the previous day. He had come 250 miles from Cape Columbia and would reach the pole in another 225 miles. Any joy from this landmark was short-lived because snowstorms stopped him for a whole day on April 15.

Stranded! Uemura had stopped in front of an expanding water channel, when suddenly he heard ice creaking and groaning behind him. The ice broke, and he was adrift. The ice floe was large enough for his camp, sled, and dogs, but would it crack apart itself or would an ice bridge form?

Uemura spent a day floating helplessly. Knowing the temperature should drop at dusk, he waited. Soon he found that he could move forward, but it took over two hours to reach solid ice. Uemura made up for lost time and traveled twenty-four miles on April 21 and another thirty-six miles the next day.

The sled teetered on the edge of open water. The dogs had crossed the thinly frozen channel safely but had slowed on the far side. As they slowed, the heavy sled full of supplies began to break through the thin ice. "Yah!" Uemura yelled. "Go! Go!" The dogs sprinted again, and the sled pulled up onto the firm ice. It was the last tense moment. Later that day, at 6:30 P.M. on April 29, Uemura and his dog team reached the North Pole after traveling 477 miles in fifty-five days. He spent three days at the pole and checked his position using a sextant. The pilot who flew him and his dog team back to Greenland also confirmed his position and victory.

Uemura returned from the North Pole to his home in Tokyo, Japan. The son of a farmer from the Kyogo Prefecture west of Osaka, he now lived with his wife, Kimiko, in Tokyo. Besides being the first to solo to the North Pole, Uemura is considered the first to have trekked across the middle of Greenland.

Now Uemura was famous and welcomed, but it had not always been so. Earlier, when he had become the first man to walk the 1,750-mile north-south length of Japan, his countrymen had not honored him but considered him crazy. His thirty-seven-hundred-mile kayak trip down the Amazon found no place in Japanese tradition. His solo climbs of Mont Blanc in 1966, Kilimanjaro, and

Aconcagua had been criticized by older men who told him to get a decent job. The tide had turned somewhat in 1970 when he became part of the first successful Japanese team to climb Mount Everest. His solo to the North Pole had finally and firmly established him as the first Japanese adventurer.

Uemura had climbed Mount McKinley in 1970 just before climbing Mount Everest. He decided to climb it again solo and in winter as preparation for a trip to Antarctica. He celebrated his forty-third birthday, February 12, 1984, on the summit of Mount McKinley after the first-ever successful solo climb in winter. However, the day after that, he lost radio contact. Three days later, he was spotted from an airplane at 16,400 feet. That was the last time he was sighted, and his body was never found. His eight books in Japanese, however, still stir his countrymen, and today he is an undisputed national hero.

BEN ABRUZZO
Ballooning Across Oceans

Atlantic Ocean

Benjamin Lawrence Abruzzo sat in his home reading a story in the latest issue of *National Geographic*. As a balloonist, the story of Ed Yost's 107-hour and 2,745-mile journey had caught his interest. Ben himself was an expert balloonist, but he flew hot-air balloons, which rise by heating air. Since the propane must be stored on board, hot-air balloons can fly for only a few hours. In contrast, Ed Yost had flown a gas balloon, which rises because the helium gas inside is lighter than air. The balloon descends when the balloon cools under clouds or at sunset, or when some of the gas is released through a valve. Yost's flight lasted more than four days and beat the previous time and distance records by twenty hours and 578 miles. His balloon, *Silver Fox,* had made it farthest across the Atlantic and had crashed into the sea conveniently near a large ship for rescue. In spite of setting two new world records and falling only seven hundred miles short of Portugal, Yost had failed.

The article depressed Abruzzo. He hated failure. Born on June 9, 1930, in Rockford, Illinois, he had failed in physical fights in elementary school. In fact, he had been beaten up so many times by the time he was in the sixth grade that he asked for weights for his birthday. He worked out daily. At 160 pounds, he found he could beat up each of the bullies that had clobbered him, so they would not pick on him anymore. He also became fit enough to be a lifeguard at the beach, where he met Patricia Steen. He married Pat in 1952 upon his graduation from the University of Illinois.

Ben had also initially failed in business. After his two years in the air force at Albuquerque, New Mexico, where he had earned the rank of first lieutenant, he had decided to settle and work in Albuquerque. He had failed in used car sales and in his uranium mining investments and ended up with a debt of $40,000. Instead of filing for bankruptcy, he worked hard doing odd jobs until he had paid back the entire debt and could support his family. Then he bought land to start a ski resort at nearby Sandia Peak. Between the resort and nearby properties he had developed, he became a millionaire.

"Did you read the story about Ed Yost?" came a voice over the phone. Abruzzo recognized the inquirer as his friend Max Anderson, another millionaire, whom he had met skiing at the resort in 1966. Recalling the depressing article, Abruzzo told his friend that he had read it.

"What would you think about you and me flying the Atlantic?" asked Anderson. Abruzzo and Anderson had won several balloon competitions in their jointly owned hot-air balloons. Abruzzo responded immediately, "Let's do it!"

Albuquerque is the balloon capital of the world for hot-air balloons, but no one there made helium balloons. In April, Abruzzo and Anderson visited Ed Yost in Sioux Falls, South Dakota, the only place to get helium balloons in America at the time. Yost, who with Don Piccard, had made the first balloon crossing of the English Channel on April 13, 1963, had been so shaken by his record-breaking disaster in the Atlantic that he had said he would never attempt to cross the Atlantic again. Yost agreed to build a helium balloon for his two visitors for $50,000. Later changes cost another $5,000. They named the balloon *Double Eagle,* commemorating Lindbergh's airplane, *Lone Eagle,* that first crossed the Atlantic.

In early June, Yost took them up for a training flight over the Texas panhandle. This flight in a small helium balloon cost them another $3,000 but earned Abruzzo and Anderson their licenses. They marveled at the quietness of the ride. Instead of propane tanks blasting in their ears, they could hear footsteps across wooden porches and the lowing of cattle, thousands of feet below.

Abruzzo worked on learning the principles of helium balloons. He quizzed himself constantly with questions such as how much ballast should he jettison to halt a descent of five feet per second? Meanwhile, Anderson worked on North Atlantic weather patterns and navigation. On July 1, both men needed a break, and they entered their hot-air balloons in the first Pikes Peak Balloon Race. Abruzzo won the race.

On September 9, a large crowd gathered to watch the liftoff from Marshfield near Boston, Massachusetts. When the balloon was filled with 101,000 cubic feet of helium, its top stood nine stories above the gondola hanging below it. The loudspeaker blared the "Star Spangled Banner" through the evening darkness. His mother-in-law gave Max his favorite German chocolate birthday cake. Anderson would be forty-three the next morning.

The ground crew cut the ropes at 8:16 P.M., and the balloon began to rise. Pat Abruzzo called after Ben, "I love you. God be with you both. I'll see you in France." Both wives were crying as Pat turned to embrace Max's wife, Patty. Both women had flown in hot-air balloons with their husbands and could laugh over close calls. However, little was known about helium ballooning compared to the knowledge of airplanes that Lindbergh had had available. Both women supported their husbands in this venture, but both knew the dangers.

All ten previous attempts had failed, and five people had died. The first attempt was made by Donaldson, Ford, and Hunt in 1873, but their balloon *Daily Telegraph* took them only forty-five miles. In the second attempt, two men in *Small World* reached midocean in 1958. Ten years later, two other men ditched their balloon *Maple Leaf* near Halifax. In 1970, the *Free Life* and its crew of three were lost at sea in midocean. Sparks unsuccessfully flew *Yankee Zephyr* in 1973 and *Odyssey* two years later. During the intervening year, Tom Gatch disappeared beyond Bermuda in *Light Heart,* and *Spirit of Man* exploded off the New Jersey coast, killing its pilot, Bob Berger. The most recent attempts had been made by Thomas in *Spirit of '76* and Yost in *Silver Fox.*

After the balloon left the lights of Boston behind, it entered clouds. Air currents carried the men over the White Mountains of New Hampshire. Abruzzo charted positions obtained by radio from air traffic controllers. At an altitude of about 2,700 feet, they were on a collision course with 5,267-foot Mount Katahdin in Maine. They hoped the winds, which would be diverted around it, would carry the balloon around it safely too. It was eery knowing that the danger was near but being unable to see through the clouds to adjust correctly.

Abruzzo began yodeling through a megaphone. He explained to puzzled Anderson that he could count the seconds for the echo to bounce back off the mountain as a gauge of distance. After fifteen minutes, the skies cleared, and they could tell from maps that they had passed the mountain. It was 3:00 A.M., and Maine's northern wilderness spread before them. Three hours later they crossed into Canada.

Suddenly the balloon rushed downward. Abruzzo threw ballast overboard but could not check the descent. They could see they were only 150 feet above the ground and about to crash. Dumping out more ballast, they heard tree branches breaking beneath them as they slowed. Part of the antenna hanging below them broke off as they began to ascend from the Gaspé Peninsula of Quebec. The morning sun should have made the balloon rise, but instead they had almost crashed. The two men guessed that they had been trapped in a rotor, a wind that rushes over the crest of a range and drops down the other side. After two more rotors, they were over the Gulf of St. Lawrence. They ballasted out of a fourth rotor only eighty feet above the water. They had used far too much ballast.

By the time they crossed into Labrador, it was raining. Both men were soaked, but Anderson wore wool on the advice of his Minnesota relatives. Abruzzo had worn down ski clothing and was soaked. So far north and at high altitudes, he began shivering. Snow fell as they continued in clouds over the Atlantic. Abruzzo enjoyed his view of the Canadian shore as the balloon began its flight over the Atlantic. It was dark again and cold. Abruzzo had slept only three of the twenty-five hours since Boston. He alternated three-hour shifts as pilot with Anderson. His coldness had hindered his sleep, and he fought both cold and weariness for control of his mind.

Storm clouds, piled thousands of feet high, towered above the balloon. *Double Eagle* entered a blizzard as the cloud engulfed it. Shielded from the warm sun, the balloon dropped three-fourths of its height to two thousand feet. At this altitude, more rain entered the gondola.

The entire balloon shook twelve hours later as a cyclone caught it. The cyclone off Greenland gripped the balloon for over six hours and sent it in a circle five hundred miles across. Abruzzo suspected what was happening, but radio contact was lost. The sea churned and frothed below them. Abruzzo looked into the maelstrom and saw great icebergs littering the sea. If they went down, could they possibly survive?

As they neared Iceland, a navy helicopter came to the rescue. They realized that they would have to ditch the balloon. Landing in the sea, they released the balloon. They huddled in the gondola, a tiny boat in a restless sea with waves twenty-five-feet high. The helicopter hauled in Anderson and then Abruzzo on the rope. Abruzzo was near death. After hospitalization and almost losing his foot to frostbite, he limped for months. They had failed.

Abruzzo and Anderson asked Ed Yost to design their second balloon as he had their first. The balloon held 160,000 cubic feet of helium. Both balloon and gondola included several improvements. They also brought along a third crew member, Larry Newman, to share the watches. Meanwhile, they kept close tabs on other attempts to cross. Reinhard and Stephenson ditched their *Eagle* near Halifax later in 1977, but Cameron and Davey almost took the record. Their *Zanussi* came down just 110 miles short of the French coast.

Slowly, the balloon inflated to its eleven-story height, but as liftoff time approached, it still looked slack. They found problems with the pump, and hours of work still did not correct the problem. The balloonists finally launched in the darkness three hours late and without completely filling the balloon. *Double Eagle II* rose quietly into the night sky at 8:43 P.M. on Friday, August 11, 1978, over Presque Isle, Maine.

Abruzzo, Anderson, and Newman floated leisurely, ten thousand feet above the earth. New Brunswick and Newfoundland passed below them. On the third day, a downdraft brought them down to thirty-fivehundred feet. They threw out ballast and rose to their preferred altitude of fifteen thousand feet, where they put on their oxygen masks.

As Iceland neared, dangers increased. Ice building up on top of the balloon increased its weight by three hundred pounds. The extra weight dropped the balloon over two thousand feet, but as the sun dawned, the ice melted, and the balloon rose again. Next, a low pressure storm caught them but veered north before engulfing them. As soon as the storm turned away, high cirrus clouds blocked the sun. The cooling effect reversed the air expansion, and the balloon began to descend. After descending all the way to four thousand feet, it hovered at the top of a bank of cumulus clouds. Just as they began to descend into these clouds, which would block even more sunlight, they slowed and began to climb, rising to a trip high of 24,950 feet.

Irish airport radars picked up the balloon on the night of August 16. When they notified Abruzzo by radio, the entire crew celebrated—they had reached Europe! They did not land yet, though, because they hoped to reach Paris. Breezing across Ireland, Wales, and England, they gradually descended to eleven thousand feet. If Abruzzo let out helium too fast, they would veer south to Brittany; if too slowly, they would drift east to London and Belgium. They needed to stay at the altitude with winds that would carry them in the right direction.

Crossing the English Channel, they now floated over France. They dropped some ballast in a field near Evreux and then began to see cars lining the farm roads below them. Hundreds of people had turned out to see the landing and welcome them. They skimmed a corn field and then touched down in a barley field outside the town of Miserey at 7:49 P.M. on August 17.

Abruzzo and his two friends had spent 137 hours airborne and had traveled 3,105 miles across the Atlantic. Besides the first-ever ocean crossing, they had also set a new distance record for manned balloon flight. As they touched down, crowds swarmed them. The three balloonists felt like Charles Lindbergh when he had crossed the Atlantic in an airplane and landed at Le Bourget airport not far away. Crowds greeted them, as they had Lindbergh, in the grand French tradition.

However, the landing and the crowds ruined the barley crop. The balloonists learned that the field belonged to Roger and Rachel Coquerel, and they reimbursed them for the crop loss. The mayor of Evreux gave a speech, and then the celebration moved on to Paris. The balloon found its way to the National Air and Space Museum in Washington, D.C.

Albuquerque also welcomed the heroic trio. Over sixty hot-air balloons hovered over their route from the airport to the civic center. The mayor, governor, and state congressmen turned out for the welcome. Abruzzo was overwhelmed that Albuquerque had "turned itself inside out" for them.

Pacific Ocean

Ben Abruzzo and Max Anderson joined forces again with a 34,500-cubic-foot helium balloon. Racing against sixteen other balloons for 560 miles, they captured the 1979 James Gordon Bennett Cup in *Double Eagle III*. Beginning from Long Beach on the Pacific Ocean on May 27, they flew across four states to Utah's border with Colorado.

The following year, Max Anderson and his son Kristian became the first to cross the North American continent. They launched their *Kitty Hawk* from Fort Baker on San Francisco Bay on May 8. They crossed the Sierra Nevada and then the Continental Divide in the Rocky Mountains of Wyoming. After the Black Hills, the Mississippi River, Lake Michigan, and Lake Huron, they floated over Ontario and Quebec, slipped across northern Maine, and became snagged in trees in New Brunswick. After a Canadian rescue helicopter fanned them out of their tree, they had a proper landing on May 12 at St. Felicite, Quebec. They had made the first transcontinental balloon flight and set a new distance record of thirty-four hundred miles.

Abruzzo hoped his own plans for *Double Eagle V* would go as well as his friend's. At 3:05 A.M. on November 10, 1981, Abruzzo's

400,000-cubic-foot balloon lifted off with a four-man crew. Larry Newman joined Abruzzo once again, together with two new balloonists: Ron Clark and Rocky Aoki. As they rose from Nagashima, Japan, the dawning sun sent a glow across Mount Fuji.

After six hours, the balloon had reached an altitude of nineteen thousand feet, but ice had begun to accumulate. Having to drop ballast to maintain altitude in the first two hundred miles of the trip frustrated Abruzzo. Concern heightened in the evening as the cooling gas contracted, and they dropped even more rapidly. After a low of forty-five-hundred feet, the warmth of the morning sun expanded the gas again, and the extra lift helped them to rise.

The four men looked down on the blue ocean spread below them as far as the eye could see in all directions. They viewed the vast Pacific Ocean through the windows of their specialized gondola, designed by Larry Newman. By evening they achieved a new high of twenty-two thousand feet.

At 2:00 A.M. on November 12, *Double Eagle V* crossed the international date line. Abruzzo turned his calendar back one day, and lived November 11 all over again. He enjoyed a full day of stable flight at sixteen thousand feet. He did not complain about the low speed of forty-three miles per hour because the stable altitude conserved ballast, which in the end was more important than speed.

The balloon descended even in the warmth of the morning sun. During the morning of November 12, three tons of ice had accumulated on the balloon, which dropped rapidly. Abruzzo jettisoned more ballast, but they continued to drop. The crew again reviewed procedures for crashing into the ocean. The end of the trip seemed imminent, and only five hundred miles from the California coast.

Abruzzo realized how successful they had already been. Even if they had to ditch the balloon, they were making history. Their flight would go on record as the first manned balloon to attempt to cross the Pacific Ocean. They were also the first to cross the international date line, and they had already traveled over five thousand miles, which far surpassed the thirty-four-hundred-mile distance record set by Anderson. Each mile of ocean that passed below them now increased the new distance record. Yet, Abruzzo's goal had been to achieve the first Pacific crossing. He knew that these lesser achievements would not satisfy him.

The balloon continued to drop. Abruzzo continued to jettison ballast until he had dropped 825 pounds and could not risk more of their remaining supply. Even with this largest ballast drop of their flight, they lost twelve thousand feet of altitude in only two hours. They reached their lowest altitude of the entire trip—only forty-two hundred feet above sea level. Prospects looked bleak.

Chunks of ice larger than basketballs rained down around the gondola at noon. The chunks would have injured Abruzzo and his crew if they had not included a roof on their gondola. More importantly, the chunks signaled that the warmer air at lower elevations had finally begun to melt the balloon's thick icecap. Abruzzo's hopes soared as the balloon climbed to thirteen thousand feet once more. At this colder altitude, snow began to fall, but very lightly.

Dusk and then darkness enveloped them once more. The chill air sank the balloon into the clouds. From an altitude of sixty-nine hundred feet, Abruzzo listened. They could not see anything, but they could hear the roar of ocean surf crashing on Point Arena. They had just reached the California coast. They had crossed the Pacific Ocean, but they were not safe yet. They had just entered the worst storm in twenty years in this part of California.

The storm whipped the balloon along, and Abruzzo released helium to descend as fast as he dared. Breaking through the clouds, he identified the town of Willits. He released more helium to land in the valley as rain beat on their balloon and gondola. Lightning flashed around them, and the winds carried them straight for the houses of Willits.

"Watch out! Up, up! Drop ballast!" Abruzzo called. They had descended to five hundred feet but could not risk crashing into the houses in the storm. They dropped ballast and climbed again to eight thousand feet. They sighted another valley in the coastal mountains south of Covelo and began descending again. This time the storm carried them toward a brushy hill. It would do. Abruzzo detonated the explosives to sever the gondola from the balloon. The gondola fell the last few feet to the ground. They had succeeded.

In four days and five nights—eighty-four hours and thirty-one minutes to be exact—they had traveled a record 5,768 miles and crossed the Pacific Ocean. In 1997, another American, Steve Fossett, set a new distance record of 10,361 miles by flying his balloon *Solo Spirit* from St. Louis to Sultanpur, India. Distance records such as Fossett's seven-day flight across the Atlantic and Sahara will continue to be set, but Abruzzo, who died in a plane crash on February 11, 1985, will always retain the record of the first Pacific crossing.

ROY MACKAL
Into the Likouala Swamp

"Your findings from Loch Ness are very intriguing, Dr. Mackal," said James Powell. "I greatly enjoyed the lecture. I, too, have been researching creature sightings. Are you familiar with *n'yamala?*"

Dr. Mackal, having taught in the field of biology for over twenty-five years at the University of Chicago, had a special interest in cryptozoology, which is the study of hidden or unknown animals. Powell's comment immediately interested Dr. Mackal. Born on August 1, 1925, in Milwaukee, Wisconsin, Mackal was willing to follow leads even into the jungles of Africa. He listened as Powell gave the following background on the unfamiliar *n'yamala* creature.

"A Catholic missionary to what is now Cameroon found tracks of a creature the natives called *amali,*" related Powell. "The tracks, three feet around and eight feet apart, showed claw marks. As you know, the largest elephants have such a long stride—but no claws. In 1870, in Gabon, a man found similar prints of *n'yamala.* Broken elephant tusks near the prints impressed the ivory trader. What could kill elephants? In 1912, a German zoo manager heard about a hippo-killing elephant-dragon in Rhodesia called *mokele-mbembe.* In 1913-14 a German expedition to the Congo reported locations where African guides had sighted this huge wading animal. In 1938, a German scientist made similar reports. In 1976, I heard more *n'yamala* stories as I conducted crocodile research in Gabon."

Dr. Mackal and Powell decided to investigate *n'yamala* together. Powell returned to Gabon for a survey. At the village of Obongo, he interviewed the witch doctor, who correctly identified photos of gorilla, elephant, crocodile, hippo, and leopard. He could not identify the bear because bears do not live in Africa. Next, Powell showed him dinosaur drawings from a children's book. The witch doctor had never seen tyrannosaurus, stegosaurus, or triceratops, but he identified diplodocus and a plesiosaur as *n'yamala*. Tribal chiefs in other villages gave the same responses. The chiefs added that *n'yamala* lived in deep pools and lakes in remote parts of the swamp and were rarely seen.

Meanwhile, Dr. Mackal searched the literature. He found that a Dr. Bernard Heuvelmans had collected reports of strange African animals. Huevelmans classified the sightings: (1) known animals that are rare and unfamiliar in a region (manatees often surprise inland Africans who see them); (2) known animals of unknown sizes (reports of fifty-foot crocodiles may be exaggerated); and (3) unknown animals. Mackal concentrated on the third group of reports, which came from three regions: the marshes of Benin, Lake Bengweulu in Rhodesia (now Zambia), and the swamps of the Congo. The Benin reports, all from the same person, could be a hoax. The Lake Bengweulu reports dated from the nineteenth century, and lack of recent reports suggest that the creature had either died or departed to more remote locations. However, the reports from the Congo seemed promising. Hoaxes are not substantiated by multitudes of recent reports.

Dr. Mackal knew he could find out the truth only by searching in the area of the sightings. Aside from the evolutionary bias among scientists, there was no reason that some species of dinosaurs should not exist. Even evolutionists consider crocodiles to be older than dinosaurs. Likewise, the tuatara of New Zealand and the coelacanth of the Indian Ocean both represent otherwise extinct orders of animals. Dr. Mackal reasoned that if some animals survive from supposedly extinct orders, some member of the order of dinosaurs may have survived too. The possibility is strengthened by the many cultures worldwide that have legends of huge creatures, sea monsters, and flying dragons. In fact, ancient cave paintings in Africa show dinosaur figures, though secular archaeologists always label them as unknown animals because they refuse to believe that people could have seen living dinosaurs.

The Likouala

Dr. Mackal and James Powell approached Impfondo, a single paved airstrip beside an iron-roofed shelter for waiting passengers. The small Congolese plane had departed from Maya Maya Airport in Brazzaville earlier that day for the weekly flight to Impfondo. As they landed, the little terminal seemed very small in the vastness of the Likouala Swamp, a portion of a swamp that stretches across the Congo into the Central African Republic and Cameroon. Two of the three countries have national parks near their common border. These parks of the Ndoki are so remote that *National Geographic* called it "the Last Place on Earth." It is certainly the most remote jungle area remaining.

Missionary Gene Thomas greeted them on the airstrip. Pastor Thomas had spent twenty-eight years at Impfondo. He knew the area and the natives and was interested in *mokele-mbembe,* which the natives often told him about. Pastor Thomas invited natives who had seen *mokele-mbembe* to give their stories, which he translated for Dr. Mackal.

Pastor Thomas also told Dr. Mackal about the references to leviathan and behemoth in the Bible. Pastor Thomas admitted that many commentators try to explain these references as large mammals or crocodiles, but when Dr. Mackal read the passage in Job 40:15-24 for himself, he agreed that no crocodile eats "grass as an ox," and no elephant, rhino, or hippo has a tail "like a cedar." The passage probably describes a sauropod dinosaur such as apatosaurus or diplodocus.

Pastor Thomas also mentioned an archaeologist who considers a carving on the Ishtar Gate at the ruins of Babylon to be a dinosaur. This was no problem to Pastor Thomas, who knew that God had created dinosaurs just hours before He created man and that dinosaurs had survived the Great Flood on the ark.

Dr. Mackal, though an evolutionist, disagreed with his colleagues over the possibility of dinosaur survival. The numerous

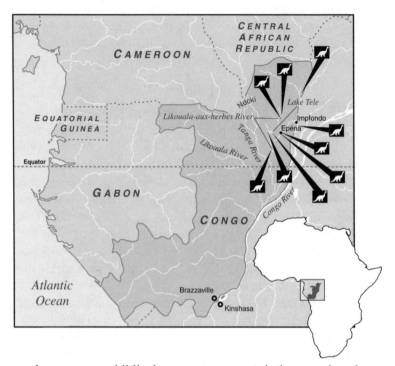

modern reports, biblical accounts, cave paintings, archaeology, and legends from many cultures had convinced him that some species of dinosaurs had coexisted with man.

Dr. Mackal heard about other strange animals besides *mokele-mbembe* from the natives of Impfondo as well. One man told him about *emela-ntouka,* or elephant-killer. The rhino-sized animal had a long curved horn, but it was not a rhino, since rhinos always lose fights with elephants because their horns break. Dr. Mackal guessed that the animal was either a new type of aquatic rhino or the horned dinosaur monoclonius. Another native told them about *ngoima,* a bird with a five-foot wingspan that swoops down from its nest in the tallest trees (one hundred feet high) to prey on monkeys. From this description, Dr. Mackal recognized a known but rare bird—the crowned eagle.

Dr. Mackal set out early on May 19, 1980. A truck brought his party three miles before its passage was blocked by a vehicle mired in the mud. From there, they began walking, hoping to reach Bimbo, an extended family outpost, before dark.

Dr. Mackal felt the muck pulling at his feet with each step. Rivers of sweat poured off him in the 90 percent humidity and 90°F temperature, even in the shade of the leafy canopy high overhead. Methane gas and sulphurous fumes rose from the swamp, causing indigestion. In the stifling heat, Dr. Mackal noticed Powell and Pastor Thomas swatting mosquitos and squishing the biting ants that swarmed on them. Only the native guide, Marien Ikolé, and the other Pygmy porters seemed tireless and maintained a quick pace, even though they carried all the gear. As dusk descended, they found Bimbo.

After several more hours of jungle trekking the next morning, the expedition reached its first village, Boleke, where the natives grew excited at seeing their first white visitors. On the way to Bossimba, they saw some forest elephants. Later, they crossed a large savanna. The Pygmies made noises to scare off water buffalo, which would attack if surprised in the tall grasses. At Botala on the Tanga River, a dugout awaited them. When Dr. Mackal saw it, he called to Pastor Thomas, "Praise be to God, your prayers have been answered."

The first-ever trek by Europeans across the most remote part of the swamp had been completed. They paddled the dugout down the Tanga into the wider Likouala-aux-Herbes. Before long they reached Epéena, where a crowd of Pygmies greeted them. They listened to a dozen natives tell of their own encounters with *mokele-mbembe.*

Nicolas Mondongo described *mokele-mbembe* as thirty feet long, with reddish brown skin and a comb like a rooster's on its head. It stood about six feet tall and ate *malombo,* a species of liana with white flowers and large nutlike apple-shaped fruit. Other natives reported *mokele-mbembe* with gray skin. Some told of a group that had speared one to death at Lake Tele, but all the natives who had eaten its meat had died.

Dr. Mackal already knew about *malombo* (landolphia). All the reports agreed on this point. In fact, the food explained many things that paleontologists could not figure out from dinosaur bones. Some thought the sauropods, such as Camarasaurus, were too heavy to move on land and must be aquatic. The long neck was for breathing at the surface. This theory ran into problems when Camarasaurus tracks were found on land, and neither could it explain how the creature could breathe. Its lungs would be unable to expand under the water pressure at even moderate depths. The second view held that Camarasaurus browsed on land like a giraffe, but how could its skeleton support the weight of a dozen elephants? If it ate water plants, why then would the teeth show so much wear? Perhaps it ate shellfish, but why would it have a long neck?

Eyewitness details resolved the riddles of the bones. The sauropods supported their weight by wading with their body near the surface, enabling them to breathe. They could walk on land to deeper water holes during droughts. Their long necks enabled them to reach the *malombo* fruits, which grew along the riverbank. The teeth would wear down from munching the hard nutlike fruit. Of course, the natives could not know about the competing theories in paleontology. Could they have made up a creature that explained the dilemmas of paleontologists? It is far easier to believe that they had seen the sauropod and that its actual habits explained the riddles.

As to its six-foot height, perhaps the larger specimens have not survived. The forest elephant of the swamp is not as large as the Indian elephant either. Further, neither elephants nor humans are as large as the mammoths and Goliaths of history. The size of sauropods may have decreased as well since the Flood.

In the next several days, Mackal and Powell heard other reports as well. One woman had seen a creature called *mbielu-mbielu-mbielu* with planks growing out of its back. She identified it with a drawing of a stegosaurus in the dinosaur book. One man even took them by dugout to the place where he had seen *mokele-mbembe*. They saw a lair in the riverbank, but since the water level was low, there was no inhabitant. With their visas about to expire, they flew to Impfondo. Most of the Pygmies preferred to return on foot, but Marien Ikolé opted for the plane ride and saw his native land from the air for the first time. From Impfondo, on February 27, 1980, they flew to Brazzaville and then home.

Return to the Likouala

In October of 1981, Dr. Mackal returned to the Congo. This time he brought three team members with him: British anthropologist Richard Greenwell and two Americans—geomorphologist Justin Wilkinson and photographer Marie T. Womack. They arrived in Brazzaville on October 27. Here four Congolese men increased the team size to eight: two security officers, zoologist Marcellin Agnagna, and military radio operator Pascal M'Beke. At Impfondo, Pastor Thomas as interpreter, Marien Ikolé as chief Pygmy porter, and two other Pygmy porters completed the team.

The expedition launched its outboard and dugout before dawn on November 17. They went upstream on the Ubangi River to get to the canal. They motored through the narrow Djemba Canal slowly, often hacking through submerged logs that blocked their way. They barely got camp pitched at the far end when the brief tropical twilight gave way to night in the jungle darkness at 7:00 P.M.

At Epéna, after a day of travel on the Tanga with quick stops at Luesso and Botala, they learned that *mokele-mbembe* had been sighted at Dzeke. A day later, they headed down the Likouala-aux-Herbes toward Dzeke.

"Mokele-mbembe!" the natives screamed. Something large had plopped into the river from the shadowy bank. The wave, almost a foot high, sloshed water into the dugout. No one had seen it clearly, but the natives knew of no other explanation than *mokele-mbembe*. No gorilla or Nile crocodile could have made such a wave. They searched the bank and then searched the water in widening circles. They found nothing. Certainly a hippo, elephant, or water buffalo could not have disappeared without a trace. In fact, no hippos had ever been spotted in that region of the river, and all tales of *mokele-mbembe* asserted that they killed but did not eat hippos.

Dr. Mackal noted *malombo* plants laden with fruit growing along the banks. He imagined the sauropod feasting; yet as a zoologist, he knew he must not jump to conclusions. At Dzeke, a native who had served in the military had kept records in French of his *mokele-mbembe* sightings. Dr. Mackal copied down the details and places. The sightings from Dzeke turned out, however, to have been from almost a year previously. Lost. The French had aptly named the Likouala-aux-Herbes. The sea of floating grass looked the same in every direction. They could not find the main channel at the confluence of the Bai. After three tries to reach the Bai, they felt hopelessly lost. They paddled up to the only high ground they could see in order to camp. Fortunately, a hermit lived there, who guided them into the main channel in the morning. However, they soon were lost again until another native guided them to Kinami, where they spent three nights.

The people of Kinami welcomed the expedition, but they wasted the next day trying to obtain information from the last village upstream. The chief of Moungouma Bai refused to see them. The following day, Dr. Mackal and Pastor Thomas visited a *mokele-mbembe* pool with a guide from Kinami. Their radars detected a twenty-foot creature on the bottom, but they could not tell for sure whether it was a large Nile crocodile or *mokele-mbembe*. The rest of the group went looking for lowland gorillas with no success. In 1963, Kinami had received its only white visitor—a Frenchman on a malaria survey. The children were enthralled at seeing their first white-skinned people. They appreciated the medical help from Dr. Mackal, too, and were sorry to see the expedition leave.

The expedition returned to Dzeke. Here, they heard some new sauropod stories and were also led to a site where *mokele-mbembe* had been seen on land. A path of broken branches six feet high through the jungle led to the river. The Pygmy hunter who brought them there said he had first thought it was a forest elephant track. However, the elephant would not leave clawed footprints and would also have come out of the river nearby. He had scouted the river and found no exit. The maker of the tracks had lived in the river.

From Boha, a strip of high ground extends to Lake Tele. Four campsites provide accommodations along the thirty-mile route. Because of the route, the men of Boha claimed ownership of Lake Tele. Native fishermen had often encountered *mokele-mbembe* at the lake but refused to share information with Dr. Mackal. The natives, already fearful of speaking about *mokele-mbembe*, had become suspicious of expeditions because the expedition led by American aerospace engineer H. A. Regusters had not respected their authority over the lake. His expedition had spent an entire month on the lake and departed only a few weeks before Dr. Mackal's arrival. Since supplies had already run low, Dr. Mackal returned to Epéna. Obtaining gas, the expedition turned back toward Impfondo.

A black mamba hanging from the branches overhead fell onto Dr. Mackal's shoulder. They had seen mambas, cobras, and other vipers often but had not had contact. Dr. Mackal froze. He expected to feel the fangs any moment, but the falling mamba toppled harmlessly into the water of Djemba Canal.

Stuck on a log, the dugout would not budge either forward or backward. Shouted orders in three languages clashed, but the dugout remained stranded. Low water because of the dry season hindered progress. They had hacked through fallen trees from 6:00 A.M. to 3:00 P.M., but gained only five miles. Half the distance remained, but only three hours of light.

Greenwell, the British anthropologist, jumped overboard. Feeling the obstruction underwater, he guided the dugout over the down-slanted end. To avoid getting run over by the freed craft, he grabbed the front and let it pull him forward, risking the crushing impact of the next log. None of the Pygmies or Congolese men would enter the snake-and-crocodile infested waters. At the next logjam, Greenwell repeated his performance, with water reaching up to his chest. Greenwell freed the dugout many times this way as they continued.

Darkness descended. Night had fallen at 6:00 P.M. after torrents of rain had soaked them. Caught in the jungle at night, they proceeded by flashlight for several hours. Soon, even the last flashlight went dead. Dr. Mackal collected the flashlights and checked each pair for a working battery. Eventually, by trial and error, he found two that worked together. The feeble light died in a half-hour, but by then Dr. Mackal had found another functional pair. Meanwhile, Greenwell waded in the swamp in the pitch-dark to free the dugout again.

The fires of Mweti welcomed the expedition, and they all slept soundly. They returned to Impfondo the next day, December 1, 1981. They thanked Greenwell profusely for his efforts. The Congolese security officer, who had frequently called Greenwell a delicate Englishman because of his fussiness, now complimented him. "Englishmen are very delicate," he said, " but they are also very strong and very brave."

Mackal's expedition had not seen a *mokele-mbembe* but had explored and collected data for future expeditions. In fact, their Cuban-trained Congolese zoologist, Marcellin Agnagna, returned with an all-Congolese expedition in 1983. With help from Boha, they arrived at Lake Tele on April 28 after a two-day trek. On May 1, they spotted *mokele-mbembe* and observed it for twenty minutes. They considered it to be a small sauropod. Whatever this zoologist saw, his sighting confirms that some previously unobserved species of large animal is alive and well in the Likouala.

PIOTR CHMIELINSKI
Kayaking the Amazon

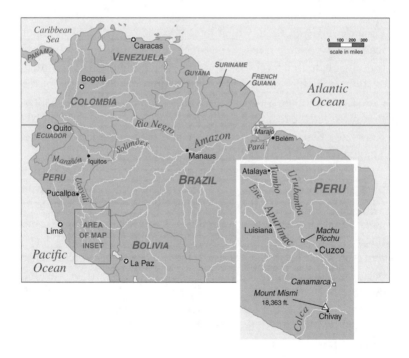

Colca River Canyon

"Pass the big rock, paddle hard left to avoid the hole, then run straight for the clear." Piotr Chmielinski shouted to be heard above the thundering river. He had just scouted a rapid, where Peru's

Colca River squeezes through a narrow chute and causes dangerous rapids with a whirlpool-type hole in which a rafter could easily get pinned and drown. The six kayakers launched one by one into the surging torrent. Following the instructions, they avoided the massive boulders, glimpsed the churning white vortex, and passed into calm water. The raging waters became calm rarely and briefly along the fifty-mile stretch. The river drops an average of sixty feet per mile with sections as steep as one hundred feet per mile.

Chmielinski had come to Peru in 1981 to explore the world's deepest canyon. When he had left Poland in 1979, eight friends had accompanied him. The team was in the process of kayaking twenty-three rivers in eleven North and South American countries. Thirteen of the runs would be first descents. Last year they had run the Rio Paquare in Costa Rica, which later became one of Central America's most popular rivers. They had achieved six other firsts by running uncharted rivers as explorers for the Mexican government.

Two from the group had returned home without running the Colca, and another waited in Arequipa because of illness. Andrzej Pietowski led the team consisting of Chmielinski, Stefan Danielski, Krzysztof Krasniewski, Jerzy Majcherczyk, and Jacek Bogucki. The team hoped to make the first descent of the Colca River.

River conditions can range from calm, flat water to vertical plunges hundreds of feet down. Navigable rapids are rated from Class 1 to Class 6. Calm water is not rated, though it could be considered Class 0. Lofty waterfalls, being unnavigable, are not rated either, though Class 7 could be invented for them. Class 1 represents the least dangerous rapids, suitable for typical family outings. Amateurs typically run Class 2 rapids but portage the more dangerous Class 3 rapids. Class 4 rapids must be scouted even by experts. Class 5 rapids require expert skills just for survival; any mistake can be fatal. Class 6 rapids often result in death even for experts. Some Class 6 rapids that look navigable have never been survived.

Ahead, the roar from Landslide, the first Class 5 rapid, warned Chmielinski to scout. Barren cliffs soared overhead. Steep canyon walls boxed them in. Rock piles in the uncharted Colca Canyon reminded the kayakers of the frequent rock falls from the cliffs. The crash of falling boulders often woke them at night. After Landslide, more Class 5 rapids challenged them, culminating at a long series which they named Canoandes after their expedition. Twice before, they had tried to climb out of the canyon instead of facing the boulder-strewn walls of water. However, the precipitous crumbly slopes had defied climbing.

The rafters still faced the most dangerous rapids—Class 6. Because they were sick and out of food, climbing out of the canyon was unthinkable. The kayakers launched into Reparaz. They rowed furiously through the rapid unable to see. White blanked out everything: seething white rapids beneath, walls of white billows all around, and blankets of white spray overhead. A few days later, another Class 6 rapid blocked progress. Paddling to the side and clinging to the sheer cliffs on narrow ledges, they guided their craft with ropes through two-thirds of the canyon. Finally, they ran out of ledges and took to the river for the final churning maze of currents. When they saw the end of the canyon, they named the final rapid Poles Canyon.

A friendly couple, Antonio and Anna Vellutino, took them in and nursed them back to health. Unable to return to Poland, Chmielinski and some others settled in Casper, Wyoming, and became American citizens. Chmielinski's notes and maps guaranteed future expeditions some knowledge of what to expect and how to approach the most difficult rapids.

The Colca beckoned again in 1983. *National Geographic* funded the second and third Colca expeditions in May and June for a report. Chmielinski, born on July 17, 1952, in Solcina-Rzeszow, Poland, served as leader for both trips. He had been kayaking over ten years now, ever since 1972, when he had watched kayaks on Poland's longest river, the Vistula (Wisla in Polish). Pietowski and Bogucki again joined the expedition as did Zbigniew Bzdak, who had been sick during the first run. Bzdak, a nuclear physicist from Krakow and Chmielinski's best friend, served as photographer. Alvaro Ibáñez from Arequipa became the first Peruvian to attempt the run.

Tim Biggs, a short, muscular South African of British descent, had also joined the team. Biggs had earned an excellent reputation for kayaking. Once, alone, he raced an eight-man paddling team.

The race lasted twelve hours, and Biggs won. Someone who can outrow eight men for twelve hours deserves respect, and the Poles gladly offered him the dubious honor of front kayak. The Poles had originally met Biggs leading wild parties on the Apurímac. However, since then, Biggs had accepted Christ as his Savior. Chmielinski and Bzdak noticed the change in Biggs. Now he read the Bible as diligently as he had once partied.

In May 1985, two years after their successful run, Alvaro Ibáñez decided to lead the first all-Peruvian run. Within one minute of launching, the flooded Colca flipped the raft. All four team members went under, and only two survived. Ibáñez washed ashore, and the only female team member swirled by just out of his reach. Ibáñez jumped back in to save her. He was never seen again. The girl's body was later found by helicopter.

In July Chmielinski led his fourth run to search for Alvaro's body. The team included several other Poles and Antonio Vellutino, Alvaro's brother-in-law. They did not find the body but did retrieve eleven pieces of his equipment including his helmet, life jacket, and sleeping bag.

A second Peruvian expedition ran the Colca in 1989. This time Antonio Vellutino brought his son Duilio. Duilio had taught himself to kayak using a kayak that Chmielinski had given his father. He had developed a style that fought the current with youthful strength and enthusiasm. But treacherous Reparaz swept Vellutino from the raft, dunked him, and whipped him wildly. Shaken to the core, he vowed to conquer Reparaz.

Duilio Vellutino's chance to face Reparaz again came two years later. In 1991, Vellutino and Pietowski accepted the third and fourth kayak positions on Chmielinski's fifth Colca trip. The team selected Jerome Truran as lead kayaker. As a former kayaker on the British National Team, he executed his maneuvers flawlessly and remained calm in the worst rapids. Truran's Canadian wife, Morna Fraser, also a world-class kayaker, followed him. Chmielinski captained and steered one of the two rafts from the back right position. Bogucki and American Joe Kane would man the wet seats (front), while big Johnny Moscarillo from Virginia manned the ejector seat (back left). The back positions bounced like a roller coaster, and only the man steering had time to brace himself. Robin Moore, a professional river guide from West Virginia, captained the crew of the second raft consisting of Bzdak and two other men.

The team ran Gutter Rapid on the second day out. The ripping of raft fabric on sharp rocks shattered their well-laid plans. The virtually bottomless raft took on water, and they were tugged and shoved at the mercy of the current. Beyond, progress slowed further. They spent most of the third day drying and patching the three-foot gash, and on the fourth day they advanced only one mile through Landslide.

Canoandes Rapid sucked Fraser's kayak into a hole on day seven. Fraser executed an Eskimo roll to escape. Her head made a circle with the kayak as the center axis. Since half of the circle is underwater, swift rocky waters make such rolls dangerous. Fraser performed it superbly.

The rafts fared worse. The hole sucked them down, and the river thrashed the helpless victims. The raft bucked both Americans into the raging waters. Kane went limp as he swirled but suddenly broke through the surface and caught a rescue line thrown by Pietowski. Moscarillo washed up downstream. Chmielinski, still in the bucking raft, held a rescue line from Truran. It took fifteen minutes of pulling to rescue the raft from the hole.

Only the hardest two rapids remained. On day nine, they reached Reparaz. Too tired to think clearly, they camped, huddling beside the frothing torrent. They slept fitfully, with the roar of Reparaz filling their dreams and stealing their sleep. After scouting, they ran Reparaz late the next day. The five quick turns blurred together. Vellutino had fulfilled his vow. The victory carried them all the way through Poles Canyon on the eleventh day.

They had conquered Colca Canyon, the deepest canyon in the world. Colca Canyon is about ten thousand feet deep but thirteen thousand feet below the mountain peaks on either side. It is much deeper than the Grand Canyon, which yawns up to eighteen miles wide but is only 4,700 feet deep from its South Rim to the Colorado River (though 5,800 feet deep from its North Rim). Colca Canyon also exceeds Hells Canyon, which drops 8,032 feet to the Snake

River. Colca Canyon, fifty miles long, is also longer than the forty-mile Hells Canyon.

The Amazon

Chmielinski and his long-time friend Bzdak agreed to join the first Amazon expedition in spite of its eccentric leader, François Odendaal. Odendaal, a South African researching butterflies in the American West, had planned the trip for six years. When his British film sponsors backed out, he contacted columnist Joe Kane at the *San Francisco Chronicle*. Kane flew to Lima six weeks later with Odendaal. Kane, the only American, earned a spot on the team by raising additional funds. He was in good shape, running five miles and doing two hundred pushups daily, but at this point had never been in a kayak before. In 1985, Kane's part in Chmielinski's final run of the Colca River was still six years in the future.

Chmielinski and Bzdak had remained in Arequipa after searching the Colca for Alvaro. Sergio Leon, a naturalist from Costa Rica arrived in Arequipa after an eighteen-hour bus ride from Lima. They collected supplies for three weeks. Fast-food dishes were limited to "no cooking required" and a few luxuries that needed boiling water. Kate Durrant, the team's British physician, arrived next.

Soon Tim Biggs and Jerome Truran arrived, both professional kayakers from South Africa. When the world had protested South African apartheid policies, South Africans had been barred from international races. Biggs, the man who outrowed eight men, had quit racing and turned to exploring. He had also recently married. Truran had continued to compete by using his dual British citizenship. He won gold medals in 1980 and 1982 competitions and a silver medal in the World Championships of 1981.

Finally, Odendaal arrived with two cameramen from South Africa: Fanie Van der Merwe and Pierre Van Heerden. The ten-person team from six nations was complete. Some of the less-experienced kayakers showed their agnosticism with foul language and drinking bouts. In spite of this, Tim Biggs, the only born-again Christian, maintained a testimony for the Lord.

Everyone but Odendaal knew that success depended on the river skills of Truran, Biggs, Chmielinski, and Bzdak. Truran and Biggs had been on previous expeditions led by Odendaal. On Odendaal's Limpopo River expedition, everyone had deserted but Johan Smit who had drowned a few days later. On the second attempt, Odendaal left in anger just before the hardest rapids but later claimed success as the expedition leader. Biggs overlooked the ineptness of his friend and enjoyed participating in the expeditions. He begged Odendaal to learn basic kayaking skills before going to Peru, but Odendaal refused. In contrast, Odendaal's incompetency made his arrogant boasting impossible for Truran to take. Truran came as a hired hand, with respect only for Biggs.

On August 26, 1985, they walked toward Mount Mismi. Shrouded in mists, its rocky summit soared to 18,363 feet above sea level. Approaching Chivay, Chmielinski looked down the Colca River Valley. In the distance, Sabancayo's 19,606-foot snow-ringed summit belched smoke, and the dark shaft of Colca Canyon stirred memories. Crossing the river at Chivay, they reached the last outpost of civilization, Lari. They hired burros and two Quechua Indian guides. With upset stomachs and dizziness from altitude sickness, they trudged through a blizzard to a 17,000-foot pass, high in the Andes. They had walked three days to this pass on the Continental Divide. Behind, snow melted into the Colca drainage and the Pacific, only one hundred miles away for the Andean condors circling overhead. Ahead, runoff trickled toward the Atlantic, two thousand air miles away.

The next morning, Chmielinski viewed the icefall at the farthest source of the Amazon, high on Quehuisha, one of several peaks on Mount Mismi. They planned to follow the trickle from that icefall along its winding course for forty-two hundred miles. The trickle grew successively into the Apacheta stream, Lloqueta, Challamayo, and Hornillos Rivers—all small creeks too shallow for kayaking. The following day, with Mount Mismi still visible in the distance, the Hornillos deepened to form the Apurímac at La Angostura. With enough water for kayaking, the river party would no longer have to hike beside the creek. Biggs prayed aloud for the Lord's help.

Mystery shrouds the Apurímac Canyon, which bows only to the Colca in depth. The name *Apurímac* is Quechua for "Great (Apu) Oracle (Rimac)," describing its thunderous rapids. The Quechuas are descended from the Incas and count the river as their ancestral home. Inca ruins such as Mauccallacta and Canamarca dot the area. Even the most famous Inca ruin, Machu Picchu, stands nearby— high on a pinnacle over the Urubamba River to the east. Below Canamarca the only remaining Inca bridge hangs across the Apurímac. Woven from grass, it can support many pack animals at once.

Chmielinski, Truran, Biggs, and Odendaal kayaked easily for two days as the Apurímac snaked lazily across the treeless Andean plateau. Soon, boulders the size of buildings blocked the river. Frequent portages drained their strength, and tiredness prompted them to take dangerous risks. Odendaal, inept and out of shape, portaged constantly. The other kayakers carried Odendaal's gear to lighten his kayak for him. Biggs coached him through rapids. Chmielinski sometimes beached his own kayak and waded back to portage Odendaal's kayak for him. Nearing the Black Canyon portion of the Apurímac, Chmielinski recalled the serious accidents, sickness, and food shortages during his trip with Biggs in 1983. Theirs was the only previous descent of Black Canyon, and it had taken them ten days to run those twenty miles. Odendaal decided to walk along the river and meet them at the far end.

Enter Black Canyon. Biggs recognized the spot that had given him the biggest scare of his life in 1983. Now the funnel caught his kayak in an instant replay. The kayak flipped, and Biggs felt the raw power of the river dragging him under. He knew he had only seconds before the current pinned him under the boulders. "Dear God, don't let me go like this," he prayed. His hands searched the boulders above for cracks. Summoning all his strength, he pulled himself up. A glimpse of sky and a breath of air, but the river sucked him back down and slammed him into another boulder. Quickly, he found small toeholds and finger holds and pushed against the river until his head surfaced. He heard Chmielinski and Truran shouting, but the rescue line floated out of reach. The current wrenched his foot from its small hold. He felt himself going down again. His fingers gripped tiny ridges on the boulder, and he slowly hauled himself to the top. Heart racing and exhausted, he collapsed on the boulder.

Chmielinski had a close call shortly after. With his kayak stuck in a hole, he bailed out. The river ricocheted him through three rapids, which Truran described as "pinball." Chmielinski broke his nose on the bumpers. Later in their six-day passage, he broke his nose a second time. A gold panner told them of two Swiss kayakers heading for the Atlantic. The Swiss had started at La Angostura and passed about two weeks earlier. They met Odendaal, just below Black Canyon, but cameraman Van der Merwe had already flown back to South Africa from Cuzco.

The river continued to be rough. The kayakers spent much extra time waiting for and helping Odendaal. Slow and inept, he jeopardized them all. Truran rebuked him: "Men without kayaking skills belong on commercial trips, not wild uncharted rivers." Odendaal demanded Truran's dismissal for insubordination. Chmielinski pleaded, "What expedition dismisses its most skilled member?" Odendaal temporarily relented. Biggs began coaching Odendaal on Eskimo rolls, ferry glides, and reverse ferry glides. Odendaal improved, but growing proud, he misjudged a rapid. The current sucked him under and dragged his face across the rocks. Biggs cleaned and bandaged his friend's bloody, swollen face, wondering how they would survive the unknown parts ahead.

The support crew had hiked along the rim of the canyon sixty-two hundred feet above the river. They met the kayakers at Pillpinto and again for the visit to Cuzco. Funding improved here when millionaire Jack Jourgensen of Wyoming joined the team. Chmielinski got two rafts out of storage and also visited a whitewater company to ask about conditions ahead.

The local guide said he had rafted twenty-five miles on three occasions, but recent revolutionary encounters stopped him. Raids by the Sendero Luminoso (or Shining Path) had escalated recently. The town Villa Virgen had been destroyed first by guerillas and then by the military. The Red Zone, two hundred river miles to Luisiana, was under martial law. He added that beyond that first twenty-five miles, little was known.

Only five attempts had ever been made to run it. In 1953, a Frenchman, Michel Perrin, and Teresa Gutierrez, his Peruvian girlfriend, had portaged eighty miles, searching the fearsome rapids for navigable water. Teresa had drowned. About 1975, J. Calvin Giddings had led his five-man team through the awesome gorge, which he named the Acobamba Abyss. One portage lasted five days without a sign of navigable water. The next year, a German expedition ended within minutes of starting when their leader drowned. A few years later, John Tichenor, an American rafting guide, had led three trips on short sections but did not try the complete descent. The guide concluded by saying, "Since you are going to try it, I can send a guide with you for the first twenty-five miles, but that is the last exit."

As they prepared to enter the river, alarming news arrived. Falling rock had crushed the leg of one of the members of the Swiss expedition ahead of them. The Swiss team had quit. Second, the promised guide had skipped town. He wanted no part of running the Apurímac.

Chmielinski, with his usual military organization, captained the fourteen-foot *Riken.* Durrant and Leon rode the front wet seats, while Kane rode the ejector seat. Inexperienced and fearful, they all eagerly followed Chmielinski's commands, though they found it difficult to overcome their natural impulses. They wanted to sit in the bottom but soon learned that the supply-weighted bottom catapulted bodies more quickly than their seats on the edge of the tube. They learned that leaning over the side for rowing as Chmielinski directed worked best.

Jourgensen captained the other raft, the sixteen-foot *Avon.* Odendaal ignored Bzdak, the most experienced rafter. Van Heerden added to the mayhem. Kane described the *Avon's* progress as "an exercise in floating anarchy." Biggs and Truran were glad to be kayaking.

Chmielinski coached Kane as they scouted rapids. A series of Class 5 rapids extending a half-mile took two hours to scout. Cliffs squeezed the river's width from fifty to fifteen feet in a chute, followed by a low waterfall with a standing "surfer's wave," and then widened back out into a boulder-strewn maze. Chmielinski identified the best route and directed the paddling. They shot into the chute and slammed into a boulder. The raft threatened to flip, with one end tipped high. All rafters moved toward the high end, and they pulled through. Chmielinski returned upstream to guide the *Avon* through.

Chmielinski still seemed fresh, even with his extra work scouting and helping Odendaal. When it was his turn to cook, he made the most elaborate meals and kept a neat, orderly kitchen. He considered himself a slave until all were fed. When Odendaal had asked for help with the accounts, Chmielinski had taken over the books and carefully recorded all supplies. He knew how much of each item they consumed daily and stayed up late each night making notes by candlelight. The records had aided planning in the remote sections of the river. He also had the foresight to map the route for the benefit of future expeditions. In spite of his extra work and late nights, he was always first to rise, first packed, and first on the river. Brave and unintimidated, he resembled a military commander conquering the river.

After twenty-five miles, the expedition reached the last exit described by the local river guide. Leon and Durrant left for Cuzco to bring supplies downriver. Odendaal would kayak. Now one raft, the *Riken,* would suffice. Bzdak and Van Heerden rowed in front. In back, Jourgensen sat between Kane and Chmielinski. They entered the unknown.

Waves eight feet high hid the kayaks from Chmielinski's view. The raft accidentally ran over a kayak, trapping Biggs underneath until Bzdak pulled him free. Odendaal dumped twice. They entered a canyon only forty feet wide with cliffs five hundred feet high. They camped among the boulders, squeezed between the river and the cliffs. One night Bzdak crushed a scorpion; the next night rainstorms came. Would the rain-swollen waters flood them out? Thunder and lightning shook boulders free from the towering rain-soaked cliffs. Wearing helmets, they listened all night to the crash of boulders around them. The end of the Swiss expedition took on new meaning.

Acobamba Abyss enclosed them. The walls narrowed to thirty feet. Light could not reach the river even at midday. Biggs and

Truran kayaked the first dangerous rapid leading to a chute and a whirlpool. They got into rescue position at the chute. The others tried to line the raft through the rapids, but it flipped. The line broke as they flipped it back over. The raft floated uncontrolled and unmanned toward the brink of the chute. Truran dove in, swam to the raft, and climbed aboard. Teetering on the edge of the chute, he caught a rescue line from Chmielinski—just in time.

Even after Truran's heroic raft rescue, they had yet to get the raft down the chute. Bzdak and Kane edged out over the chute along the left wall on a narrow ledge fifteen feet above the whirlpool. "Don't look down!" Bzdak told Kane as they lowered themselves to a small rock.

Chmielinski sent the raft over, and Bzdak reeled in its line. Kane took the line as Bzdak jumped from the ledge into the raft. Each rafter followed, crawling across the ledge, down to the rock, and jumping in. Last, Chmielinski threw Odendaal and his kayak across the top and jumped in after them. They paddled left, missing the whirlpool; then right, grazing a rock that could have upended them; a wave crashed over them, and then they were free.

The expedition had gained only one mile that day. After portaging most of the next day also, the team advanced only two additional miles. The third day, Truran scouted a half-mile rapid and named the four parts: Ballroom, Milk Shake, Liquidizer, and Dead Man. Tired of portages, they ran it.

An unexpected wave at the crest made them airborne. The raft jackknifed, spun, and entered backwards into Ballroom. Waves swept Jourgensen overboard. They watched him go under twice after turning pale and limp. With one hand, Bzdak grabbed the overweight fifty-two year old and heaved him into the raft as they surged into Milk Shake. They began to flip but regained control in Liquidizer. As they plunged five feet over a falls into Dead Man, they lost control again. They bounced off rocks and both canyon walls. Spinning 360 degrees, Kane stared down into the largest hole he had ever seen. With momentum built from the wild descent, they shot across it.

The day ended after an advance of only one mile. They spent most of the next day lining the raft through Class 5 rapids. Bzdak stayed in the raft to steer and troubleshoot.

The next morning, a crosscurrent at the top of a rapid caught the raft and flipped it. Currents pinned Van Heerden to boulders at the edge of the hole, which would soon funnel him under. Chmielinski and Bzdak caught the raft but crashed into the boulder where Van Heerden flailed helplessly.

Meanwhile, Kane tumbled until he could not tell which way was up. The frigid water winded him, and he resigned himself to drowning. He surfaced downstream, choking on water. Truran called, but he went under again. He careened off more rocks and blacked out. He spluttered alert as he surfaced near Truran, who draped him over his kayak and rowed ashore. Kane's ordeal had badly shaken him. All the rafters were surprised to see each other alive and longed for the end of the canyon. Yet another one-mile day had passed.

How much more? The sixth day they lined the raft through more rapids. Durrant and Leon had brought two burros with supplies down to the river. Leon and Van Heerden left to return the burros. Durrant replaced Van Heerden, paddling through the rough rapids of the seventh day. On the eighth day, Jourgensen went overboard and submerged three times before Bzdak could grab him. The ordeal crushed his spirit. He had had enough white water for a lifetime. On the tenth day, Leon and Van Heerden arrived with supplies. Jourgensen left funds with Odendaal and departed. After two more days, the canyon finally ended.

Gunfire followed them for three days. Now, six gunmen, all shooting, descended the canyon. The rafters pushed off, realizing that they were the targets. They had entered the Red Zone, the area closed due to revolutionaries. Bullets whizzed across the raft as the swift current carried them through unscouted Class 5 rapids. Suddenly, the raft hit a hole and flipped. The men climbed back in, and Truran rescued Durrant from a whirlpool. They had escaped this time.

A submachine gun confronted the rafters. Two Shining Path activists had been just out of sight as they stopped to scout. Now they were caught. The rifleman took Chmielinski's watch and hunting knife. He showed his Polish passport and explained that the raft was not military and contained no weapons. After taking five cans of tuna and a fishing net, the revolutionaries let them go. They ran the rapid unscouted.

Abruptly, they traded desert tarantulas and cacti for jungle vines, monkeys, and parrots. They lit no fires for their first two nights in the Amazon basin and took turns keeping watch. Finally, at Luisiana, the Red Zone ended. Peruvian marines surrounded them and checked passports. "What were you doing in the Red Zone without permission?" they asked. "Don't you know the Shining Path hanged five civilians upriver a week ago?" The marines watched them all night, and the rafters griped among themselves. Some complained about Odendaal, while others complained about having to cook in the rain.

Chmielinski, organized, uncomplaining, and methodical as always, rebuked complainers. He felt sorry for Odendaal, who agreed to kayak separately with Biggs and go ahead to Atalaya to extend the visas. As for cooking, everyone depended on the food, even in rain when stoves malfunctioned.

Whirlpools forty feet across endangered them, but Truran coached Kane daily in kayaking. Tributaries increased the river power, and many boats plied it. The Apurímac became the Ene, the Tambo, and finally the Ucayali. The river became the Ucayali, when the mighty Urubamba joined it near Atalaya. After ten days and 250 miles, the team regrouped for a week at Atalaya.

Odendaal, extending visas in Lima, decided to return to London to present his descent of the Apurímac to the Royal Geographic Society. Without Odendaal to worry about, Biggs returned home to his wife. Leon and Van Heerden had stored sea kayaks in Pucallpa and departed as well. Truran had come mainly for the white water, which was now all behind. He was the only one on the expedition who had never fallen into the river. The master kayaker still hoped for a gold medal with the British white-water team, but he must begin training now. Kane regretted his leaving; this man had often saved his life.

Although not as dangerous as the Black Canyon or the Acobamba Abyss, the Ucayali demanded respect. At Atalaya, they heard about an Italian who had brought his family to Peru for adventure. A whirlpool had claimed his shirt, his canoe, his son, and his wife. He was now a derelict, penniless. Besides whirlpools, the expedition occasionally saw the alligator-like caimans and deadly poisonous bushmaster water snakes. Fortunately, they saw neither piranhas nor the tiny dreaded fish candiru—a human parasite.

Chmielinski rejoiced when Kane agreed to kayak with him, while Durrant and Bzdak booked passage on riverboats to meet them when possible. The kayakers paddled twelve hours every day with a five-minute break each hour. Knowing Kane's inexperience, Chmielinski took most of the gear. The fuel, stove, extra paddles, and canned foods filled his boat and covered the decks. Even with that, Kane developed a wrist condition—tenosynovitis.

Some four hundred miles beyound Atalaya, Chmielinski and Kane arrived at Pucallpa, where they got the sea kayaks that had been stored for them by Leon and Van Heerden. Another eight hundred miles brought them to Iquitos, where the river joins the two-mile-wide Marañón. They had already enjoyed dolphins in the river, but now they began to see sharks.

Chmielinski took stock. They were camped two days and one hundred miles below Iquitos, still 230 miles short of the Brazilian border. Somehow they had to reach the border by midnight Christmas Day, when their visas would expire. In the morning, Christmas Eve, they began paddling again. By dusk, they had paddled sixty miles and decided to paddle through the night. Tired, they became separated in the darkness.

Chmielinski hit the thug's hand with his paddle, but a second canoe approached. The canoers had surprised him in the dark and demanded money. Ruddering with the paddle, he had turned the kayak quickly and with powerful strokes far outdistanced the two-man canoe. The river divides Peru from Colombia just before entering Brazil—an area of illegal drug traffic. He had looked for Kane for three hours but could not return upstream now. With less than twenty-four hours to reach Brazil, he left supplies for Kane with a Peruvian border patrol and paddled on. He reached the Brazilian border at 11:00 P.M. Chmielinski had rowed 230 miles in forty hours. Kane joined him the next day, knowing he could not have kept pace.

At the Brazilian border, where the river becomes the Solimões, they resupplied and began their two-week journey to Manaus. Only five miles beyond Manaus, the largest city in the interior, the brown water of the Solimões and the black water of the Negro meet but do not mix. The Negro is the sixth largest river in the world and four times larger than the Mississippi. When it hits the even larger Solimões, they flow side by side for six miles before mixing. This stretch, called the Meeting of the Waters, marks the start of the Amazon proper.

Durrant and Bzdak met the kayakers about five days later. Jacek Bogucki, a Colca veteran, met them, and they hired Captain Deomedio and his fifteen-year-old grandson Afrain to motor along the final eighteen hundred miles with the kayakers. For accommodations, the entire team now slept in the anchored boat. The captain told them about pirarucú—a ten-foot-long fish.

At the delta, Chmielinski chose to paddle the Pará. Just as they had started at the most distant headwaters, they would paddle down the longest arm of the Amazon delta. Two days beyond Belém, they paddled into open ocean beyond Marajo Bay. It was February 19, 1986.

Chmielinski and Kane had traveled the entire Amazon—from source to sea. Six of the original ten had quit by Atalaya. Bzdak and Durrant had provided motorized support to the end. Kane had walked or paddled to the end. Chmielinski ran the whole river—forty-two hundred miles. By contrast, the first run of the Green and Colorado Rivers by John Wesley Powell covered nine hundred miles. The Apurímac drops thirteen thousand feet in three hundred miles—five times more steeply than the Colorado River drops through Grand Canyon. The steepness and the dangers made for an extraordinary feat.

On returning to his Wyoming home, Chmielinski moved to Washington, D.C., where it would be easier to write his article for *National Geographic*. In August, Joanna, whom he had married in

1984, in the Vatican was finally able to leave Poland and join him in Washington.

After his fifth run of the Colca Canyon in 1991, Chmielinski and his partner Dr. Hugh Granger began an environmental lab that studies pollutants. With a masters degree as a mechanical engineer and certified as an industrial hygienist, he now works on environmental problems such as his three-month study of the kinds of contamination caused by the 1993 bombing of New York's World Trade Center. For relaxation, he leads kayaking trips on the Potomac and Gauley Rivers. His son Maximilian, age six, is already learning to kayak, and younger Alexander is bound to follow suit.

In 1997, Chmielinski was able to visit the twenty-five-year anniversary celebration of the kayaking club, Bystrze, of which he was one of the eight charter members while in school in Krakow. From 1975-77, the club had run many rivers in Eastern Europe, Greece, and Italy in preparation for the trip to the Americas. Since then some 3,000 students have been members, and current membership is about 450. The club runs rivers all over the world, including Japan and Africa.

REINHOLD MESSNER
The World's Fourteen Highest Peaks

Messner is most famous for the way in which he climbed Mount Everest. But his other two great adventures are even more amazing. He first climbed the three Big Walls in the Alps and then extended the concept worldwide to include Aconcagua and Nanga Parbat. His ultimate goal was to climb the world's fourteen peaks that exceed 8000 meters in elevation. Two lesser adventures in New Guinea and Africa are also included here as examples of his preparation for the great one and as background for Patrick Morrow.

The Alps

Reinhold Messner clung to the sides of the icy cliffs called the Grandes Jorasses. The Walker Spur on these cliffs led to Walker Point, a 13,805-foot pinnacle among the various subpeaks of the massif forming Mont Blanc. Messner climbed with three friends in August of 1966. Roped in pairs—Messner with Fritz Zambra, and Sepp Mayerl with Peter Habeler—they used their crampons, ice axes, and ice pitons even though it was summer. At the top, Messner rejoiced at his personal victory: his first climb of the hardest of the three famous climbs in the Alps.

Messner's personal victories had accumulated for about twenty years. His first climb—at the age of five in 1949—had been with his father up the Sass Rigais. Five years later, on the East Face of the Kleine Fermeda, his father had first permitted him to lead the way up a Class 3 pitch. In 1960, on the North Face of the Sass Rigais with his brother, Günther, he had pounded in his first pitons. Three years later, he had climbed his first Class 6 face, the Tissi Route on the first Sella Tower. The same summer, he had climbed his first ice face, the North Face of Similaun. In the summer of 1965, Messner had set his first record. With Günther and two other men, he had made the first-ever ascent of the Class 5+ route up the North Face of the Grosse Fermeda. In 1966, he soloed the Class 6 Solda route on the South Face of the Piz-de-Ciavàces.

*   *   *   *

On January 29, 1968, Messner climbed another step up a narrow snow-choked fissure. He pounded in a piton for stability. He and two friends had spent two nights wet and shivering in small overhang caves on the face of Monte Agnér. The peak rises in the Dolomites, a range of the Alps in the South Tirol region of Italy. Born at Bressanone, Messner grew up in this German-speaking region ceded from Austria to Italy in 1919. Now, as the sun set on their third day, they made the last scramble to the summit. This climb was more than a personal victory. It was the first-ever winter climb of Monte Agnér.

Messner also developed his style in the Alps. On the Dirupi di Larsec in May of 1967, Messner and his brother decided that technical aids could take the sport out of climbing. Even an amateur could succeed on difficult climbs with rope ladders, bolts, and drills. One might as well land on the summit with a helicopter.

On the other hand, Messner did not ignore safety. Messner and his companions often admitted defeat on a given day due to weather or weariness. Knowing when to turn back is part of safety, and Messner had never fallen in his climbing career. He also would not ignore the most advanced clothing or flashlights. Messner decided he would use ropes and pitons to limit the length of potential falls but would use as few pitons as possible. Messner was a free climber. His challenge was to find the best natural route up the rock face.

Climbers classify pitches much as rafters classify rapids. Climbers do not rate stretches of easy walking or impossible smooth rock faces. Everything in between gets classified from 1 to 6. Class 1 involves steep scrambles, and Class 2 adds the use of hands. Climbers rope together for safety at Class 3 and they belay one another with ropes for Class 4 pitches. Class 5 designates the most difficult technical pitches, subclassified from 5.1 to 5.9 and now up to 5.14. Climbers also use grades to rate routes based on the toughest pitch, length of technical portions, and difficulty of retreat in case of blizzards or injury. Grades 1 through 6 range from technical portions of a few hours with easy retreats to multiple days of extreme climbing, which may be fatal even for experts. By 1969, at the age of twenty-five, Messner had achieved fifty first ascents in the Alps and twenty solo ascents. What would be next?

*   *   *   *

Lightning sliced the sky. Messner and Peter Habeler waited for the thunder and the rain of stones from the lightning-struck summit of the Matterhorn. They huddled on the difficult North Face of the 14,690-foot peak at the end of July in 1974. The ledges could not hold the large amounts of falling snow, and the sliding drifts poured over them. Pulling themselves onto the summit, they had achieved another of the three classic ascents of the Alps—and in very difficult conditions. They descended quickly because of lightning danger.

Distress signals flashed from the Eigerwand, a sheer wall of rock almost six thousand feet high from base to summit. Messner and Habeler, in spite of bad weather, set off at 5:00 A.M. on August 14, 1974, to see whether they could help. Rain-swollen waterfalls poured over ledges and drenched them as they ascended the Class 5 pitch called the Difficult Crack. Roped together and taking turns at the lead, they soon reached the distressed party. One of the pair had fallen forty meters and broken a leg. As they spoke, a helicopter hovered while a rescuer jumped out on a rope. He splinted the broken leg, and the helicopter hauled up each man on the rope. Messner and Habeler, their help unneeded, continued up more Class 5 pitches: the Ramp, the Spider, and the Exit Cracks. In their haste to help the injured man and to avoid afternoon rockslides, they passed parties that had been climbing for several days. They reached the top at 3:00 P.M., setting a record of ten hours for the climb.

Messner had now scaled all three of the classic big walls: the Matterhorn North Face, the Grandes Jorasses, and the Eiger North Face (Eigerwand). These are considered the classic climbs because they lead to major Alpine peaks, combine high-elevation climbing with extreme technical difficulty, include both rock and ice climbing, and lack easy escape routes if the climber gets in trouble.

Nanga Parbat

Reinhold and Günther Messner gazed at the tallest rock face in the world. The Rupal Face of Nanga Parbat rose 14,700 feet above them—over two-and-three-quarters miles straight up. The summit itself, the ninth highest peak in the world, climbs to 26,656 feet. As the brothers gazed on the immense wall, they realized that it was almost three times higher than the Eigerwand.

A red signal rocket climbed into the sky, telling Messner and his brother that weather reports looked bad. They had joined Dr. Karl Herrligkoffer's expedition and reached base on May 15. Within a week the expedition had established three advanced camps at 15,500; 18,000; and 20,000 feet. Blizzards had raged for three weeks and trapped the brothers in Camp 3 for ten days. They had established Camp 4 at 21,000 feet by June 15 and Camp 5 shortly after, but storms had forced them down again to Camp 4. Now the eighteen-man expedition would end defeated, unless some climber would risk a solo climb.

Messner took the risk. Soon he saw Günther climbing below. He waited, excited at his brother's company. They traversed steep snow fields using crampons. Mists shrouded them as they attained the South Shoulder. As they gained the last three hundred vertical feet to the snow-domed summit on August 27, 1970, they broke through the mists and looked down on a sea of white clouds. Although the mountain had been climbed once before by an easier route, they were the first to climb the steepest face in the world. But the hardest part was ahead.

Coldness crept over the brothers, and their wet boots made them shiver. They found a niche at the South Shoulder at dusk. They needed rest but had not planned an overnight and had no sleeping bags. The next day, while two other climbers reached the summit safely, the brothers began to descend the easier Diamir Face. They descended all day and slept again. After a short rest at the lower altitude, Günther felt better, so they continued by moonlight. About 8:00 A.M., they crossed a steep snow field separately. Messner had gone ahead to look for water, and they planned to meet at the first spring.

"Günther!" called Reinhold. Messner had found a spring where he had drunk and rested, but his brother had not come. He crossed a fresh avalanche and ascended a rock ridge. Surely his brother had gone up the ridge? Sometimes, in his tiredness, he thought he heard someone. He searched and called, "Günther!" He returned to the spring. By nightfall, he had found nothing. Exhausted, he dropped on the snow.

Messner feared the worst but could not give up. A whole day had passed since he had seen his brother. He retraced his path to where he had last seen him. Could those be tracks at the edge of the avalanche path? He began digging frantically. He called and dug all night. As daylight warmed the snow, he saw more avalanches and sank into despair. He knew Günther had died. Avalanche, lack of food, and exposure now threatened his own life. His boots were frozen lumps; he collapsed again.

Messner bathed his blue frostbitten feet in a mountain stream. He stumbled along, unable to feel his feet. At evening, he fell asleep until late afternoon. Local shepherds fed him, but they could not understand him. He trudged farther and slept under a tree. His boots would not fit on his swollen feet now. Blood oozed from his black toes. He tried using his axe and a stick as crutches but made little progress. Finally, two men took turns carrying him piggyback to the next farm for the night.

A Pakistani officer found Messner the next day and brought him to his expedition. Dr. Bulle Oelz amputated four of the frostbitten toes. Messner had three more amputations at Innsbruck—only his three smallest toes on his right foot remained. After six weeks in the hospital, Messner was released. He began lecturing, writing books, and teaching high school math to pay debts. Later, he returned to search for Günther's body—with no success.

New Guinea

Dani tribesmen surrounded Messner and his friend Sergio Bigarella. The bush pilot left after helping them unload their gear at the highland jungle village of Ilaga in New Guinea. They wondered if the Dani would kill them and eat them—as they had done to missionaries two years earlier.

"Ndugundugu!" Messner blurted out the only word he knew. The word meant "snow," but for this jungle tribe it also referred to the snowy peaks. Messner sighed with relief when the naked men began pointing toward the mountains they had seen from the air. Using gestures and presents, he hired twenty-five men as porters and guides.

Messner and Bigarella first glimpsed the snowy peaks after two days of pushing through dense jungles. At the jungle edge, they offered rewards to five volunteers who would enter the strange terrain. The rest departed. Three days later, they set up Base Camp just below the thirteen-thousand-foot snow line. Messner provided warm clothing for the Dani. The tribesmen wore the clothes but not the boots, which upset their balance and prohibited their toes from gripping slippery logs and rocks.

Messner, Bigarella, and the five porters made an advanced camp on the ice near New Zealand Pass. Before dark, the porters ran back to Base Camp, fearful of the cold and ice. Crossing the pass in the morning, they climbed Puncak Jaya. This 1971 climb became the second time in history that this peak had been climbed, the first being led by Heinrich Herrer in 1962. The peak's three names are Ndugundugu (Dani), Puncak Jaya (Indonesian), and Carstensz Pyramid (European, after its Danish discoverer of 1623).

Messner also climbed Puncak Sakarno before returning to the advanced camp. At Base Camp the next day, he discovered that the Dani porters had eaten all but one day's food rations. They trekked the remaining five days through the jungle, hungry and weak.

South America

"What are the three classic mountain faces worldwide?" Messner wondered. Using the criteria for the Alpine classics, he realized that many world-famous walls, such as El Capitan in California, would not qualify because they fail to lead to a major peak, lack high altitude, or retain ice and snow only seasonally. Messner also decided that one peak should represent each major range: the Himalayas, the Rockies-Andes, and the Alps. The Eiger North Face is the largest sheer drop in the Alps. The South Face of Aconcagua forms the largest face in the Americas and leads to the highest peak in the Americas. Finally, Nanga Parbat's Rupal Face is the biggest wall in the world and is on one of the 8000-meter Himalayan peaks. Messner mused, "Nanga Parbat in 1970. Now, Aconcagua."

Messner blinked at a dead body before him. This time he stood just below the summit of Aconcagua. As he pondered the body, he recalled that a Japanese climber had died here a year ago. This mountain, too, had claimed its share of lives, and the South Face was its most difficult side—a rock wall thirteen thousand feet high from base to crown. Messner's team suffered no casualties, but Messner alone made the summit on January 23, 1974. They had toiled for a week with mules to the Base Camp and another week to establish Camps 1 and 2. The passage of the Class 6 overhang at Broken Towers had been the most difficult pitch, and the dreaded White Wind had made the conditions as bad as the pitch. A few months later, when he climbed the Eiger North Face, he had climbed all of the Big Walls.

Himalayas

Messner heard a faint cry through the driving wind and snow. His partner for the summit of Manaslu had turned back earlier in good weather because he knew they could not make it by nightfall. A storm had blown in from the south, and Franz must be directing him to the tent.

Messner had reached the summit of Manaslu on April 25, 1972, by the South Face. At the summit he had found a piton left by a Japanese climber on the first ascent in 1956 from the northeast. The second ascent, also Japanese but on the northwest ridge in 1971, had let it remain. Messner had retrieved the piton to prove his success.

Messner moved toward the faint calls and shouted but heard no answer. Soon he saw an ice slope that he had recently left. "I'm walking in circles—lost," he thought. Icicles hung from his face, and his lips cracked. He sat in the snow and slept. He awoke in the night, the storm still raging. He recalled the storm arriving from the south, which meant he would have to walk into the prevailing winds to reach the tent. He found the rock outcrops near Camp 4, and after four tries, he located the tent.

Franz was not there! His calls must have been cries for help! Two men, recently arrived from Camp 3, went out to search. They heard shouts but could not find him. Lost, they slept in a snow hole. Only one of the two men returned to the tent and retreated with Messner to Camp 2 for medical help. Messner had reached his second major Himalayan summit (after Nanga Parbat), but two men had lost their lives. The same blizzard killed four Korean climbers, a Japanese climber, and ten Sherpas in an avalanche on the north side of the mountain.

*　　*　　*　　*

Blizzards blew again in 1974, this time on Makalu. Continuous snow at Camp 4 for a week slowly weakened the team's spirit until they gave up. Again in the spring of 1975, Messner was on an expedition that admitted defeat to the famous South Face of Lhotse. These failures convinced Messner that expeditions were not the best method. He considered the problems carefully, and within two weeks of leaving Lhotse, he left for Hidden Peak.

"No chance," scoffed the experts. "You'll die up there." Mountaineering theories, like other theories, were not open to new ideas. Messner had proposed a lightning ascent of a Himalayan peak. He invited Peter Habeler, an old friend and a fast climber. Supplies for two climbers would be minimal. Without bottled oxygen, they would not need porters to lug a bottle per day per person up to the high camps. Without climbers of varying ability bringing up supplies, they could save the weight of fixed ropes and the time required to attach them. In fact, since the rock on Hidden Peak was crumbly, they brought no ropes at all. They had only the bare essentials.

Messner hired porters and the required liaison officer as far as the base of the mountain. However, only a dozen porters were needed for their little party. At the base of Hidden Peak on August 8, they paid off the porters and sent them home after only two weeks' trek from Skardu, Pakistan. They bivouacked the next night at twenty-three thousand feet. The next day, August 10, 1975, they climbed the northwest face to the summit and returned to the bivouac. They had completed the second ascent of Hidden Peak in history and the first ascent of its most difficult face. They returned to Base Camp two days later and then to Skardu. They had succeeded on the first-ever Alpine-style climb in the Himalayas. They had shortened the time required for mountaineering expeditions from months to days by dispensing with no fixed ropes, bottled oxygen, and the succession of high-altitude camps. Best of all, they had opened the Himalayas to Alpine-style climbing.

In 1977, Messner, Peter Habeler, American Michael Covington, and German Otto Wiedemann attempted the South Face of Dhaulagiri. Halfway up they were peppered by small avalanches and turned back in defeat. Messner added the still unconquered route to his two other defeats on 8000-meter peaks: Makalu South Face and Lhotse South Face. In spite of three failures, Messner had climbed three Himalayan peaks with altitudes in the Death Zone— over twenty-six thousand feet.

Kilimanjaro

"Taylor fractured his ankle when he fell on the Icicle. Barber carried him over a mile to his sleeping bag and went for help." Messner listened to the rescue man's story. "Barber reached us three days later. We found Taylor still alive, surviving on the snow covering his sleeping bag. So the Breach Wall remains unclimbed. I can loan you whatever extra gear you need. Why don't you try it?"

Messner knew that the Americans Rob Barber and Henry Taylor ranked among the world's top climbers. He also knew that the previous attempt on the Breach Wall by British climber Doug Scott had also failed. Climbing the Breach Wall on Mount Kilimanjaro would be a never accomplished challenge, unlike the usual route which had been first climbed in 1889 by Hans Meyer and Ludwig Purtscheller.

Messner had already climbed the challenging Mount Kenya in 1972, and now in 1978 he had simply wanted to ascend Mount Kilimanjaro—a simple climb in preparation for high altitudes on his upcoming attempt on Mount Everest. Excited by the challenge, Messner and his partner, Konrad Renzler, headed for the Breach Wall in the morning.

The Icicle soared above them. They scanned the ice anxiously— a thick tower of ice twenty-five stories high enclosing a thundering waterfall. After two days, they had reached the base of the Breach Wall and had climbed Diamond Glacier well before dawn to avoid rock fall. Now, they pounded in ice pitons and climbed the Icicle. Arriving at the summit of Mount Kilimanjaro after twelve hours of climbing, they had achieved the first ascent of the Breach Wall.

Everest

Winds over one hundred miles per hour ripped one of the tents pitched on the South Pass. Messner and two Sherpas huddled in their sleeping bags, trying to keep warm in the -50°F temperature. Following the route of Sir Edmund Hillary, the expedition had established Camp 1 on March 27, Camp 2 on April 2, Camp 3 on April 13, and now Camp 4 on the South Col. After two days in the storm, they retreated. On the way down on April 27, a ladder across a crevasse fell under Messner's weight. As he plunged into the crevasse, he grabbed the guide rope. Hand over hand, he pulled himself up. He thought of Dawa Nuru, the Sherpa who had died in a crevasse just nine days earlier.

On May 7, Messner and Habeler were alone at Camp 4 on the South Col. Four days earlier, three expedition members and a Sherpa had reached the summit using oxygen. Meanwhile, another Sherpa had a stroke, and a large party brought him down to Camp 1. By May 5, the first summit party had descended to Camp 2, and a second summit attempt had turned back in defeat. Now, they were the only expedition members above Camp 2. Even their three Sherpas had descended.

Messner and Habeler climbed four hours to Camp 5 by 10:00 A.M. They rested but could not stop for the night without sleeping bags. As they climbed, they reviewed history. In 1880, climbers believed that twenty-one thousand feet was the limit for human existence. By the turn of the century, twenty-three thousand had been reached, and in 1909 the Duke of Abruzzi increased the record to 24,600. Mallory, Somervell, and Norton set a new record in 1922 at twenty-six thousand. Two years later, Norton and Somervell reached twenty-eight thousand feet without oxygen, but there the record stood for fifty-four years. Since then the summit had been conquered but always with oxygen. Doctors, climbers, and government officials had all assured them that they would die if they did not bring oxygen bottles.

Messner and Habeler plodded toward the summit for four more hours. They reached the summit of Mount Everest on May 8, 1978, about 1:30 P.M. without using bottled oxygen. Like Hillary, they had been supported by a large expedition, but unlike Hillary, they had not used oxygen. Oxygen usage reduces Everest's 29,029-foot challenge to the equivalent of twenty-thousand feet. So in a very real sense, they were the first men to succeed in reaching the 29,028-foot peak. They had experienced the true conditions on the highest mountain in the world.

Messner's vision dimmed after the two-hour descent to the South Col. By morning, his eyes itched from snow blindness. His minimal vision turned the descent to Base Camp into a dangerous nightmare, but they made it. Three other expedition members reached the summit in the next week.

Several climbs intervened before Messner's next attempt on Mount Everest. Two months after reaching Everest without oxygen, he began climbing Nanga Parbat. On August 9, he reached the summit by ascending the Diamir Face. This climb became his first solo ascent in the Himalayas, and the first ever solo ascent of an 8000-meter peak. In 1979, he climbed the world's second highest peak, K2. Later, he left for Ama Dablam but gave up the summit to rescue New Zealanders.

"He's planning what?" Messner had heard clearly but refused to believe his ears. Naomi Uemura, the great Japanese explorer, was planning the first solo climb of Mount Everest in 1980. Messner had been thinking of doing that for years. Now he would have to race Uemura for it. Knowing that permits would all be taken for the good-weather periods of the next two years, Messner applied to go during monsoon season.

When China began permitting climbs on eight peaks, Messner obtained the first permit in Beijing. Returning to China with his gear, he came to Lhasa, the capital of Tibet, where he visited the Potala Palace. Leaving Lhasa on June 27, 1980, he hired yak drivers to establish Base Camp at the foot of Mount Everest. The following week, he toiled up the mountain on a practice run. He reached the North Col on July 22. After that, monsoon winds and rains prompted a temporary retreat. While waiting, he surveyed the area around Shisha Pangma.

As weather improved, Messner set out for Mount Everest again. In most years, four to ten days of good weather interrupted the monsoon season. Taking advantage of this, he returned to Base Camp at the Rongbuk Glacier on August 15. The next day he reached his advanced base, from which he had climbed to the North Col. On August 17, he again climbed to the North Col, left supplies, and returned to the advanced base. The following day soft snow concerned him as he began his solo ascent, and he returned to the North Col.

Messner felt himself falling into a crevasse. Sweat broke out on him as he switched on his headlamp. His fall had been broken by a tiny snow bridge that could collapse at any moment. His light could not reach the bottom of the abyss surrounding his temporary safety. Looking up, he saw the hole which his fall had left twenty feet above him. He was trapped, alone, and sweating, but his mind stayed calm. "If I get out of here, I will give up climbing," he thought. Then he thought of his crampons in his rucksack, but the ledge was so small that he could neither turn nor take off the rucksack. Across the hole, his light spotted a ledge spiraling upward. He let himself fall and leaned on the far side. Kicking a step, he stood on his new platform. He worked himself up the ramp.

The sunlight renewed his desire to climb. Jumping the crevasse at the point where he fell, Messner completed his ascent to the

North Col, where views of Cho Oyu to the west greeted him. Thin air forced him to pause every fifty paces, but he pressed on up the northeast ridge, supporting himself with ski poles. He bivouacked at 7800 meters (25,590 feet). The night passed fitfully as winds whipped his one-man tent on the exposed snowy ridge. The high elevation took its toll, and his rests increased to every fifteen paces and then to every ten paces. He bivouacked the next night about 8230 meters (27,000 feet).

Messner kept to the right of the snow cornices on the last ridge. He reached the mist-enshrouded summit at 3:00 P.M. on August 20, 1980. The climb of the Norton Couloir had been slow and laborious. Now, he photographed his last steps to the top, where the Chinese had anchored an aluminum tripod in 1975. After resting, he descended to his tent and gear at dusk. Taking only the ski poles, he descended to the advanced base and then to main Base Camp. In Kathmandu, he celebrated his Everest solo—the first—on his thirty-sixth birthday, September 17.

8000 Meters

Cold winds tore their breath from them and stung their faces with ice crystals. The 1981 monsoon had arrived two weeks early, and the three mountaineers found themselves caught two thousand feet below the summit of Shisha Pangma. They descended one thousand feet where Messner bivouacked with Friedl Mutschlechner. Dr. Bulle Oelz had descended another three thousand feet because of altitude sickness. The storm continued, but Friedl glimpsed stars through the clouds once and insisted that they try again the next morning. Friedl, anxious to reach the top on his first climb to twenty-six thousand feet, provided inspiration for Messner. When they rejoined Dr. Oelz, he was shocked that they had reached the summit in the monsoon. Which peak next?

Winds howled across the frozen white slopes of the third highest peak in the world, Kanchenjunga. The icy blasts shook the two small tents. The team slept fitfully until 5:00 A.M., when they jumped at the sickening sound of ripping nylon. The wind tore the tent apart and scattered their belongings. The night grew colder, and snow covered their sleeping bags. At dawn, they began gathering their

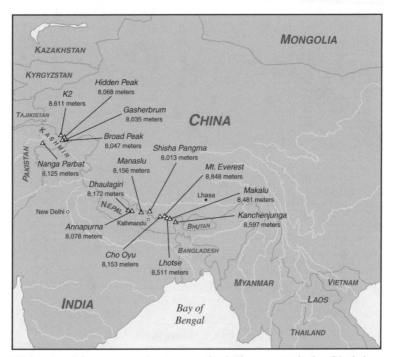

things, unable even to shout over the boisterous winds. Glad that they had reached the summit yesterday, they were weakened and miserable. Messner suffered from an abscess on the liver and Mutschlechner from frostbitten fingers. Hallucinations began as they descended to Camp 2. Messner considered this 1982 climb his second most dangerous after Nanga Parbat.

Later in the year, Messner climbed Gasherbrum with two top Pakistani climbers, Nazir Sabir and Sher Khan. As they climbed, they discovered the last bivouac of a team of four Austrians who had been missing for a week. They recovered a diary and later found one body on the way to the summit.

Only one month later, Messner joined the Pakistanis for the climb of Broad Peak. Beautiful weather made the trip memorable, but the successful climb also set a new record. This was the third 8000-meter peak that Messner had climbed in one year. No one had ever climbed even two in the same year before, and Messner referred to his success as his hat trick.

A huge boulder dislodged and slid downward toward the roped climbers. Picking up speed and careening off ice chunks, it began bounding down the slope. The boulder headed straight for Messner. Messner and Hans Kammerlander were attempting the first winter ascent of Cho Oyu. Messner, hoping for his fourth summit in 1982, knew the boulder could crush him and tear them both off the mountain to fall thousands of feet in a double death. The boulder bounded to one side of Hans Kammerlander but continued on a beeline for Messner. At the last second, Messner dodged aside, feeling the wind in the boulder's wake. This icy slope on the south face had again exposed them to the northeast winds, and soon deep snows forced a retreat. However, Messner did climb the peak the following year with Kammerlander and the top German climber, Michl Dacher. He reached the summit but did not make four in one year.

Messner loved to prove his critics wrong. They had said "impossible" to Everest without oxygen, to a Himalayan solo, and to climbing three in a single year. Messner made them eat their words. Now, his idea to climb two 26,000-foot peaks on the same trip without returning to Base Camp received the same scorn. In 1984, he and Hans Kammerlander met in June for a traverse between the summits of Gasherbrum I and II. Their success after a week in the Death Zone received little publicity, but Messner regarded it as his greatest achievement. Only climbers understand the difficulty of the feat.

Messner sat in his recently acquired medieval castle, Schloss Juval. Could he be the first to climb all the world's 8000 meter peaks? All fourteen are in the Himalayas, and most are in the country of Nepal or on its border with Tibet, a province of China. A few are in Kashmir, a region claimed by both Pakistan and India.

Messner had climbed more of them than any other man. He reviewed his successes: Nanga Parbat in 1970 and 1978 (solo); Manaslu in 1972; Hidden Peak in 1975; Mount Everest in 1978 and 1980 (solo); K2 in 1979; Shisha Pangma in 1981; his 1982 hat trick: Kanchenjunga, Gasherbrum, and Broad Peak; and Cho Oyu in 1983. All ten were climbed without oxygen masks, and only four to go!

THE FOURTEEN 8000-METER PEAKS

Mountain	Other Names	Elevation (m)	Elevation (feet)	Location
Mount Everest	Chomolungma Sagarmatha	8848	29,028	Nepal-Tibet
K2	Chogori	8611	28,250	Kashmir
Kanchenjunga	Kangchanfanga	8597	28,208	Nepal-India
Lhotse		8511	27,923	Nepal-Tibet
Makalu	Makalufeng	8481	27,824	Nepal-Tibet
Dhaulagiri		8172	26,810	Nepal
Manaslu	Kutang	8156	26,760	Nepal
Cho Oyu		8153	26,750	Nepal-Tibet
Nanga Parbat	Diamir	8125	26,660	Kashmir
Annapurna	Morshiadi	8078	26,504	Nepal
Hidden Peak	K5, Gasherbrum I	8068	26,470	Kashmir
Broad Peak	Falchen Kangri	8047	26,400	Kashmir
Gasherbrum	K4, Gasherbrum II	8035	26,362	Kashmir
Shisha Pangma	Gosaithan	8013	26,287	Tibet

In the decade ending in May of 1960, all thirteen of the known peaks exceeding 8000 meters had been climbed. Messner knew that Shisha Pangma (also spelled Xixapangma and known as Gosaithan in India) was identified as an 8000-meter peak in 1963 and was promptly climbed the following year.

Mountain	first climbed	expedition	climbers
Annapurna	June 3, 1950	French	M. Herzog, L. Lachenal
Mount Everest	May 29, 1953	British	E. Hillary, Tenzing Norgay
Nanga Parbat	July 3, 1953	German/Austrian	H. Buhl
K2	July 31, 1954	Italian	A. Compagnoni L. Lacedelli
Cho Oyu	Oct. 19, 1954	Austrian	H. Tichy, S. Jöchler, Pasang Dawa Lama
Makalu	May 15, 1955	French	J. Couzy, L. Terray
Kanchenjunga	May 25, 1955	British	G. Band, J. Brown
Lhotse	May 18, 1956	Swiss	Luchsinger, E. Reiß
Manaslu	May 9, 1956	Japanese	T. Imanishi, Gyaltsen Norbu
Gasherbrum	July 7, 1956	Austrian	Moravec, Larch Willenpart,
Broad Peak	June 9, 1957	Austrian	Buhl, Schmuck, F. Wintersteller, K. Diemberger
Hidden Peak	July 5, 1958	American	P. Schoening, A. Kaufmann
Dhaulagiri	May 13, 1960	Swiss	K. Diemberger, A. Schelbert, Nawang Dorje
Shisha Pangma	May 2, 1964	Chinese	6 Chinese and 4 Tibetans

Messner stood entranced and daunted by the immensity of the never-before-climbed Northwest Face of Annapurna. He knew that this mountain was the first 8000-meter peak to be climbed—after many unsuccessful attempts and twenty-five deaths. Chris Bonington had first climbed the South Face. One of his men had also died. Messner wanted to give up.

"Let's try at least," begged Reinhard Patscheider. Messner acquiesced: "OK, I'll go on and search out a Base Camp." Two days later Messner and Hans Kammerlander bivouacked within reach of the summit. They fought a storm along an exposed ridge to the top and descended the following day. A second group failed to reach the summit when Patscheider fell thirteen hundred feet down a hanging glacier before stopping at the brink of the icefall. Incredibly, he survived. Only three peaks to go.

Lightning flashed to the right and again to the left while the thunder roared around them. Electricity streaked between their gloves and coat sleeves; sparks flew off their crampons and ice axes. Messner and Kammerlander knew they were in trouble. Their hair stood on end as they climbed toward the summit of Dhaulagiri. Having failed on two previous attempts, Messner was not going to give up. They pushed upwards as arcs of lightning crossed the sky, piercing the stormy darkness. At the summit, it looked like a scene from *Night on Bald Mountain,* and they did not stay long. Two peaks to go.

The year 1986 ended the quest for Eight Thousanders. The remaining peaks, Lhotse and Makalu, were the fourth and fifth highest peaks in the world. Marcel Ruidi had just died descending Makalu—his tenth Eight Thousander. Could Messner do it? Two of the highest peaks, each almost twenty-eight thousand feet, in one year? Messner had made three previous unsuccessful expeditions to Makalu. Even now, he had to set out from Base Camp three times for the summit before he finally made it. Messner had also unsuccessfully attempted Lhotse before—twice. He reached its summit on October 16 and realized his goal of climbing all fourteen Eight Thousanders and doing so without oxygen.

Messner also trekked across eastern Tibet in 1986 and then across Bhutan and Tibet in 1987-88. These journeys spurred an interest in trekking as a break from climbing. He crossed the Negev and Patagonia in 1989. Late in 1989, his trekking took him back to Antarctica. His ninety-two-day trek on skis with German Arved Fuchs, completed on February 12, 1990, made them the first to cross the width of Antarctica. His only major climb during these treks was Vinson Massif in Antarctica in December of 1986 to complete the Seven Summits. (See Patrick Morrow.)

PATRICK MORROW
Climbing the Seven Summits

Mount McKinley

Patrick Morrow, a twenty-four-year-old Canadian, looked at icy Muncho Lake along the Alaska Highway. Born in Invermere, British Columbia, on October 18, 1952, he and his family had lived in Kimberly for most of his life, so an icy lake in spring seemed ordinary. Five days out of Calgary, Alberta, Morrow and driver Bernhard Ehmann arrived on May 18, 1977, at Denali National Park and two days later at Base Camp. They hoped to climb Mount McKinely, the coldest mountain in the world.

Morrow and Ehmann knew the dangers of mountaineering, but Mount McKinley was far higher than other peaks they had climbed. They soon learned that four people had died on Mount McKinley the previous year. In addition, there had been five frostbite victims, twelve cases of snow blindness, two cases of pulmonary edema (lungs filling with fluid, prompted by altitude), and seven of cerebral edema (brain swells, extreme altitude sickness).

Morrow and Ehmann struck out on a new route they called the Southwest Rib. Though caught in snow, they continued and finally made a camp after twenty hours of continuous climbing. After two-and-a-half days, they finally reached the top of the rib, which connected to the main route on the West Buttress. Instead of continuing up, however, they returned to Base Camp for supplies. After a few days' rest, they returned to where they had left off.

For their second segment, Morrow and Ehmann selected the Messner Couloir. This vertical gully, over a mile high, had been climbed only once before—by famed climber Reinhold Messner the previous year (see Reinhold Messner). Morrow and Ehmann camped at its base on June 8, and by noon of the second day on this steep part, only one thousand vertical feet remained.

Ehmann's backpack toppled and slid down the rock slab. They heard it crashing and bouncing down the couloir. Half their gear was gone, and Morrow knew they would have to turn back. Or would they? If they were willing to descend the easier West Buttress route by the light of the midnight sun, they might still summit. They agreed to try this plan.

The Indian name for Mount McKinley is Denali, "the Great One," which explains why the park containing the peak is called Denali National Park. As Morrow arrived on the highest summit of the Great One, a sea of flags of many nationalities greeted him. At thirty degrees below zero, frost covered everything, but the alpenglow of the midnight sun was beautiful.

From the South Summit, Morrow looked across at the lower North Peak of McKinley and remembered what he had heard about the first climb. The first climbing party had reached only the North Peak 850 feet lower. When Hudson Stuck, Harry Karstens, Robert Tatum, Walter Harper, and two young Indians named Johnny and Esaias reached the true summit on June 23, 1913, they saw the flag planted by the earlier party flying on the North Peak. This proved that the earlier group had not climbed the right peak. Morrow now stood on the correct summit at midnight on June 9. He returned to Base Camp by the twenty-third day of his adventure.

Aconcagua

Morrow jumped at an opportunity to climb Everest. As a freelance outdoor photographer, he took a nine-hundred-mile bike ride through the coastal mountains of British Columbia and then climbed Mount Hoge in Kluane National Park in the Yukon Territory. But as the Everest trip neared and the publicity grew, he knew they would need some practice climbs. Canada had only once before obtained a permit for Everest (1975), and the expedition had fizzled because of complications before it ever left Canada. It was important to do it right.

Morrow and three other men arrived in Argentina in January of 1981 to climb Aconcagua, the highest mountain in the Western Hemisphere. Aconcagua stands in Parque Provincial Aconcagua, one of Argentina's provincial parks. Aconcagua was first climbed in 1897 by Matthias Zurbriggen, but Morrow's group would be using a harder route called the Polish Glacier route.

On their way up, Morrow's party met the survivors of a three-day disaster. One man had slipped on ice and had fallen on a rock that ripped open his chest. A helicopter blew up as it attempted to rescue them, and eventually, the weakened companions had to leave their dying friend and descend as best they could.

Snowbound, Morrow and tent mate Gordon "Speedy" Smith relaxed and talked. This was the first time that Morrow considered the idea of climbing all the Seven Summits, the highest mountains on the seven continents. If they climbed this one, it would be his second. They knew he would need to climb Kilimanjaro and Everest to achieve his goal. They had both read *I Come from the Stone Age* by Heirich Harrer of Austria. Harrer had been on the international team that had made the first ascent of New Guinea's Puncak Jaya (Mount Jaya) in 1962. Morrow would have to decide whether to climb Kosciusko in Australia or Jaya in New Guinea. Morrow considered Mont Blanc in the Alps of France the highest mountain in Europe, but Speedy insisted that Russia's Mount Elbrus was higher. Neither knew the highest peak in Antarctica.

At the summit, which they reached on February 9, they met a tour group. The strongest man on the tour had become delirious with a cerebral edema. Morrow and teammate Roger Marshall tied him on their rope to help him descend. Though he still slipped over cliffs several times, each time the rope saved his life. Morrow was sure that a weaker man could not have descended in that condition,

Besides the disaster and the edema, they would also see other dangers on Aconcagua. When the infamous white winds, which can reach up to 160 miles per hour, came they found it difficult to pick their route across the glaciers. This storm sent avalanches onto part of the tour group, which managed to survive, but the same storm killed three Koreans on a different route. Their fourth teammate, Dave Read, went snow-blind. Marshall and Smith helped him, while Morrow watched after the tour group.

Meanwhile, Dick Bass, who owned the Snowbird Ski Resort in Utah, mentioned to one of his summer employees that he would like to climb Mount McKinley. The employee, Marty Hoey, was the only female climbing guide on Mount Rainier and Mount McKinley. She laughed in his face, and Bass took it as an insult and a dare. Had he not climbed the Matterhorn back in 1949? Marty ate her words when the fifty-one-year-old Texan climbed Mount McKinley in the summer of 1981. Bass also decided to climb the Seven Summits. He did not yet know that he would have to race Morrow to be the first.

Within the year, Bass met Frank Wells, a forty-nine-year-old corporate president from California whose youthful climb of Africa's Kilimanjaro and Europe's Mont Blanc had sparked the same Seven Summits goal. They immediately flew to Russia with two friends and attempted Mount Elbrus. With guides, everyone reached the summit except Wells.

"It must be God's will," exclaimed Bass. Marty Hoey had just called to invite Bass and Wells on an Everest expedition with the Mount Rainier climbing guides. For practice, Hoey agreed to guide them up Mount Rainier and then Aconcagua in January of 1982. Bass reached both summits, but Wells was still too out of shape.

Mount Everest

Morrow made another training climb for his Everest attempt in September of 1981. Muztagata (24,757 feet) in the Kunlun of China became his first 7000-meter summit. The highlight for him was descending on skis.

Arriving in Nepal in late July, Canada's Everest expedition established Base Camp in Sagarmatha National Park on August 15. Sagarmatha is the native name of Mount Everest. They threaded their way through the dangerous Khumbu icefall and began carting supplies up to Camps 1 and 2 in the Western Cwm.

Avalanche! Snow came flooding past. Morrow could not see or hear a thing. He tried to shelter behind a sérac that he knew was close. Waves of snow kept pulling him back. The wind ripped his breath away and strove to tear his fixed rope from the mountain. He wondered if any of the team would survive.

It ended as suddenly as it began. Morrow had not been in the worst part of it. He immediately helped uncover one teammate who had been buried to his chest. When they saw a foot sticking out of the ice, they promptly rescued a teammate who had been spun and buried upside down. Next, they began to search for the three missing Sherpas. They dug along the fixed rope and finally uncovered a hand. It turned out to be Pasang Sona, but even CPR could not revive him. The other two Sherpas were never found. The total was three deaths by August 31.

Just two days later, séracs collapsed along their route through the icefall. The first ice boulder barely missed them. The fixed rope snapped, and Dave Read felt the ice beneath him slide into the crevasse. He found himself wedged between two great blocks of ice. He reached for a hat and found Sherpa Tsering. As they struggled to get free, another man heard them and helped them out. Blair Griffiths was less fortunate; he had been crushed between ice slabs. After this fourth death, six of the original twenty-two team members decided to go home.

Morrow and expedition leader Bill March established Camp 3 on the slopes of Lhotse at the end of September. On October 4, Dave Read and two other men went up to establish Camp 4 on the South Col, but one had to descend when his oxygen regulator malfunctioned.

The next day, one of the three who had established Camp 4, Laurie Skreslet, climbed with two Sherpas, Sungdare and Lhokpa Dorje, to the summit of Everest. They set a record eight-hour roundtrip to the summit from the South Col. It was Sungdare's third time to the top, but Skreslet became the first Canadian ever on the summit. His success broke the team's depression.

Morrow headed up to Camp 4 on the next day with three other climbers and two Sherpas (Lhakpa Tschering and Pema Dorje). The following morning, he began toward the summit with a partner and the two Sherpas. Morrow, moving more slowly, soon fell behind.

Morrow caught up with the others at a steep section. Another faulty oxygen mask forced his partner to turn back. Morrow roped himself and the two Sherpas together for safety. Resting every five steps, they soon reached a dead body.

The body was Hannelore Schmatz, who had reached the summit in 1979 with American Ray Genet and Sungdare, two days after her husband Gerhard Schmatz of Germany. Exhausted, the three had bivouacked on their descent at twenty-eight thousand feet. Genet had died in his sleep, and Sungdare went down for more oxygen to help Mrs. Schmatz. This sacrificial effort resulted in frostbite and the loss of four toes; the oxygen helped Mrs. Schmatz, but only briefly, before she died. Gerhard offered a reward to any climber who could get her body down, but for three years no climber had been up to the task at such a high elevation.

Seeing the body of Mrs. Schmatz reminded Morrow and the Sherpas of the seriousness of their undertaking. They continued thoughtfully across the corniced ridge. Their ice axes occasionally sliced through the ice into the empty space below. On the summit at noon on October 6, 1982, all three celebrated their first time on Everest. The grand one-hundred-mile views would later become part of Morrow's traveling exhibit assembled from his four thousand expedition photos. As they descended, Morrow twice caught snow-blind Pema Dorje with the rope as he started stumbling off the crest.

Summit	Continent	Range	Elevation	Country
Mount Everest	Asia	Himalaya	29,028 ft.	China-Nepal
Aconcagua	S. America	Andes	22,834 ft.	Argentina
Mount McKinley	N. America	Alaska	20,320 ft.	United States
Kilimanjaro	Africa	none	19,340 ft.	Tanzania
Mount Elbrus	Europe	Caucasus	18,510 ft.	Russia
*Puncak Jaya	Oceania	Carstensz	16,503 ft.	Indonesia
Vinson Massif	Antarctica	Ellsworth	16,067 ft.	none
* or Mount Kosciusko	Australia	Snowy	7,310 ft.	Australia

Morrow had looked up a few details before his climb of Everest. He now knew the highest peak on Antarctica. Morrow knew he was now one of only 132 people who had ever climbed Everest, of those, none had climbed Vinson Massif. Morrow could still be the first on the Seven Summits.

Morrow had also investigated the highest peak in Europe to see why he had disagreed with his friend Speedy White. Mount Elbrus is certainly higher than Mont Blanc, it was not always considered part of Europe. It lies in the Caucasus Mountains which form the boundary between Europe and Asia. Since Mount Elbrus in Russia drains into the Black Sea, it is now universally acknowledged as part of Europe and therefore Europe's highest peak. Mount Elbrus was the first of all Seven Summits to be climbed when F. Crauford Grove made the first successful ascent in 1874. Morrow reckonized that he would have to climb Mount Elbrus, instead of Mont Blanc, but he had not yet resolved the dispute over Australia's highest peak.

The Race Quickens

Although Morrow did not want a race to the Seven Summits, he did have to consider his ability to find sponsors. If others finished first, it would be harder to find sponsors. He knew of six other men also seeking to climb the Seven Summits. Three of the six were Americans: Dick Bass, Frank Wells, and Gerry Roach. Gerhard Schmatz, a German, had started climbing the Seven Summits after his wife's death on Everest. The last two, famed climbers Naomi Uemura and Reinhold Messner, seemed to be the most serious rivals. (See chapters on these two men.)

Japanese adventurer Naomi Uemura had been in the race the longest. He had climbed Mount McKinley and Mount Everest in 1970 and had also climbed Kilimanjaro, Aconcagua, and McKinley solo. Like Wells, he had climbed Mont Blanc in the days, when it was considered the highest peak in Europe.

Reinhold Messner had been in the race almost as long. He had made the second-ever ascent of Puncak Jaya in 1971 (and later climbed Mount Kosciusko). He climbed Aconcagua in 1974 and pioneered a new route on Mount McKinley two years later. In 1978,

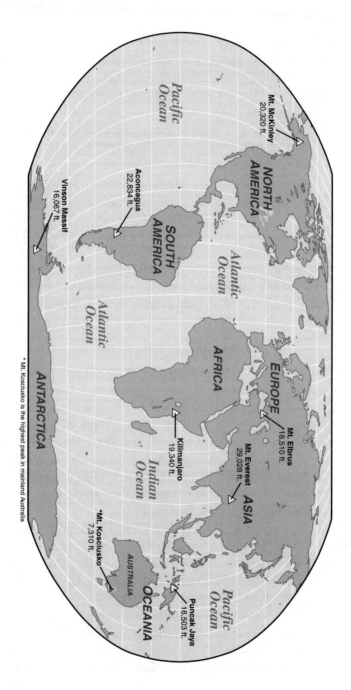

he set two records: a new route on Kilimanjaro and Mount Everest without use of oxygen. Messner had also climbed Mont Blanc but knew that he would need to climb Elbrus as well as Vinson Massif to finish his Seven Summits. Motivation to plan these last two climbs came when he heard about Bass and Wells in 1982.

Morrow, with his wife, Baiba, attempted Mount Elbrus but reached only the lower eastern summit on July 25, 1983. After failing on Elbrus, Morrow went to Africa and climbed Mount Kilimanjaro on August 17, 1983. In spite of some armchair geographers who insisted that there was no snow on the mountain, Morrow hauled skis to the top for some enjoyable glacier travel. Kilimanjaro dominates Kilimanjaro National Park in Tanzania, and it has several summits. The highest is named Kibo, but the second highest, Mawenzi, is a more difficult climb.

Meanwhile Bass and Wells had taken their families on a safari to Africa and summitted Mount Kilimanjaro while Morrow was attempting Elbrus. On their way home, they had stopped in Russia to climb Mount Elbrus while Morrow was climbing Kilimanjaro. Bass and Wells had now eached climbed four of the Seven Summits. A few weeks later, Reinhold Messner ascended Mount Elbrus in a blizzard, making his sixth summit.

Morrow himself had just visited Australia and climbed Mount Kosciusko during his fifty-four-hour layover in Sydney. The peak is in Kosciusko National Park in the province of New South Wales in the Snowy Mountains of the Australian Alps. Morrow knew that Bass, Wells, and Roach had all determined to do Kosciusko rather than Puncak Jaya, but after his hike to the top, Morrow decided to do some research.

Morrow found four possible views. First, Mount Kosciusko, at 7,310 feet, is the highest mountain on the mainland of the continent of Australia. Second, Big Ben, rising 9,003 feet on Heard Island in the Indian Ocean, is the highest peak owned by the country of Australia. Third, Australia's continental shelf includes New Guinea but not Heard Island to form a region sometimes called Australasia. Puncak Jaya, at 16,535 feet on New Guinea, is the summit of the continent of Australasia. Fourth, Oceania consists of Australia and the Pacific Islands (except those linked to Asia by the continental shelf or adjacent seas such as the China Sea and the Sea of Japan). Puncak Jaya is also the highest peak in Oceania, far surpassing New Zealand's Mount Cook (12,349 feet), and Hawaii's Mauna Kea (13,796 feet). In fact, Puncak Jaya is the highest mountain on any island in the world.

Morrow considered the options. When the world is divided into seven continents, most of the islands are classified with them. Madagascar is part of Africa, and Great Britain and even Iceland are considered Europe. If Mount McKinley were transported from Alaska to Long Island or Cuba, it would still be the highest peak in North America. Even the country of Australia includes Tasmania, and both New Guinea and New Zealand are usually grouped with the continent of Australia. Ignoring these islands would be like saying that Japan is not in Asia.

Such thoughts convinced Morrow that first option was not adequate and that islands should be included. Puncak Jaya should rank as one of the Seven Summits rather than Kosciusko. This decision seemed satisfying because Puncak Jaya is the only one of the peaks in question with an elevation similar to the other six of the Seven Summits. Since Puncak Jaya is also a remote and difficult climb, it is worthy to be included in the Seven Summits. Morrow had not needed to hike up Mount Kosciusko.

Vinson Massif

"How are you getting to Antarctica?" Morrow asked Wells on a long-distance phone call. They swapped stories of their hundreds of letters and phone calls and the discouragement from the American and British bases. Wells told him he had finally found Giles Kershaw, an independent pilot who had the most flying experience over Antarctica. Kershaw would take them for $200,000. Between the expense and Kershaw's busy schedule, Morrow would have to wait until early 1984.

As Morrow waited, Kershaw landed Bass and Wells on the icy plain five miles from the base. Chris Bonington and Rick Ridgway guided them, their photographer Steve Marts, and Japanese climbers Tae Maeda and Yuichiro Miura to the top. Bonington made the summit from Camp 2, but fierce winds drove the others back. After four days, Bass and Ridgway made the summit, while the others finally re-established Camp 2. The following day, the last four men made the summit.

Since the first ascent in 1966 by Schoening and Evans (see Pete Schoening), only one other group had climbed it, a group of German and Russian geologists in 1979. The Bass and Wells expedition became the third party in 1983. Morrow was glad that Bass and Wells were the only ones who had climbed it that were in the race for the Seven Summits.

Morrow soon learned that two contestants were out of the running. Wells, who had promised his wife he would not attempt Everest a third time, bowed out of the race after celebrating his sixth victory with his family on Mount Kosciusko. Naomi Uemura had tragically disappeared on Mount McKinley in February 1984. Bass, Roach, Schmatz, and Messner remained as rivals to Morrow in the race.

In August, Morrow and his wife headed for Puncak Jaya in New Guinea. They thought they had the correct permits until they arrived in Jakarta in Indonesia. After getting the runaround between Jakarta and New Guinea, they finally settled for a visit to some famous tribal areas. They could not get permission to climb.

Bass had only Everest left, and he got in with a Nepalese cleanup expedition on Everest. Red tape, however, postponed the attempt on the summit, and by the end of October, his good friend Sherpa Yogendra died. The expedition collapsed, and his third attempt on Everest had failed.

Now Morrow got his chance to catch up. Organizing had been a first-class headache. He had had to raise $250,000 for the trip to Antarctica and scramble for backers and other climbers to share the fare. Insurance was almost impossible to get and very expensive when he finally found it. He had to contact several countries just to find one that would sell fuel, another major expense. Many governments had refused any involvement at all and discouraged all private visits.

Morrow arrived on November 17, 1984. Giles Kershaw, the ace British pilot, flew them to Antarctica. They reached Antarctica at an Argentinian base and staked the plane to the ground. The famous gale-force winds of Antarctica flipped the plane upside down anyway. If it had not tangled with a snow tractor, the winds would have also blown it into the ocean. Kershaw's expertise enabled them to limp back to South America, but the need for additional repairs precluded any climb of Vinson.

In 1985, a Norwegian team asked mountaineer Chris Bonington and photographer David Breashears to join their expedition to Everest. The promise of funding enabled them to secure a place for Bass on the climb. As Bass climbed, he meditated on his wife's words: "Never let your guard down; remember how much you have to come home to; I love you."

Bass reached the summit on April 30, 1985, where his climbing partner, David Breashears, greeted him with a hug. Bass was the oldest man (age fifty-five) to climb Mount Everest and the first to ascend the Seven Mainland Summits. Bass prayed, "Thank You, Lord, for getting me here safely. And I pray You will get me down as well. Without You nothing is possible."

Bass knew he could not have done it without Breashears, a true friend. The strong twenty-nine year old was such an expert climber that he had been the first to provide live television coverage from the summit of Everest. Bass relied on his trail breaking, fixed lines, and expertise. Morrow and Messner both respected Bass for his drive to summit Everest at his age. However, both knew that Bass was only an amateur climber and that he had elected to climb Mount Kosciusko rather than remote Puncak Jaya. Bass had won the title for the Seven Mainland Summits, but Morrow and Messner were not interested in the mainland summits. While Bass was at Everest, Messner attempted to reach Antarctica but without success.

Morrow went through the Antarctic headache again. This time it cost $400,000 to organize the trip. He became part owner of Adventure Network, an adventure tour company, and flew with Sir Edmund Hillary and astronaut Neil Armstrong to the North Pole for publicity. They stopped on Ellesmere Island on the way back to climb Ad Astram, a five-thousand-foot peak at a temperature of -56°F. A group of Korean researchers and an American climbing team signed on for an Antarctic trip. Funding found, schedules had to be coordinated.

Giles Kershaw flew Morrow to Antarctica the second time in early November of 1985 along with the Korean and American teams that were Morrow's clients. Kershaw himself became part of Morrow's climbing team, when the oldest member, sixty-four-year-old Bill Hackett had to descend from Camp 2 and give up his fifth summit because of a torn neck ligament. The team pitched Camp 3 in the saddle between Vinson and Mount Shinn.

Two days later, on November 9, 1985, Morrow's group of nine reached the summit. It was a great celebration. After photos, Kershaw left his pink flamingo on the top. Morrow and Martyn Williams spent two hours on top. During the next days, the weather grew worse. The Korean group put only three people on top. Of the American climbers, only two reached the top, but one of them was Gerry Roach, who had just completed the Seven Mainland Summits.

Puncak Jaya

Steve Fossett, who had been with Morrow on Vinson, invited Morrow to climb Puncak Jaya (also spelled Jaja, and Djaja). As with many peaks, the native name *Puncak Jaya* has displaced the European name, *Carstensz Pyramid*. Morrow and Fossett obtained the first permit to climb Puncak Jaya since 1975. Morrow's wife, Baiba, also came. The remainder of their team consisted of three students from the University of Jakarta: Adi Seno, Titus Pramano, and Yura Katoppo. Pramano was the leader of the university climbing club and had climbed Jaya before; all three were in their twenties.

Morrow and company arrived at the mining town of Tembagapura at eleven thousand feet. Having been at sea level only twenty-four hours before, Morrow felt queasy. By nightfall, their ten porters hauled their supplies to Base Camp at 13,200 feet. The next day, they placed Camp 1 at the foot of the Meren Glacier. The porters left immediately after they were paid. In shorts and T-shirts, they shivered in the daily downpour at this high elevation.

The following day the team crossed the glacier and set up Camp 2. They also got used to the daily weather. Mornings were always clear, but as the sun heated the jungle, water vapor would collect into clouds. By midafternoon the downpours would begin and turn into electrical storms by nightfall. As the night cooled, clouds would empty and disperse, clearing again by morning for the cycle to begin all over again.

This climb was Morrow's favorite of all the Seven Summits. The craggy peaks beyond the glacier reminded him of his climbs back home in British Columbia. Several routes had ratings of 5.7 or more on the North American scale, which does not exceed 5.13.

On May 7, 1986, the six climbers left at 5:00 A.M. for the summit. Katoppo still felt sick and decided to return to camp. In four hours, they had reached the ridge leading to the summit. Clouds soon enshrouded the view of the distant sea. Four rappels enabled them to cross the knife-edged ridge.

At the top, they sank knee-deep in snow. By now they were cloaked in fog. The drizzle turned into a downpour just below the summit ridge. The last rappels were made in darkness. At the end of this fifth day of the climb, candles in Katoppo's tent welcomed them back.

In August, Morrow returned to Mount Elbrus and climbed the true western summit. He had now completed the Seven Summits.

Messner and his two friends, Dr. Bulle Oelz and Wolfgang Thomaseth, climbed Vinson Massif in forty-eight hours with only one bivouack in December of 1986, having hired none other than Giles Kershaw to reach Antarctica. Messner became the second on the Seven Summits and the fourth on the Seven Mainland Summits. Since even Morrow had used oxygen masks and fixed ropes on Everest, Messner became the first to free climb the Seven Summits. On June 22, 1990, American Geoffrey Tabin became the fourth on the Seven Summits after third place Oswald Olz of Switzerland. Nevertheless, Pat Morrow retained the title of first on the Seven Summits.

WILL STEGER
Dogsleds Across Antarctica

The Arctic

Frigid winds tore at Will Steger's clothing and drove the blinding snow into his face. Snowflakes swirled along the base of the drift. A ridge of snow thirty feet high loomed out of the blizzard ahead; Steger veered left. At the next snow ridge, he veered right. At each of hundreds of ridges, he made an instant decision, trying to maintain a northerly course. He felt like a rat running a maze, but his prize was the North Pole.

Ski tracks! Steger could not believe his eyes. Here in the middle of the Arctic Ocean, over two hundred miles from even the most remote research station on Canada's Ellesmere Island, he had stumbled across ski tracks. He followed the tracks. Soon his dogsleds caught the hardy skier, Jean-Louis Etienne, who was about to make camp.

Etienne, a Frenchman, explained that he hoped to make the first solo ski trek to the pole. Naomi Uemura had made the first solo trip by dogsled two years earlier, but Etienne skied with no dogsleds and planned five airdrops for his solo ski record. Steger, from Minnesota, aimed for the first unsupported expedition to the North Pole—no air support or supply caches. They relaxed; it was not a race.

In the morning, Steger invited Etienne into his tent to talk. Together they lamented the exploitation of polar lands. They both dreamed of crossing Antarctica to draw attention to the need for preserving the last wild continent. Etienne's medical training pleased Steger. Etienne had specialized in sports medicine. Steger's extensive experience with sled dogs impressed Etienne. Steger bred and trained his own dogs in northern Minnesota near Ely, and in 1985 he had mushed five thousand miles from Minnesota's northern border to Point Barrow, Alaska, on the Arctic Ocean. Steger and Etienne exchanged phone numbers.

Will Steger was born August 27, 1945, in Richfield, Minnesota. He and seven teammates had left from Canada's Ellesmere Island on March 8, 1986. Even with forty-nine dogs, their 1,350 pounds of equipment had to be moved in stages. Each day, after moving half of the equipment, they returned for the other half. As they used up supplies, they moved more swiftly. By April 2, they evacuated New Zealand team member Bob McKerrow, whose ribs had been cracked in a sled accident. The plane removed the injured man and seven unneeded dogs but did not drop off anything so as not to jeopardize their goal of carrying all their own supplies. Three days after meeting Etienne, they flew out twenty-one more dogs.

On April 14, Steger's team came to a lead—a channel of open Arctic Ocean water. They found a narrow place to jump, but when Ann Bancroft jumped, the ice broke, and she plunged into the ten-thousand-foot-deep waters of the frigid Arctic Ocean. As she splashed into the freezing water, she turned and grabbed the ice floe. She pulled herself out quickly and changed into dry clothes. She still hoped to be the first female to the pole. Two days later, Bob Mantell flew out with badly frostbitten feet.

On May 2 after fifty-six days and five hundred miles, the remaining six teammates arrived at the North Pole and became the first unsupported party to reach it since its discovery. Besides Steger, the team included Minnesotans Paul Schurke and Ann Bancroft, Alaskan Geoff Carroll, and Canadians Brent Boddy and Richard Weber. Etienne, born December 9, 1946, arrived at the pole several days later on May 11. Etienne knew that Steger's team had succeeded when he found their sled tracks at the pole.

After two years of correspondence, in the spring of 1988, Steger and Etienne joined forces for the first crossing of Greenland from south to north. The trip covered sixteen hundred miles in sixty-two days. Three other men accompanied them: Geoff Somers of the United Kingdom, Keizo Funatsu of Japan, and Victor Boyarsky of Russia. The group mushed across Greenland, learned to share and communicate, and became good friends.

In 1995, Steger returned to the Arctic, hoping to cross it from Siberia to Canada. On March 11, his team encountered miles of open water and returned to Cape Arcticheskiy in Siberia, where a helicopter flew them across the open channel on April 2. The helicopter lift meant that the trip would not be a complete crossing on the ground, but they headed for Canada anyway. The team consisted of five people: Will Steger, Victor Boyarsky, Takako Takano, Martin Hignell, and Julie Hanson. On April 21, they arrived at the North Pole. On June 16, they switched to canoe-sleds brought by their air-support team. They canoed the last one hundred miles of open water to Canada's Ellesmere Island, arriving July 3. The canoeing reminded Steger of one of his first adventures: kayaking the length of the Yukon River with a friend at age nineteen and then kayaking the three-thousand-mile Mackenzie River the following year. However, the icy landscape reminded him more of the adventures of his boyhood hero Edmund Hillary.

Antarctic Crossing

Three sleds raced down the icy mountainside, each pulled by twelve powerful Huskies. Steger tensed, knowing that it was his fastest speed ever. Suddenly, his sled slid sideways. He tried to correct it but spun out of control. At breakneck speed, the sled careened into snowdrifts and overturned. The abrupt crash sent dogs flying. Boyarsky, roped to the sled, flew over the top and barely escaped the runners of the rolling sled. Funatsu's sled crashed too, but Somers, with British discipline, controlled his dogs enough to avoid disaster.

Sled repairs occupied the next day, August 9. The media had covered the departure from Seals Nunatak at the tip of the Antarctic Peninsula on July 27, 1989. Steger laughed as he remembered the camera crews scrambling to get out of the way as the straining dogs pulled free unexpectedly. The team consisted of the five adventurers

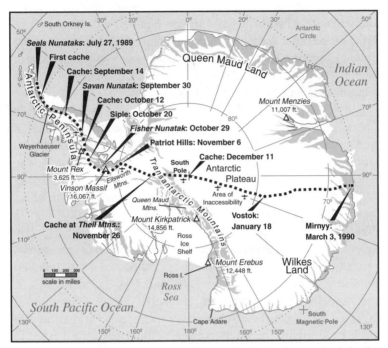

who had crossed Greenland together and Qin Dahe, a glaciologist (glacier specialist) from China. So far, the zero-degree temperatures had been mild.

Somers, who had the most experience with crevasses from his work for the British Antarctic Survey, warned the team about the crevasses that riddle the Antarctic Peninsula. Thin crusts of ice often hide these faults. Any dogs, men, or sleds that venture onto the crust fall through the ice into the chasm. Crevasses 150 feet deep spell certain death, equivalent to falling from a fifteen-story building. However, small crevasses can also cause deaths. Jagged ice scrapes the victim, and the fall wedges him into the narrow fissure at the bottom. Somers cautioned them to stay roped together or to the sled at all times. Even when checking dogs, they should straddle the dog line. He told of a partner who had dangled upside down for fifteen minutes while being rescued but who would have died without the rope.

Boyarsky felt ice breaking under him as he walked forward to untangle the dogs. He instantly regretted his folly of not straddling the dog line. He caught himself with his elbows, and dangling on the brink of death, groped for a hold in the ice. His searching hand found a line attached to his heavy sled, and he quickly pulled himself up.

Qin Dahe beckoned the other sleds to hurry. Somers, lying on the ground, strained to hold three dogs from falling to their deaths. With help from Steger and Funatsu, he hauled up two dogs that had hung suspended by their harnesses in the chasm, but the third harness came up empty. Cautiously, they peered over the brink. Steger shuddered as he glanced at the icy blue depths fading into inky blackness. Then he spotted Spinner rigid with fright and crouched on a tiny ledge twenty-five feet down. As Etienne rappelled down the crevasse, Spinner got excited and almost slipped into oblivion. Etienne put the panicked dog in an extra harness and attached it to a rope. With the dogs rescued, the team members held their breath as the half-ton sleds crossed the crevasse on the remaining snow bridge.

The August 20 dog rescue made the team appreciate their dogs even more. They had trained seventy dogs for Antarctica. From these, Steger, Funatsu, and Somers had each selected twelve of the strongest for a dog team. They had also chosen Fuzz, Rex, Garret, Brownie, Apak, and Godzilla as reserves to wait in Punta Arenas. Unfortunately, the last two had died of heat exhaustion in Cuba's tropical July weather on the way south.

Toughness and drive are essential for a six-month trek in the windiest and coldest climate in the world. All but fourteen dogs had been bred on Steger's Minnesota farm, and none were Alaskan Iditarod dogs. Dogs bred for the annual thousand-mile Iditarod race have enough toughness and endurance for several weeks of Alaska's winter, but speed is the key to the race. Crossing Antarctica would not be a race, but its length would match four Iditarod races and under much colder conditions.

Steger knew his homebred team well: Sam, Tim, Ray, Buffy, Panda, Zap Junior, Hank, Yeager, Tommy, Chuchi, Bly, and Gordie. The pacesetters Sam, Tim, and Ray alternated as lead dogs. The two 110-pounders, Panda and Gordie, boosted the average weight of Steger's dog team to ninety pounds. Besides many of Steger's special breed, Funatsu had selected five dogs from the last surviving Antarctic dogs bred by Admiral Byrd. Funatsu's team included Bjorn, Kutan, Odin, Casper, Monty, Herbie, Rodan, Kuka, Arrow, Aukluk, Chinook, and Kinta. Somers had included several dogs leased from Krabloonik Kennels in Snowmass, Colorado, together with many of Steger's special breed: Thule, Soda Pop, Spinner, Sawyer, Huck, Chewbakie, Kaviaq, Floppy, Jocky, Jewback, Pup, and Jimmy. Somers had chosen obedient and lighter dogs, averaging only sixty-five pounds. Because of their obedience, Somers's team was the best behaved; his lead dog, Thule, was the only female dog on the expedition.

Hours after the dog rescue, they came to the site of the third food cache, placed by Somers in January. They searched for two days, but deep snows had covered it. They had to push on one hundred miles to the next cache at the Weyerhaeuser Glacier with only twelve days of human food and eight days of dog food.

Two days after they resumed progress, they encountered more crevasse incidents. When Huck fell seventy feet from his harness onto a ledge, Somers rappelled down for the rescue. Later, Sam and Yeager dropped from Steger's sight. No other sleds were in sight to help, so Steger peeked over the brink. Both dogs still hung in their harnesses, but their stiffness and whimpers reminded him that they shared the hardships at the North Pole. The whines broke his heart, and energy welled up in him as he contemplated the abyss. After untangling the lines, he hauled them out single-handedly. The next day, Steger and Boyarsky rescued Buffy from yet another crevasse.

Flying? Swimming? Sledding? For two days, thick fog melted into the fresh powdery snow to erase the horizon. Falling flakes acted as lumps in the milk shake through which they seemed to swim. *Whiteout* aptly described the visual effect. Boyarsky described the lack of contrast saying, "You never know if the next step is a hole or a wall."

The six men needed to reach the next cache. They continued through the snow, which hindered movement but aided sleep.

Huskies dig snow hollows as windbreaks and let the snowfall cover them for insulation. On ice, when they cannot dig, they curl up and depend only on their double coat—fuzzy down covered by thick fur. At the top of the glacier on August 31, a three-day whiteout delayed the search. Since they could find no sign of their cache under the deep fresh snows, an air-support crew brought a few boxes from their next cache. They hoped this strategy would not shortchange them later.

The long sunrises and sunsets of the slowly lengthening days sent rainbows of colors across the horizons of icy mountains. Soon they spotted the three peaks of the Eternity Range— Faith, Hope, and Charity—rising from the plateau elevation of sixty-five hundred feet. At this elevation, the famous Antarctic winds hit with full force. On September 10, after days of holing up in blizzards, the weather worsened. Winds blasted them at ninety miles per hour, and the temperature dropped to -40°F with wind chills of -150°F. Steger made popcorn, his favorite blizzard pastime. The popping surprised Boyarsky, who had never had any in Russia.

With so far to go on limited food, they pushed on through the blizzard. Facing the frosty winds, the mushers could not always see their lead dog, much less the lead sled. Soon Etienne and Funatsu could not glimpse Somers and Dahe ahead of them. They waited for Steger and Boyarsky to catch up. The storm had already erased the tracks from Somers's sled, so the four men waited in an emergency shelter.

They all knew the gloomy whiteout stories from Scott's South Pole expedition. They also recalled stories shared several days earlier. Boyarsky had recalled a blizzard in 1976, when his Russian group took snow tractors between Antarctic stations. He and a comrade had tried to cross the 150 feet between the sleeping and cook cars but got lost in between. They searched for an hour on hands and knees, miraculously missing the crevasses and finding a cable that guided them back. Dahe had related an event from 1983, when he had worked at Australia's Casey Station. Their meteorologist went out for routine measurements, and they found him in the morning frozen to death. He died between two buildings, sixty feet from the one he had left and forty feet from the other.

An hour and a half later, relief flooded over them when they saw Somers. He and Dahe, realizing that they were not being followed, had stopped and set up camp. Then, tying together all their ropes, Somers had searched in widening circles until he found them only 150 feet behind.

On September 14, they found their cache, reduced slightly by their early pilfering. Of course, they could not supplement their diet by hunting. Seals and penguins inhabit the coast, but little lives in the interior of Antarctica. Only a few bugs and plants live within a thousand miles: mites, lice, midges, springtails, mosses, lichens, and two rare flowering plants.

Steger faced a decision. Two days earlier on September 24, the worst storm yet had raged. Winds reached hurricane force at one hundred miles per hour. They had been snowbound for thirteen days in September and had made little progress toward their cache still forty-five miles away. The dogs were weakening on the strict rations because crossing drifts four feet deep required extra energy. Some dogs suffered from icicles on their fur, and it was still snowing. They dumped one hundred pounds of gear to lighten the sleds, but still the dogs grew weaker. Sawyer, exhausted, had to be laid on the sled, adding seventy pounds to the lightened load. On September 29 they advanced four miles toward the cache at Savan Nunatak, still seventeen miles away. Only two days of dog rations remained, and snow must be covering the cache anyway.

Steger radioed for air support, but the blizzard delayed landing for a day. The pilot, unable to sight the cache, told them to bypass Savan Nunatak (a nunatak is a rocky mount standing out as an island in the ice). The small plane had to carry extra fuel for its long flight, which limited supplies to three reserve dogs and lots of dog food. They sent the fifteen most exhausted dogs, including Sawyer, to Punta Arenas.

Steger considered cooperation and adaptability the keys to success. Steger refused to let self-confidence or resignation interfere with cooperation. He often inspired himself with Amundsen's story, but he also encouraged communication—a difficult task when team members spoke French, Chinese, Japanese, Russian, and English. Only Steger and Somers used English as a mother tongue, but

Funatsu and Etienne had become fluent in this second language. Steger especially admired the efforts of Boyarsky and Dahe, who had begun speaking English quite recently. Concerning adaptability, Steger said, "Human strength lies not in resistance but in giving in. If we are to survive Antarctica, we must give in to nature, not fight it." Fritdjof Nansen had also said that polar success depended on "conforming the personal will to the Almighty will." Indeed, Steger prayed for good weather at times but always accepted whatever weather came. On October 9, Steger counted blizzards on forty of the last fifty days.

The men reached Mount Rex for their next food cache on October 12. Mount Rex is at the end of the Antarctic Peninsula. From here on they would be on the continent proper. Much of the continent receives less than an inch of precipitation annually. If it were not already covered with a solid sheet of ice, it still would be a desert. They expected less snow and fewer crevasses. Going would become easier if they could tolerate the bitter cold and constant wind—little consolation for suffering men. After months of freezing and thawing, their fingers and lips had become cracked and painful. Sunburn from the twenty-four-hour daylight compounded the pain.

Etienne searched the ice fields with binoculars. They were about to camp the evening of October 20, but they knew Siple was near. Soon he spotted an antenna from the American research station seven-and-a-half miles away. Snow covered the rest of the station, which had closed in 1986. During their two days at Siple, they dug out the cache from twelve feet of snow and mourned the death of a lead dog, Tim.

Temperatures dropped below -40°F with wind chills of -100°F. They endured conditions harsher than those reported by Amundsen and Scott, but finally the weather cleared. Somers found their next cache at Fisher Nunatak on October 29. Now they could see the beautiful Ellsworth Mountains, the highest peaks on the continent. The soaring peak of Vinson Massif, sixteen thousand feet above sea level, dominated the skyline. Seeing the peaks reminded Steger of his three first ascents in Peru's Cordillera Blanca. He had been twenty years old, and two other climbers had fallen to their deaths.

Steger edged his sled down a steep glacier. They had crossed many crevasses in the Heritage Mountains and ascended Horseshoe Pass, only to look down the far side at steep cliffs blocking their progress. The men had scouted the entire five-mile summit ridge looking for a way down. Five men had resigned themselves to backtracking for many days around the base of the range, but not Steger.

Steger descended the glacier in wide switchbacks until it became too narrow to traverse. He covered the sled runners with extra harnesses as friction brakes and then mushed his dog team down the sixty-five-degree slope. At the base, even with the brakes, it took a quarter mile to cruise to a stop. The other men watched in amazement and then followed, their sleds leaving great snow plumes in their wakes. Looking back, they could see that if they had skidded too far left they would have plunged over a one-thou-sand-foot cliff to their deaths. Steger's extensive experience with dogsleds in the Arctic had come to their aid, negotiating a difficult route where others saw no hope.

The expedition team pulled into the Patriot Hills base the next day, November 6, and they enjoyed heated huts and fresh food. A plane flew in twelve of their well-rested dogs. They also met Reinhold Messner and Arved Fuchs, who hoped to ski across Antarctica from the Filchner Ice Shelf to the Ross Ice Shelf via the South Pole. Limited airplane fuel moved their start to the inner edge of the Ronne Ice Shelf on November 13.

Could it be that in 1989 a continent remained that had never been crossed? Ernest Shackleton had made the first attempt in 1914, but ice crushed his ship *Endurance* even before he reached the shore, and his crew spent fifteen months in lifeboats before being rescued. In 1957-58, Edmund Hillary and Vivian Fuchs crossed Antarctica in Ferguson snow tractors. In 1981, Ranulf Fiennes and two com-panions crossed in snowmobiles. Messner and Fuchs planned the first man-haul (humans on skis pulling small sleds). However, these expeditions crossed Antarctica at its narrowest width. The six-man Trans-Antarctica team was the first to attempt to cross the longest distance by any means. They had already crossed the remote

Antarctic Peninsula, but the other infamous wilderness awaited them—the Area of Inaccessibility.

Sastrugi cluttered the landscape. These wave-shaped drifts frozen in place make for difficult travel. In clear weather, the seas of windblown waves, spires, and pinnacles took on the beauty of Bryce Canyon, Utah. However, Steger, Funatsu, and Somers mushed up the crests and down the troughs in a whiteout unable to see the terrain. The uneven terrain caused the sleds to lurch, shift, tip, and even overturn. Once, an overturned sled pinned Somers to the ground.

Boyarsky became point man when crossing sastrugi during whiteouts. He skied in front and maintained a straight course. Very strong, he could keep pace ahead of the sleds all day without a break, guiding the dogs and watching for especially dangerous slopes. Easygoing and calm, he never complained about frostbite from facing the winds. He provided stability, and he also diligently recorded meteorological observations.

The expedition found the supply cache in the Thiel Mountains on November 26. They drank in the sight of rocky ridges: the last mountains and exposed rock for the next eighteen hundred miles. The blue icefalls along the base of the range added to the glorious scene. After a climb of several days, they reached the Antarctic plateau at ten thousand feet above sea level. The high elevation deepened the blue of the sky.

Steger heard a deep roar. Was it thunder? Or was the Messiah returning? He had experienced snowquakes before as snow settles a few inches, but here the trembling and settling of vast snow fields caused a sound like thunder. He had also seen sun halos and diamond dust in the Arctic, but never matching the uniqueness of Antarctica. Steger saw sun halos often here—and even double halos. Diamond dust, caused by airborne ice crystals, created rainbow arcs, and even a triple arc once met his astonished gaze.

Banners welcomed the six men to the candy-cane-striped barbershop pole set up to mark the South Pole. That day, December 11, they toured America's Amundsen-Scott research station at the pole and held a question-and-answer session for the crew. The station could not accommodate them because they discouraged private expeditions in Antarctica (due to lawsuits resulting from a tourist air crash taking 275 lives at Mount Erebus). They managed the welcome after Russia officially asked the American base to greet Boyarsky as a diplomat.

For three days the six men camped by the base, rested, and took photos. Steger and Etienne had now attained both poles. They celebrated their personal victories, though they knew that Arved Fuchs had done as much in a single year. Somers took a fifteen-second walk around the world. By walking a circle around the pole, he crossed all time zones and longitude lines.

The Area of Inaccessibilty is the region farthest removed from every coast. Only once had it ever been crossed before, and Russian researchers in snow tractors had made that crossing. The expedition entered the region and made good time across the Antarctic Plateau to their scheduled rendezvous with a supply plane at 86° S on the day after Christmas. Christmas was white but uneventful—like the flat, icy horizon around them. Each man relaxed with his allotted four pounds of personal items. Somers usually embroidered, Steger made drawings, and Funatsu sang from his book of Japanese folksongs. Boyarsky and Dahe made scientific measurements and took breaks gazing at a family photo (each had a wife and son). Funatsu and Dahe also brought spices to flavor foods. Etienne usually read books or made radio contact with the outside. By radio, they learned that Messner and Fuchs reached the South Pole on New Year's Eve.

An airplane rendezvous on January 8, 1990, brought new supplies. Since all the time zones meet at the South Pole, time gets confusing. So far, they had kept Chilean time because Punta Arenas served as their support base. However, growing distance made radio contact with Punta Arenas difficult. Since they moved toward Vostok, a Russian station, they set their watches ten hours ahead, the time in both Vostok and Moscow.

Qin Dahe, initially unfamiliar with skis and dogsleds, became a competent skier and also learned to mush when necessary. The son of a veterinarian, he had studied glaciology and married a physician. Because he was educated, the cultural revolution in China during the 1970s had forced him and his wife to work in rice paddies for a time. Afterwards, he had become accustomed to digging samples at high altitudes in the Himalayas before serving at China's Great Wall Station in Antarctica. Now, he dug holes five feet deep in the ice to obtain snow samples all across Antarctica. The first snow samples from the Area of Inaccessibilty excited him greatly. The samples would be checked for pollutants affecting Antarctic snowfall.

Weather in the Area of Inaccessibility proved cold but clear. At eleven thousand feet of elevation, the air was thin and temperatures were low. The plain of ice seemed to extend forever, but they reached Vostok on January 18. The Russians rolled out the red carpet: showers, food, and even real meat. After a four-day rest, they set a fast pace toward the small Soviet base, Komsomolskaya. They reached their cache at the base on February 2 in a temperature of -58°F, the lowest of the entire trip. On February 14, two days after Messner and Fuchs completed their 1,550-mile, ninety-two-day Antarctic crossing, they watched the first sunset of the season. Two days later they reached Pioneerskaya.

After four days, the team reached the last cache and celebrated Somers's fortieth birthday one day late. Somers's conservative and cautious pessimism had helped them, forcing them to analyze worst-case scenarios. Steger always responded to Somers's anger without rebuke or defense, knowing that "a soft answer turneth away wrath." Etienne admired Steger as the only one who never argued with Somers: Steger "can convince people to work together, and he has the appetite to commit to long, hard jobs," he said.

"Has anyone seen Funatsu?" Boyarsky asked about 6:00 P.M. Spacing themselves out along 340 feet of rope, they searched for him in wide circles until dark. Next, they set off flares, but without result. Earlier that day they had sighted the ocean only thirty miles away. Disaster had struck within a day of victory. They could not sleep. They waited for full daylight to search because sight would be essential if Funatsu were incoherent or unconscious. They already missed his kind and generous spirit, his calmness and courtesy, and his attention to details.

Funatsu found himself alone in a whiteout. He had left the tent to feed the dogs at 4:30 P.M., dressed warmly but casually for the

-25°F temperature. Before he had finished the feeding, the temperature dropped, brisk winds kicked up, and snow fell thickly. He had seen a ski that he had placed as a marker and walked to it. Unable to see his second ski, he had veered off course. He had tried to return to the first ski, battling into the wind, but could not find it. Adrenaline coursed through him as he realized he was lost in the whiteout. He began shouting, but the howling winds drowned his efforts. He knew he could not be more than one hundred yards behind camp. His toes ached with the cold. He searched the ground.

Sled tracks! Funatsu followed the tracks, but they soon ended where the blizzard had drifted over them. If he headed in the direction the tracks pointed, he risked another disorientation. He stopped. With pliers for fixing dog collars, he broke through hard surface ice and hollowed out a ditch like the dogs make. Snow covered him in seconds, but he could not get warm without his blizzard gear.

Soon darkness came, but the storm continued. Every half-hour he kicked his feet or jumped up and down, worried that he was losing energy, trying to warm up. Funatsu saw the flares, but they looked distant through the snow and darkness. He knew he could not reach the camp that night and had resigned himself to a night in the snow. It was March 1, only sixteen miles—an easy day of sledding—to the end of their journey at Mirnyy. What if he died in the whiteout? He thought of the shame both for him and the expedition. Funatsu was the youngest man on the expedition, born November 19, 1956, only thirty-three years of age. He hated becoming a burden.

Funatsu reviewed the events that brought him to Antarctica. As a boy, his dad had taken him to see the *Kainan Maru,* the ship of Nobu Shirase (1860-1946). Shirase was the first Japanese to set foot on Antarctica. Funatsu soon adopted two more childhood heroes: pole conquerors Roald Amundsen and Naomi Uemura. Three years after receiving his master's degree from Kobe University, he had begun his own adventures: bicycling across the Sahara and then across the United States. He had stayed in America to work, first training Iditarod sled dogs in Minnesota, where he met Steger, then for an Outward Bound school, and finally for

Krabloonik Kennels in Colorado, when Steger invited him to Antarctica.

Now, Funatsu struggled for his life only one day short of a successful adventure. He tried to look on the bright side as he always did. Few people see Antarctica, few of those explore, and few of the explorers get to experience a night lost in a whiteout. He knew such an experience would strengthen him and teach him the survival skills he hoped to teach to others. If he just sat tight, the search must find him eventually. But would he be alive?

At dawn, the blizzard still raged as Funatsu rechecked the ground for the sled tracks without success. Soon he braced himself for the possibility of a second night in the snow with no food. His feet felt strange—numbed from frostbite. Meanwhile, after asking God for help, his friends had resumed their searching and yelling at 6:00 A.M.

Funatsu heard something and wondered at the strange wind sounds. Louder and closer, now it sounded like people calling his name. Funatsu stood up and with snow flying, he yelled, "I am here." Steger rushed toward him and hugged him like a long-lost brother at an airport terminal. Everyone cried for joy. Funatsu had been outside fourteen hours and lost in the blizzard for thirteen of those. Funatsu thanked God for life and apologized for making "big trouble." Etienne acknowledged that God had answered their request.

On March 3, 1990, the blizzard abated. They reached Mirnyy about 7:00 P.M., after 220 days of mushing. The British had told them it was impossible to cross the Antarctic Peninsula, especially in winter. The Americans and the French had warned them that it was impossible to cross the Area of Inaccessibility. The Russians told them that they would not be able to cross from Vostok to Mirnyy as winter approached. At Mirnyy, over one hundred people awaited their arrival, including Boyarsky's wife, Natasha, who had been flown in as a special surprise. Cheers greeted them as mushers and skiers passed under the finish-line banner. It was a great finale—the Trans-Antarctica team had accomplished the impossible.

Later that day, Steger telexed his alma mater with the admonition: "Look beyond personal gain to your responsibility as God's stewards of the earth." On March 7, they sailed on an icebreaker for nine days to Perth, Australia. From there, they stopped at their six national capitals for receptions. In Beijing, Qin Dahe's biography had already been written, and autograph seekers swarmed him. Somers gave a speech to the Royal Geographic Society and then took Thule home to Keswick, where she had seven puppies. Funatsu brought Kinta and Monty to Osaka to begin his own dog breed for his Outward Bound school. Etienne published a book in French and began educational tours with his new ship, *Antarctica*.

APPENDIX
Notes and Summaries

How do you get to be an adventurer? Do you have to be male, big and strong, rough and tough? Perhaps you were surprised that one of these adventurers is a woman and another is a man only five feet, three inches tall and 135 pounds. Adventurers come from various nationalities and many walks of life. Size, strength, money, or political connections may be of help to an adventurer, but none of these things is necessary. What, then, does it take to be an adventurer?

Adventurers require faith and a willingness to launch out into the unknown. In the words of one great adventurer, Reinhold Messner, "Adventure is not made up of distant lands and mountain tops, rather it lies in one's readiness to exchange the domestic hearth for an uncertain resting place" (*Reinhold Messner: Free Spirit*, p. 25). In this sense, Jesus Christ is the greatest example because He voluntarily exchanged the glories of heaven for the sin-scarred earth where He had no place to lay His head. Jesus showed His faith in God through prayer, and He set the example for man.

Adventurers also need good character. Again, Jesus Christ is the perfect adventurer because His character was perfect. The Bible says that He was "without sin" (Heb. 4:15; I Pet. 2:22). The modern adventurers in this book are not perfect, and their faults should be avoided. Most are not born-again Christians; yet each has some character strength that can inspire Christians. You will find among these adventurers models of courage, self-discipline, cooperation, and persistence. Model yourself after the worthy qualities in the life of each adventurer: "Whatsoever things are of good report; if there be any virtue, and if there be any praise, think on these things" (Phil. 4:8).

Finally, adventurers need knowledge. Many people think of adventure as a vacation—no work and no study—but they do not think of the years of preparation. Adventurers are not goof-offs; they are neither lazy nor dumb. An adventurer must read history and geography to know what challenges are worth attempting that have never been done. He must know science to recognize and survive natural dangers. He must know math and logic to reason correctly and to make quick decisions in solving life-threatening problems. He must develop persuasive speech skills to obtain financial backing. He must develop writing skills to record his adventures in a marketable form so that he can go on more adventures. Of course, Jesus again is the model because He knows everything (Col. 2:3); He is the master of all these subjects. No modern adventurer knows them all, but each recognizes the value of such skills and seeks to develop them. A Christian, too, should study these subjects to become a better steward of his God-given skills. The Bible says, "Giving all diligence, add to your faith virtue; and to virtue knowledge" (II Pet. 1:5).

As you read the exciting accounts of the lives of the great adventurers of our times, do not fail to learn the lessons of faith, virtue, and knowledge. It is essential, however, to recognize that misplaced faith results in death (as Robert Scott learned; see chapter on Amundsen). It is essential that each person trust the Lord Jesus Christ for forgiveness from sin. It is only He that enables us to turn from sin and to develop virtue and knowledge. The Bible says that Christ is the only way to heaven, so any other faith is misplaced in the light of eternity. "Neither is there salvation in any other: for there is none other name under heaven given among men, whereby we must be saved" (Acts 4:12). Indeed, "He that hath the Son hath life; and he that hath not the son of God hath not life" (I John 5:12).

Many adventurers are not easy to obtain information on, even in secular literature, and some of the books that are available include objectionable elements such as foul language or false philosophy.

Great Adventurers of the Twentieth Century provides a useful summary for teachers and saves them the time of censoring. Each adventurer provides a teacher with an interest-catching true story that can introduce a geographical unit. Of course, the book also provides inspirational true stories for students to read and enjoy. The book is arranged by adventurer in chronological order of first major adventure.

Pastors and teachers looking for examples of a character quality or a world record will find the following chart helpful. Each adventurer has multiple positive character qualities, but the chart includes an obvious one that helped him succeed. Of the twenty-one adventurers, twelve went on foot (five climbers, four trekers, a hunter, and two spelunkers), five by animal-powered vehicles (horse, camel, and three dogsleds), and four by nonmotorized vessels (sail, kayak, bathyscaph, and balloon). The chart below serves as an index to the type of travel as well. For further information on an individual, consult the bibliography.

Adventurer	Birthplace	Birth date	Feat	Type	Year	Character
Selous	England	12-31-1851	greatest safaris	hunt	1909	courage
Peary	USA-Penn.	5-6-1856	North Pole	dogsled	1909	determined
Amundsen	Norway	7-16-1872	South Pole	dogsled	1911	steward
Casteret	France	8-19-1897	traverse sump	cave	1922	daring
Tschiffely	Switzerland	1895	Argentina to USA	horse	1927	careful
Tilman	England	2-14-1898	Nanda Devi	climb	1936	spartan
Heyerdahl	Norway	10-6-1914	cross Pacific	sail	1947	confidence
			cross Atlantic	sail	1970	
			Indian Ocean	sail	1978	
Shaffer	USA-Penn.	11-8-1918	Appalachian Range	trek	1948	committed
Hillary	New Zealand	7-20-1919	Everest	climb	1953	available

Schoening	USA-Wash.	7-30-1927	Hidden Peak	climb	1958	strong
			Antarctic peaks	climb	1966	
Piccard	Belgium	7-28-1922	Mariana Trench	dive	1960	attentive
			Gulf Stream	dive	1969	
Ryback	USA-Mich.	3-19-1952	Pacific Crest	trek	1970	endurance
			Continental Divide	trek	1973	
Wilcox	USA-Ohio	8-18-1937	Flint-Mammoth connection	cave	1972	efficient
Davidson	Australia	Sept. 1950	outback solo	camel	1977	adapts/flexible
Uemura	Japan	2-12-1941	North Pole solo	trek	1978	not discouraged
Abruzzo	USA-Ill.	6-9-1930	Atlantic crossing	balloon	1978	persistence
			Pacific crossing	balloon	1981	
Mackal	USA-Wisc.	8-1-1925	cross Likouala	swamp	1981	analytical
Chmielin-ski	Poland	7-17-1952	Colca	kayak	1982	disciplined
			Amazon	kayak	1986	
Messner	Italy	9-17-1944	Everest solo oxygenless	climb	1980	innovator
			the Big Walls	climb	1974	
			all 14 8000ers	climb	1986	
Morrow	Canada	10-18-1952	Seven Summits	climb	1986	resourceful
Steger	USA-Minn.	8-27-1945	North Pole unsupported	dogsled	1986	cooperation
			cross Antarctica	dogsled	1990	
			cross Arctic	dogsled	1995	

Subheadings under most adventurers aid those looking for a story on a particular region. The chart below lists those adventurers with an entire subheading on a particular continent or ocean.

Africa
  Selous (East and South Africa)
  Mackal (Likouala, Congo)
  Messner (Kilimanjaro)

Antarctica
  Amundsen (South Pole)
  Schoening (Ellsworth Range)
  Morrow (Vinson Massif)
  Steger (transcontinental)

Asia
  Tilman (Karakoram and
    Nanda Devi)
  Hillary (Mount Everest)
  Schoening (K2, Hidden Peak)
  Messner (Himalaya, Karakoram)
  Morrow (Mount Everest)

Australia and New Guinea
  Davidson (Australian Outback)
  Messner (Himalaya, Karakoram)
  Morrow (Mount Everest)

Europe
  Casteret (caves of France)
  Piccard (Mediterranean)
  Messner (Alps)

North America
  Tschiffely (Central America,
    Mexico, USA)
  Peary (Greenland)

  Tilman (Baffin Island)
  Schaeffer (Appalachians)
  Ryback (West U.S. ranges)
  Wilcox (Mammoth Cave)
  Morrow (Mount McKinley)

South America
  Tschiffely (transcontinental)
  Chmielinski (Colca, Amazon)
  Messner (Aconcagua)
  Morrow (Aconcagua)

Arctic Ocean
  Peary (North Pole)
  Amundsen (ship , balloon)
  Uemura (North Pole)
  Steger (transoceanic)

Atlantic Ocean
  Heyerdahl (transoceanic)
  Piccard (sea floor)
  Abruzzo (balloon across)

Indian Ocean
  Heyerdahl (around Arabia)

Pacific Ocean
  Heyerdahl (transoceanic)
  Piccard (Mariana Trench)
  Abruzzo (balloon across)

BIBLIOGRAPHY

Frederick Courteney Selous

Baker, Daniel B., ed. *Explorers and Discoverers of the World.* Detroit: Gale Research Inc., 1993. Pages 485-88 are on Roosevelt's travels.

Bull, Bartle. *Safari: A Chronicle of Adventure.* New York: Penguin, 1992. Chapter 3 (pp. 93-121) "I Mean to Be Like Livingstone" is on Fred Selous. Chapter 5 (pp. 157-83) "Bwana Tumbo" is on Roosevelt.

Dictionary of National Biography. Supplement for 1912-21. Oxford University Press.

Robert Edwin Peary

Baker, Daniel B., ed. *Explorers and Discovers of the World.* Detroit: Gale Research Inc., 1993. See pages 281-83.

Dolan, Edward F. *Matthew Henson: Black Explorer.* New York: Dodd, Mead, and Company, 1979.

Mountfield, David. *A History of Polar Exploration.* New York: Dial Press, 1974. See "North Pole," pp. 155-65.

Peary, Robert E. *Nearest the Pole.* New York: Doubleday, 1907.

————. *The North Pole.* New York: Frederick A. Stokes, 1910.

————. *Northward over the Great Ice.* New York: Frederick A. Stokes, 1898.

————. *Secrets of Polar Travel.* New York: Century, 1917.

Roald Engelbregt Graving Amundsen

"Amundsen's Attainment of the South Pole." *National Geographic,* February, 1912, pp. 205, 207-8

Antarctica: Great Stories from the Frozen Continent. New York: *Reader's Digest,* 1985. See especially pages 184-99 for Amundsen and Scott expeditions.

Chapman, Walker, ed. *Antarctic Conquest: The Great Explorers in Their Own Words.* See "Roald Amundsen," pages 235-252 an excerpt translated by A.G. Carter from Amundsen" book in Norweigan *South Pole.*

Norbert Casteret

Burgess, Robert F. *The Cave Divers.* New York: Dodd, Mead, and Company, 1976.

Casteret, Norbert. "Discovering the Oldest Statues in the World." *National Geographic,* August 1924, pp. 124-52.

————. "Lascaux Cave, Cradle of World Art." *National Geographic,* December 1948, pp. 771-94.

————. "Probing Ice Caves of the Pyrenees." *National Geographic,* March 1953, pp. 391-404.

Courbon, Paul, Claude Chabert, Peter Bosted, and Karen Lindsley. *Atlas of the Great Caves of the World.* St. Louis: Cave Books, 1989. See pages 15, 179, and 186.

Hogg, Garry. *Deep Down: Great Achievements in Cave Exploration.* New York: Criterion Books, 1962. Chapter 3 covers Casteret as first to enter the Caverns of Montespan through the sump.

Pinney, Roy. *The Complete Book of Cave Exploration.* New York: Coward-McCann, 1962. Casteret is discussed on pages 51-53, 83, 133-34.

Aime Felix Tschiffely

Obituary. *New York Times.* Jan 6, 1954. p. 31

Obituaries on File. New York: Facts on File, 1979. See page 595.

Tschiffely, A. F. "Buenos Aires to Washington by Horse: A Solitary Journey of Two and a Half Years, Through Eleven American Republics, Covers 9,600 Miles of Mountain and Plain, Desert and Jungle." *National Geographic,* February 1929, pp. 135-96.

————. *Tschiffely's Ride.* London: William Heinemann, Ltd., 1933.

Who Was Who 1951-1960. 3rd. edition. London: Adam and Charles Black, 1967, p. 1102.

Harold William Tilman

Madge, Tim. *The Last Hero.* Seattle, Wash.: The Mountaineers, 1995.

Neate, Jill. *High Asia.* Seattle, Wash.: The Mountaineers, 1989.

Tilman, Bill. *The Seven Mountain-Travel Books.* Seattle, Wash.: The Mountaineers, 1983. The seven books combined in this volume follow. All but the first (published by G. Bell) were published by Cambridge University Press. They are *Snow on the Equator* (1937), *The Ascent of Nanda Devi* (1937), *When Men and Mountains Meet* (1946), *Everest 1938* (1948), *Two Mountains and a River* (1949), *China to Chitral* (1951), and *Nepal Himalaya* (1952).

Tilman, Bill. *The Eight Sailing/Mountain-Exploration Books.* Seattle, Wash.: The Mountaineers, 1987. The eight books combined in this volume are *Mischief in Patagonia* (Cambridge Univ. Press, 1957), *Mischief Among the Penguins* (Rupert Hart-Davis, 1961), *Mischief in Greenland* (1964), *Mostly Mischief* (1966), *Mischief Goes South* (1968), *In Mischief's Wake* (1971), *Ice with Everything* (George Harrap, 1974), and *Triumph and Tribulation* (Nautical Pub. Co., 1977). The last four Mischief books were originally published by Hollis and Carter.

Thor Heyerdahl

Heyerdahl, Thor. *Aku-Aku.* Chicago: Rand McNally, 1958.

———. *Kon-Tiki.* New York: Rand McNally, 1950, 1964. (originally published in 1950)

———. *The Ra Expeditions.* Garden City, N.Y.: Doubleday and Company, 1971.

———. *The Tigris Expedition.* Garden City, N.Y.: Doubleday and Company, 1981.

———. "The Voyage of Ra II." *National Geographic,* January 1971, pp. 44-71.

———. "Tigris Sails into the Past." *National Geographic,* December, 1978, pp. 806-27.

Earl V. Shaffer

Brown, Andrew H. "Skyline Trail from Maine to Georgia," *National Geographic,* August 1949, pp. 228-51. References to Shaffer's trek are limited to page 219.

Ross, Cindy. "Earl Shaffer Revisited." Article for Long Distance Hiker site on internet. Update on Shaffer.

Shaffer, Earl. *Walking with Spring.* Harpers Ferry, W.Va.: Appalachian Trail Conference, 1983.

Shaffer, Ray. *Uncle Earl's Trail Slides.* A videotape of a slide show given by Earl Shaffer on his hike.

Tagliapietra, Ron. *The Southern Sixers.* Greenville, S.C.: author, 1997. Includes data on the forty highest peaks.

Edmund Percival Hillary

Hillary, Sir Edmund. "The Conquest of the Summit." *National Geographic,* 106, July 1954, pp. 45-64. See also "Triumph on Everest" pp. 1-44 by the expedition leader, John Hunt.

———. "Preserving a Mountain Heritage." *National Geographic, 161,* June 1982, pp. 696-703. See also pp. 704-25.

Huxley, Anthony, ed. *Standard Encyclopedia of the World's Mountains.* New York: G. P. Putnam's Sons, 1962.

Peter K. Schoening

Bass, Dick and Frank Wells with Rick Ridgeway. *Seven Summits.* New York: Warner Books, 1986. The last chapter has corrected measurements for Vinson Massif and Mount Tyree.

Clinch, Nicholas B. "First Conquest of Antarctica's Highest Peaks." *National Geographic,* June 1967, pp. 836-63. Team leader recounts first climbs of six Antarctic peaks.

———. *A Walk in the Sky.* Seattle, Wash.: The Mountaineers, 1982. Ascent of Hidden Peak including summit, Chapter 14 by Pete Schoening (pp. 171-76).

Curran, Jim. *K2: The Story of the Savage Mountain.* Seattle, Wash.: The Mountaineers, 1995. Chapter 8 is on the 1953 expedition (pp. 95-105).

Dyhrenfurth, G. O. *To the Third Pole.* London: T. Werner Laurie Ltd., 1955. This history of the fourteen highest peaks covers K2 in Chapter 3, including the 1953 expedition (pp. 19-21).

Jacques Piccard

Piccard, Jacques. "Man's Deepest Dive." *National Geographic,* August 1960, pp. 224-39.

Piccard, Jacques. *The Sun Beneath the Sea.* New York: Charles Scribner's Sons, 1971.

Piccard, Jacques and Robert S. Dietz. *Seven Miles Down.* New York: G.P. Putnam's Sons, 1961.

Eric Ryback

Contemporary Authors, Vol. 37. Detroit: Gale Research Co., 1979. See page 473.

Edwards, Mike W. "Mexico to Canada on the Pacific Crest Trail." *National Geographic,* June 1971, pp. 741-79. Comments and photos of Ryback's trek are on pages 745-48.

Ryback, Eric. *The High Adventure of Eric Ryback.* San Francisco: Chronicle Books, 1971.

———. *The Ultimate Journey: Canada to Mexico down the Continental Divide.* San Francisco: Chronicle Books, 1973.

John Preston Wilcox

Brucker, Roger W. and Richard A. Watson. *The Longest Cave.* New York: Alfred A. Knopf, 1976. Wilcox's contributions appear in Chapters 22-32.

Courbon, Paul, Claude Chabert, Peter Bosted, and Karen Lindsley. *Atlas of the Great Caves of the World.* St. Louis: Cave Books, 1989.

Robyn Davidson

Contemporary Authors, Vol. 142. Detroit: Gale Research Inc., 1994. See pages 102-3.

Davidson, Robyn. "Alone." *National Geographic,* May 1978, pp. 580-611.

———. *Desert Places.* New York: Penguin Books, 1996.

———. "The Mythological Crucible" is part three of *Australia: Beyond the Dreamtime* (pages 169-241). New York: Facts on File, 1987.

———. *Tracks.* New York: Pantheon, 1981.

Naomi Uemura

Freedman, Lewis. "The Legacy of Naomi Uemura." Chapter 4 of *Dangerous Steps.* Harrisburg, Pa.: Stockpile Books, 1990.

"Journey to the Top of the World." *Time,* May 15, 1978, pp. 69, 71.

Kodansha Encyclopedia of Japan. Vol. 8. Tokyo: Kodansha Ltd., 1983. See page 128.

"Milestones." *Time,* March 12, 1984, p. 84.

"Newsmakers." *Newsweek,* May 15, 1978, p. 53.

Uemura, Naomi. "Solo to the Pole." *National Geographic,* September 1978, pp. 298-325.

"Why? Because It Is There." *Newsweek,* March 10, 1980, pp. 16-17.

Benjamin Lawrence Abruzzo

Abruzzo, Ben L. "First Across the Pacific: The Flight of 'Double Eagle V.' " *National Geographic,* April 1982, pp. 512-21.

Abruzzo, Ben L. with Maxie L. Anderson and Larry Newman. " 'Double Eagle II' has Landed." *National Geographic,* December 1978, pp. 858-82.

Anderson, Maxie and Kristian. " 'Kitty Hawk' Floats Across North America," *National Geographic,* August 1980, pp. 260-71.

Contemporary Authors, Vol. 115. Detroit: Gale Research Inc., 1985. See page 17.

Conniff, Richard. "Racing with the Wind." *National Geographic,* September 1997, pp. 52-67. Fossett sets new distance record.

McCarry, Charles. *Double Eagle.* Boston: Little, Brown, and Company, 1979.

Yost, Ed. "Longest Manned Balloon Flight." *National Geographic,* February, 1977, pp. 208-17. Article that inspired the adventure.

Roy Paul Mackal

American Men and Women of Science 1989-1990. 17th ed. Vol. 5. New York: R. R. Bowker, 1989. See page 82.

Chadwick, Douglas H. "Ndoki: Last Place on Earth." *National Geographic,* July 1995, pp. 2-45. Good background on the swamp, but makes light of possible sauropods. (Eye-witness interviewees would not have identified a short-tailed rhino as *mokele-mbembe,* though they may have called it *emela-ntouka.*)

Mackal, Roy P. *A Living Dinosaur?* Leiden, the Netherlands: E. J. Brill, 1987.

———. *The Monsters of Loch Ness.* Chicago: Swallow Press, Incorporated, 1976.

———. *Searching for Hidden Animals.* Garden City, N.Y.: Doubleday and Co., 1980.

Piotr P. Chmielinski

Chmielinski, Piotr. "Kayaking the Amazon." *National Geographic,* April 1987, pp. 460-73. Photos by Zbigniew Bzdak.

Judge, Joseph. "Retracing John Wesley Powell's Historic Voyage down the Grand Canyon." *National Geographic,* May 1969, pp. 668-713.

Kane, Joe. *Running the Amazon.* New York: Vintage Books, 1989.

Kane, Joe. "Roaring Through Earth's Deepest Canyon." *National Geographic,* January 1993, pp. 118-38. Photos by Zbigniew Bzdak.

Reinhold Messner

Contemporary Authors. New Revision, Vol. 35. Detroit: Gale Research Inc., 1992, page 315.

Messner, Reinhold. *All 14 Eight-Thousanders.* Great Britain: Crowood Press, 1988. Published in America by Cloudcap Press, Seattle. Translated by Audrey Salkeld.

———. *The Big Walls.* London: Kaye and Ward, 1978.

———. *The Crystal Horizon.* Great Britain: Crowood Press, 1989. Published in America by The Mountaineers, Seattle.

———. *Everest: Expedition to the Ultimate.* London: Kaye and Ward, 1979. Translated by Audrey Salkeld.

———. *Reinhold Messner: Free Spirit.* London: Hodder and Stoughton, 1991. Translated by Jill Neate.

———. "First to Ski Cross Continent," *National Geographic,* November 1990, pp. 94-95.

Smoot, Jeff. *Summit Guide to the Cascade Volcanoes.* Evergreen, Colo.: Chockstone Press, 1992. Pages 4-6 discuss ratings. Classes 1 through 6 are defined. This standard decimal system should not be confused with the rating scale for overall difficulty or the Grades 1 to 5 of technical routes.

Patrick Morrow

Bass, Dick and Frank Wells with Rick Ridgeway. *Seven Summits.* New York: Warner Books, 1986.

Huxley, Anthony, ed. *Standard Encyclopedia of the World's Mountains.* New York: G.P. Putnam's Sons, 1962. Seven summits: pp. 55, 107, 147, 192, 194, 206-8.

Messner, Reinhold. *Reinhold Messner, Free Spirit: A Climber's Life.* London: Hodder and Stoughton, 1991. Pages 230-32 are on the race for the Seven Summits.

Morrow, Patrick. *Beyond Everest.* Camden East, Ont.: Camden House Publishing, 1986.

Porzak, Glenn. "Continental Divide" appendix (pages 216-17) of *To Everest Via Antarctica* by Robert Mads Anderson. New York: Stackpole Books, 1996. Porzak finished the Seven Summits in 1994; Anderson climbed six solo but failed seven times on Everest.

Schmidt, Jeremy. "Climb Every Sponsor." *International Wildlife.* July/August 1988, pages 34-39.

Tabin, Geoffrey. Blind Corners. Merrillville, Ind.: ICS Books, 1993. See especially page 142 on summits and 159 on summiteers.

Will Steger

Baker, Daniel B., ed. *Explorers and Discoverers of the World.* Detroit: Gale Research Inc., 1993. See pages 531-32.

Etienne, Jean-Louis. "Skiing Alone to the Pole." *National Geographic,* September 1986, pp. 318-23.

Italia, Bob. *Will Steger.* Bloomington, Minn.: Abdo and Daughters, 1990.

"N. Shirase of Japan Sought South Pole." New York Times for September 11, 1946. Obituary on Lt. Naoshi Shirase, Chobu, Choku, and Nobu.

Steger, Will. "Dispatches from the Arctic Ocean." *National Geographic,* January 1996, pp. 78-89.

———. "North to the Pole," *National Geographic,* September 1986, pp. 288-317.

———. "Six Across Antarctica," *National Geographic,* November 1990, pp. 66-93.

Steger, Will and Jon Bowermaster. *Crossing Antarctica.* New York: Alfred A. Knopf, 1991.

Appendix

Messner, Reinhold. *Reinhold Messner: Free Spirit*. London: Hodder and Stoughton, 1991. Quote from page 25.

Index